OF SPECIAL NOTE
OF SPECIAL NOTE

The elements of transformation presented in this book are based on the shared stories and the personal and professional experiences of the author.

In no way does the author assume to have the answers to all questions or needs, because in situations of loss, each case is unique, and grief is a completely subjective process.

The purpose of this book is to help you the reader, through the stories within these pages and the principles and suggested activities, to transform your loss and, therefore, change your life.

PROLOGUE

A Line Between Two Numbers

A *few days ago, during one of the many and lovely conversations I have had the pleasure of sharing with Ligia, she asked me to write the prologue for her new book Transform Your Loss: Your Guide to Strength and Hope. I must be honest and say that I felt extremely honored by her invitation, but I experienced a sense of great responsibility for the simple fact that I had never done anything like this before. Her intention to carry a message of strength and hope is such that I simply felt that the task of writing the prologue was something of a commitment.*

Wow! I confess it is truly an honor for me, Ligia, but ... why me?

What she told me was enough to remind me, once again, that my experiences have not only transformed my life in a very positive manner, but they should also be shared with everyone who is willing to hear them and perhaps to learn from them.

Nearly five years ago I lost my beloved mother, a cancer victim. This loss can only be described by someone who has lost a loved one as close as a father or mother. Mom was a wonderful mother, wife, and grandmother who lived for her grandchildren. She physically left her husband, children, and grandchildren but spiritually she will live forever. The experience of seeing Mom fade away, little by little, was something very hard for us all.

About three weeks after she died, I was diagnosed with stage 3 melanoma, a type of cancer that has no identified treatment protocol. My diagnosis was also very negative, as the cancer had already spread to the nodes of my neck. This meant that, according to the statistics of this prognosis, I had between six and twenty-four months to live.

They say that normally the grieving process, after losing a loved one, is difficult, but I had almost no chance to mourn for my mother because three weeks after her passing, my own life was in danger.

Even through the process of losing my mom, twelve months before my own prognosis, I was living a happy, healthy, life, with a united family and a productive business. But now it seemed that an unexpected storm had come over us. After two operations and six months of treatment I had a relapse which ended in another operation and another year of treatment. During this process I also lost my young business. So over a period of two and a half years we lost our savings and we were practically bankrupt. It was a very abrupt and sudden change.

One night, my lovely wife Naomi and I were contemplating the tsunami we had gone through. I remember perfectly: we were in the garden and I told her that both she and I were very *fortunate people. Blessed for being part of this beautiful planet without having asked to be here; blessed for having me; blessed for having been able to have five beautiful children; blessed for having been able to sow our love in our children; blessed for the mere fact of having been talking together that night; blessed for getting through all we had been through and because, rather than destroying us, it has made us much stronger. Now, after the storm we were awaiting a beautiful sun. When I look back, I can truly say:*

My experience was a blessing!

In this wonderful book, Transform Your Loss, Ligia wishes us to understand that our experiences of pain can be transfigured and eventually be seen as something that, simply, is part of the process of life. Our life is like a book in which one chapter ends and another begins. As the wise words say, "There is a time to cry, a time to laugh, a time to live and a time to die."

Why do I say that my experience was a blessing that changed my life?

When I was operated on for the last time, before I was anesthetized, I thought that maybe I had a few months to live; it also occurred to me that I could die in the operating room. It was then that I learned to consider the beautiful gift of time and, that perhaps, I had not taken advantage of my life as I should have. I realized that life (a gift I did not ask for) is a line between two numbers: the day I was born and the day I die. This is the same for everyone: my parents, my children, my wife, my friends, all human beings without exception. A line between two numbers! This was my prayer of gratitude:

Lord, if possible, give me a little more time. And if not, then give me, please, energy to achieve all that I can with the time I have left. Thank you for giving me such a beautiful family. Thank you for the name you gave me; the month I was born in; the country where I was born; thank you for my culture; thank you for giving me the gift of my beautiful parents and my unforgettable grandparents; thanks for the time you gave me with my mother; thank you for my beautiful children; my wife; my friends; the sun, stars, mountains, the sea and the animals; thank you for teaching me through good experiences and also painful ones.

My experience made me realize that I was given a short timeline and that within that line all that there is, is a gift. This did not leave me anymore than to be grateful for the things I mentioned earlier.

I do not know what experience you are going through at the moment: a divorce, the death of a loved one, a disease, or your loss of innocence. But Transform Your Loss is more than a book; it is a tool to help the one who is ready to receive the message of hope and acceptance of this wonderful, privileged process of life. Through her good intention, knowledge and compassion, Ligia has compiled a melody of hope.

I have to finish these lines, mentioning the biggest blessing I received during my experience, my understanding of faith. I read about a lot of exceptional people throughout history and about many writers and their formidable messages. Without exception, all have taught me something positive, but the person I have received the greatest teachings from is Jesus of Galilee.

My experience was miraculous, and part of the process of that miracle was to understand that faith moves mountains. Not necessarily physical mountains, but the mountain that is blocking your happiness. Jesus, during his many miracles never said "I healed you." His expression always was "Your faith has healed you." I managed to release all of my complaints and concerns to God and that gave me peace and tranquility. That in itself was another blessing.

Friends, it is possible! And in this beautiful book you will see many testimonials from people like you and me who managed to close a chapter and open another, moving on "from suffering to peace."

It has been almost five years since Mom died and almost five from my cancer recovery. Thanks to God, today, I am free from cancer, and I am willing and able to share this with you. Today I understand that everything I have gone through is part of a divine process that I must accept. I hope that you open your mind and your heart and let Transform Your Loss: Your Guide to Strength and Hope help you understand that you can transform your loss.

I leave you with a prayer that I learned when I had the impression that the world was falling down around me. I do not remember who gave it to me, but I am sure that it was an angel:

Lord, thank you for what you have given me,
thank you for what you are giving me and I do not

realize, thank you for what you are going to give me, because for you everything is present; thank you for what you refuse me in your infinite mercy and thank you, Lord, for teaching me that your delay is not your denial. Amén!

JORGE CÓRDOBA

THE CITY THAT WE ARE

Transform Your Loss: Your Guide to Strength and Hope is a living document, enriched with a collection of testimonies on the human experience that reaffirm the experience in its entirety. It helps us understand that grief is as natural a part of life as is being born, growing and dying. It helps us understand that we live in a costume, that is the human body and that our soul never dies, but it goes to another dimension, it becomes "real life."

With this work of Ligia M. Houben's, I learned that every life is like a map. Every human being is like a city: some small, and some large. And we pass and travel along that map to our destination, our home. For some of us Heaven is our home, where our Heavenly Father lives. For others, it is a power as great as the sun, that is there and we cannot get to unless in a pure form, as a spirit.

In addition, with helping me in my job as a clinical psychologist (where I work with people who are going through the grieving process), this book has also helped me transform my spiritual perception above and beyond what is conventional. I stand by my human experience as the basis to help others through the purest of teachings, love. We are here to learn from each other. Some of us do it through small things, like silent workers, knowing that the voice of reward does not tell us we did a good job, the merit is to know that we carry out our actions inspired by that love. Let us not forget that we must live in the present, not remembering what happened yesterday or worrying about what will happen tomorrow: the important thing is to live the experience of now.

I feel that this book is a tool inspired by something divine and which can serve to help us understand the pain as something normal.

Transform Your Loss also contains a rich set of accounts of great human value that help us to perceive that we are not alone; these collective memories can help us to process the pain and to understand there is joy in the pain and that this joy can be achieved only by passing through the grief and letting go.

ALEXANDER FIUZA, PHD
Clinical psychologist

HOW THIS BOOK WAS BORN

This book comes in the wake of a television segment in which I participated and discussed the issue of losses and how to deal with them. After this program, many people asked me if I had ever written a book about loss, because they wanted a guide on how to turn their life around after going through a grieving process. Analyzing people's need for more guidance on this subject—which is so universal, yet so ignored—I decided to write this book. I was inspired because I had experienced the loss of my father at the age of twelve, and at that time I had no professional help or books to give me hope or consolation either. I am aware that this experience of loss changed my life and was the flame that gave me the desire to help other mourners to process their losses and, in turn, to transform their lives.

With the birth of this book, thirty-six years after the physical loss of my father, I give tribute to his memory, which I always carry with me:

Love does not end, it is transformed ...

But we have to be aware that when talking about losses we do not need to limit ourselves to loss by death alone. We face countless situations in our daily lives that cause us pain and grief. We live in a society that avoids talking about losses. We believe that it is logical to maintain the attitude of "I'm well and I hope that you are also all right." We can appreciate this attitude when we ask someone how they are, and are surprised if we do not hear the preconceived answer "Fine, and you?"

Although we continually face loss and go through the grieving process, we still have not become used to speaking about the topic. We realize that we are part of a society in denial of grief, as Elizabeth Kübler-Ross said when she spoke of the five stages of grief, which are applicable to all kinds of losses: denial, anger, bargaining, depression, and acceptance.

The first of these stages is precisely the denial.[1] While we remain in this stage we cannot really process our losses or understand those of others. We must recognize that sometimes we are not okay, and we need to share and process that experience. Similarly, we need to be aware that we have within us the power to move forward and transform our misfortune into a source of personal and spiritual growth.

With my desire to give you that opportunity, *Transform Your Loss* was born.

This is an interactive book that discusses and illustrates the various types of losses we face in life, how we react to them, and how we can transform them. In its final part, I offer you the tools necessary to transform your loss after you have read the testimony of those who decided to share their own stories of loss, with the intention of helping you in your moment of pain or confusion. Although most of these stories deal with the loss of a loved one, other losses that are significant in our lives have been included. Keep in mind that each of these stories is written with great feeling and in the spirit of helping you in your own process. Each of these people, including myself, went through pain and grief similar to yours after our loss. I do not say the same kind of grief, as each person's is unique.

Many of us feel that sometimes we are unable to get up and go on with life. However, a number of us have shared our stories to assure you that, although we do not know you, we feel very close to you in your loss. We have opened our souls and hearts to let you know that, like you, we have suffered, we have cried, and we have trusted—and transformed our loss. Our losses are part of life, and we must learn to deal with them and grow during the grieving process.

My greatest desire with this book is to inspire you to take the opportunity and necessary steps to transform your loss and, consequently, to change your life.

HOW TO USE THIS BOOK

It's not what happens to you that determines how far you will go in life; it is how you handle what happens to you.

ZIG ZIGLAR

I invite you to read this book through the eyes of your soul. Surely some of its sections or stories will touch you more than others. But if one of the messages, one of the ideas, even a simple suggestion, helps you process your grief and enhance your life, this project has been worthwhile. I will therefore feel honored to have contributed to the transformation of your loss, and hence to your life. All who have contributed their own stories have done so wholeheartedly and with a desire to help you and inspire your own process of transforming your loss. It is also my wish to let you know that you are not alone and that loss is a part of life. Unexpected things happen at every turn and we face them, suffer them, and the world continues to turn.

So read this book at your own pace, read it all at once or section by section. But read it as if it was written for you—which it was.

The book is divided into three sections. In the first section, I deal with what loss and grief are. I explore the different types of grief and their manifestations. This will give you the opportunity to identify your own personal situation. The second section offers personal stories about several kinds of losses, with messages of strength and hope; and in the third section, I give you the tools necessary to transform your loss. I do not intend to give you all the answers about loss, as there are many philosophies and approaches to dealing with grief. The eleven principles that I propose (in the third section) for transforming your loss are based on my personal and professional experience as a grief counselor, and on the common elements contained in the stories that were shared in the second section. In response to the principles I hope you will write your own thoughts, using the simple exercise *A Moment of Reflection*, which will allow you to communicate with your inner self and tap your internal capacity for transformation. (It would be a good practice throughout your reading of the book to keep a notebook or journal handy).

I invite you to read the book in its sequential order, as it was written for that purpose. It would be best to answer Questionnaire I, *Evaluation of Your Loss*, following this introduction, before reading the first part of the book. Then, after you have read our stories and completed the exercises and meditations, you can answer Questionnaire II, *Evaluation of Your Loss Now*, at the end of the book for comparison.

If you have suffered a recent loss, especially the loss of a loved one, you may think that this book is too demanding and that you are not yet ready to do the exercises or to accept and use the suggestions. You may still be in the acute stage of mourning. If so, just set the book aside, and when you are ready to begin this process, pick it up again and open your heart to its message. Indeed, this may be the first step to transforming your loss. But if your loss is very recent or you think you cannot deal with your grief, let alone try to transform your loss, be assured that with time, you will work out your grief, and succeed at transforming your loss.

The most important thing is to start on a path of personal and spiritual growth even in the early stages of you loss. Once you gain control of your life you can develop the potential you have within yourself to transform you loss. The desire to move forward is what can generate enough will to take the necessary steps to transform your loss and regain a sense of life. In carrying out these steps, you will integrate the loss into your life in a special way, without it causing you so much suffering, and thus learn to live a new reality. You can also decide to stay where you are, without even attempting to move forward. It is your decision. As Rabbi and thanatologist Earl Grollman says, "Grief is a process, recovery is a choice."

In order to assess where you are in regard to this loss, it could be helpful for you to answer Questionnaire I below. (The statements are not intended as judgments, only to reflect your thoughts and feelings in the present moment.)

EVALUATION OF YOUR LOSS

QUESTIONNAIRE I

Please circle the statements that you identify with.

1. I do not want to think about my loss.
2. I will never be happy again.
3. These misfortunes only happen to me.
4. Everyone else is happy.
5. Looking after my health does not interest me.
6. I do not believe in support groups.
7. I do not believe in God.
8. I do not believe in spiritual guides.
9. I feel a lot of anger.
10. I feel a lot of resentment.
11. I will never forgive those who caused this pain.
12. I do not want to talk about death.
13. Life is unfair.
14. If I occupy my time I do not need to think about my loss.
15. I do not have to share my pain with anyone.
16. I need to be strong for others.
17. From now on I will not show my feelings.

18. I do not think I will recover.
19. Nobody understands me.
20. Never again will I see my loved one.
21. Religion does not help to heal a loss.
22. Why did this happen to me?
23. I am guilty of suffering this loss.
24. Someday I will be happy.
25. I will learn to live with this loss.
26. I will get over this loss and transform my life.
27. I would rather be alone.
28. I do not want help.
29. I have internalized my loss.
30. I will be happy again.
31. Losses are part of life.
32. Everybody faces tough times in life.
33. Looking after my health is very important.
34. Support groups can provide help.
35. I believe in the possibility of something stronger than myself.
36. At certain times we need spiritual guides.
37. I have managed to distance my anger.
38. Saving up resentment is not healthy for my soul.
39. I have managed to forgive.
40. It is necessary to talk about death.
41. Sometimes life is not easy, but I still go forward.
42. Although it is difficult, I need to process my loss.
43. There is a lot that helps me share my sorrow.
44. I do not need to feign strength to others.
45. It is important to show my true feelings.
46. There will be a time when I will have recovered.
47. There are people who understand my pain.

48. I always carry my loved one in my heart.
49. The spiritual dimension helps me to find meaning.
50. I am not the only person facing a loss.
51. I am not guilty of this loss.
52. I help others with their loss.
53. I can love, starting with myself.
54. By transforming my loss, I can change my life.

PART ONE

INTRODUCTION

Each life is a full life. No one can tell us how long we will live or when we will die. The best strategy is to live each day as fully as possible. As if it were the first day, or the last day of your life. Every moment can then become perfect.

IRA BYOCK

The question that we ask repeatedly when confronted by a misfortune or a tragedy, or something else that interrupts the flow of our lives, is,
"Why did this happen to me?"

We know our life, a life to which we are accustomed, and which we feel comfortable and happy with. Then suddenly something interrupts the flow of that life. And, full of despair and confusion, we wonder,
"Why did this happen to me?"

But stop for a moment and think....This has not only happened to you, but to thousands of people who at this very moment are facing loss or tragedy or hardship.

"But...the worst loss is the worst that happens to you," says Rabbi Earl Grollman. Therefore, when we go through pain or misfortune, we do not ordinarily think about others who are going through a similar situation. We only wonder,

"How is it possible that this happened to me?"

Sometimes, by our own attitude we worsen our grieving process. There are many occasions when we face obstacles that we do not expect, especially when we feel that everything in our life is in order and we are happy that everything is going well and that life is beautiful. Suddenly something unexpected happens to us and our world collapses. We lose a loved one, we perceive that we are ill, or we are faced with a divorce. When we feel lonely and frustrated, or when we feel confused and immersed in our own pain, we ask many questions, apart from the initial one of why this happened to me.

Often full of fear and anxiety, we ask ourselves,

- What will happen to me now?
- Where am I going to go?
- Will I be able to cope with this?
- How will my life be?
- How will my future be?
- Who will care for me?
- Will I be able to find a new job?
- Will I be able to adjust to this country?

We ask many questions and we want many answers, but we may not always receive the answer we need or wish. This reminds me of a conversation I had with a minister with whom I ran a training workshop on bereavement, and who is a specialist on grief. He commented that to begin the work of mourning, it is necessary to put aside those questions; then we can move forward. With time, we will probably find the meanings and understand the questions. But, for the immediate present it is best to let go of these questions.

It is only human to ask these questions, although most of the time we will not get the answer that we want to hear in our hearts. My intention is that you can develop your spiritual dimension, and in turn, transform your loss or any area of your life that is causing you trauma, or in fact, any other situation that is causing you pain. The stories within these pages are meant to help you do this. But with our stories, we do not intend to impose our religious beliefs on you. The stories simply illustrate how others drew from their religious or life experience, and how it helped them transform their loss, and often deepened their spirituality or self-assurance. You will see that although most of these stories are meant to help you deal with your own loss, we do not assume that you will do so in the same way, but according to your own belief system or philosophy. If you wish to call your "source of strength" by the name of God, the Universe, Buddha, Tao, Spirit, or Energy, then do so. In my case I call this source God. But please use any name or term that represents spiritual strength or power that will serve to comfort you.

It is not by chance that you have this book in your hand, because you could have picked any one. Perhaps the title caught your attention, as you might be going through a loss or know someone who is. I think this is possible because we are continually facing changes and losses, some more difficult and painful than others, because life is a succession of losses. But, what has happened in your life to cause you so much pain? What is causing your pain? This book is all about the power that resides within yourself to transform your life in the way you react to the pain that has created your loss. It is worth clarifying the point that although most of the book and the stories we share are about the death of a loved one, there are also other "small deaths" we face in life that we cannot ignore and which also generate pain and suffering.[2]

Transform Your Loss is a guide to help you process and transmute the pain and the feelings of emptiness inside yourself, which are so deep seated that they likely make you feel adrift. I sincerely hope that this book and its stories will inspire you and help you in your grieving process. I do not know exactly how you feel now, but I can assure you that all of us who have shared our stories in these pages have gone through painful losses and difficult times, and have been transformed by them, even though we may have thought that our situation would never improve or if we would ever heal.

In analyzing my own life and realizing that I have suffered many losses, I know that I am not alone. In my personal and professional life, I have found that as human beings we go through losses of many kinds and that it depends on how we receive and deal with them as to what they do to us.

If you allow this process to work or evolve over time, a metamorphosis will occur within yourself, and you will be able to rise like a phoenix from the ashes, because you will realize that you have a power within you to transform your losses. My intention is not to ignore your pain or to tell you that what you are feeling does not matter. I understand your pain, because I too have gone through deep grief and despair. At the same time, I hope that with the help of the messages and stories within these pages, you can act with courage and hope, and be consoled during this stage of your loss, which at this time may seem endless. This is an opportunity to develop the power of transformation within yourself. Although perhaps at this point, you do not know how you are going to deal with today much less tomorrow, you have an internal power that will enable you to channel your loss into something positive-into something that will help you get out of the difficult situation you are now in. You have the power and ability to choose a positive course for your life regardless of your particular loss.

When one suffers a loss, one also has the option of a having a new life. I understand that facing the death of a loved one is not easy, because we miss that person every day. But remember that even if this person is not physically present, their memories will always live on. We can transform the relationship we had with that departed person, since the bonds of love will continue after they have passed from this life. Although these ties are invisible, they are as precious as gold. These bonds with our loved ones can inspire us to forge a life with a higher purpose and greater meaning. But to endure a loss of great magnitude we must be compassionate with ourselves and allow ourselves time to suffer and grieve. The tears and comforting conversations are necessary. There is no defined time for processing our grief. We each process grief at our own pace.

Entering into a process of transformation does not imply that it must be done hastily or immediately, because you are unique and some people take more time than others. But little by little, you can achieve this transformation according to your own personal situation and in your own time.

It is important to remember that we live in a culture characterized by hurry. Everything happens quickly, and we expect instantaneous results, and when they are not, we become impatient. But the bereavement process must not take place quickly, because if we rush we could fail. It is like a person who plays the piano and wants to become a great concert pianist without taking time to practice. Everything of consequence takes time, and everything takes hard work and effort, including the grieving process.

LIFE IS A SUCCESSION OF LOSSES

Courage, it would seem, is nothing less than the power to overcome danger, misfortune, fear, injustice, while continuing to affirm inwardly that life with all its sorrows is good; that everything is meaningful even if in a sense beyond our understanding; and that there is always tomorrow.

DOROTHY THOMPSON

Life is a succession of losses, and sometimes it is not easy to confront what we must live with, but we must realize that our life and the lives of others have significance, and that the meaning of life is the one we give to it.

Therefore, give yourself the value that you deserve and seize the opportunity to grow in the midst of this pain, and allow your wounds to heal. When you do this, you will feel satisfied and you will see life from another point of view. I sincerely wish you the best and hope that we can walk the long path of grief and healing together. But if you trip and fall, do not worry; we are here to help you up. And do not forget that it is human to fall, but within us lies the strength to get up again as well. Always keep in mind that

- After the darkness comes light....
- After the storm, calm....
- After the night, the day….
- At the end of the tunnel is light. This is the value of hope.

If what you have tried so far has not helped you with your pain, I ask you to give yourself another opportunity by continuing to read *Transform Your Loss*. You might find the peace and healing you need within these pages, especially by reading others' stories.

However, if you want to transform your loss, the first thing that will help is to change the way you think about it. Try to see your life through different eyes: with the eyes of appreciation, with the eyes of compassion, with the eyes of growth, and with the eyes of love. I think everything starts from here. First, in our love of ourselves and then in our love of others, as urged by Jesus of Nazareth in Mark 12, verse 3:

"Love thy neighbor as thyself."

WHAT IS LOSS?

People are like stained-glass windows. They sparkle and shine when the sun is out, but when the darkness sets in, their true beauty is revealed only if there is light from within.

ELIZABETH KÜBLER-ROSS

What does the following statement cause you to feel?

From the outside the whole world would have said we have an ideal life: A very successful career, two children and a wonderful stable marriage for more than twenty years. Recently, I realized my husband has maintained a romantic relationship with his co-worker for more than two years and I feel completely adrift. I feel betrayed and angry....I do not know whether to pretend that nothing has happened or face it....I do not want go through a divorce.

What about this one?

A month ago my daughter Josefina was diagnosed with a brain tumor. Why did this happen? She is a sweet girl of barely twelve years of age. She is only beginning her life. How unfair life can be? It should have been me who has the tumor and not her. At first she only suffered severe headaches and I wished that was all it was ..... Why does God not hear my prayers?

And how does this situation feel to you?

Yesterday was the first anniversary of the death of my mother. Although I have managed to continue with my life this year and I feel her loving presence always with me, yesterday was different. I relived the pain of the first moments. I regret that I have regressed in my grief process. Could it be that I will never surpass this stage?

You may find that the previous expressions aroused your own personal feelings, as perhaps you have gone though some of these situations, or know someone very close to you who has. Although these experiences are different in nature, they all have something in common: All represent a loss. But what exactly is a loss?

We experience a sense of loss when something or someone that belonged to us and was of great value has been taken from our lives, leaving in their place a void that we are sometimes unable to fill. This emptiness leaves us baffled, stunned, and with doubts about the next steps on our path. Loss is an experience of our own human condition. It is not really alien to us, because we experience it from a young age even though we do not realize it.

Judith Viorst, in her book Necessary Losses,[3] assures us that losses are inevitable and even necessary in our lives, as this is one way to gain maturity and a greater wisdom. Viorst states that the first loss that we experience is at birth, when we are separated from the body of our mother. Viorst also gives the example of a child losing their first tooth. Imagine for a moment this situation: the child suffers a loss (the tooth) and the parent consoles them by suggesting they put it under their pillow for the Tooth Fairy to take, who will leave a little gift. This parent gives hope to the child with the promise that the Tooth Fairy will bring a present as consolation for losing their tooth.

Sometimes what seems like a small loss to an adult can be very painful for a child. They are ashamed to walk around with a gap in their teeth and they try not to laugh so that people do not notice. Now, as adults we can analyze this loss, and although it may seem insignificant to us, for that young child it was a very big loss. But they get through it and transform it into a moment of growth. We can also take as an example the change that we suffer going from childhood to puberty. We lose the innocence of being children, but we enter a new stage in our lives that will lead us to maturity.

Each of us throughout life has been faced with such losses, and we have overcome them and continued our growth as individuals. At the same time, misfortunes occur that cause us such great pain that they seem like a wave that drags us to the bottom of the sea. Then exhausted, we are thrust back on the shore, only to be dragged into the deep again. To experience the pain of loss sometimes has extremes; like an ocean tide, sometimes it is high, sometimes it is low. So is the flow of our emotions; they are never constant. However, the challenge is to appreciate the high tide and take advantage of it to the fullest. Let's not choose to stay at low tide. Our loss, no matter how painful or difficult, is an opportunity to grow and develop spiritually. Let's not squander it, but draw strength from our being, which has an infinite potential for resistance.

This capacity for survival and transformation I have seen in a very special form in the elderly whom I visit at a care center. Every two weeks we meet, and I run a support group, or rather a growth group, for them. I say "growth" because these women who range from sixty-five to one hundred and three are an example of strength, as they continue to live to the fullest, despite all the suffering they have experienced in their lives, and the physical limitations that they now face. When they share their stories, I realize how much they love life and have the ability to continue to grow spiritually. Take the example of Luisa, who is eighty-five, and tells us:

> Each day that dawns I give thanks for being alive....I know that in life there are valleys and mountains, but in the mountains I take the strength to get out of the valleys. Therefore, when we find ourselves in these valleys, let us not forget that we are also able to climb the mountains, especially when dealing with situations in life that shake us and move the ground beneath us, as in the case of facing an illness; the loss of a stable job; going through a divorce; leaving our homeland, and worst of all, losing a loved one.

A MOMENT OF REFLECTION

And what about you? What loss are you facing? I invite you to take a break, go into your inner self, and answer the following questions, jotting down your answers in your notebook or journal to help you reflect on their meaning.

- What has been the greatest loss you have suffered?
- How much time has already passed?
- How did it happen?
- How did you realize your loss?
- How did you react?
- Who was present?
- What was your physical reaction?
- What was your emotional reaction?
- What was your spiritual /religious reaction?
- Are there any areas in your life that have not yet healed?
- How are you coping with the loss?
- Have you learned anything from this loss?

We have already said that although these losses seem different to us in the first instance, they all have something in common: they involve the grieving process. For some, the process is more bearable than others, because it is influenced by the type of loss, our personality, our history of losses, and even our religious and/or spiritual beliefs. In any case, what makes us experience such great pain is our attachment to or connection with that person or circumstance. Never forget that our life has meaning and sometimes through a loss, one finds that meaning.

When one feels the pain of a loss, one looks for consolation. This can be found in different ways: in religious or spiritual practices; in a confidant(e) who listens to us and does not judge us; in grief counseling; in support groups; writing in a journal; looking through photos; visiting the cemetery or simply taking a stroll along a beach.

In the final part of the book I offer *The Eleven Principles of Transformation*^{tm} which will give you the tools to change these painful moments into an opportunity for personal evolution, because, if we learn to accept the presence of sorrow or grief, we can assess what is really important in our lives and even have an opportunity to grow spiritually. It is very likely that you are in the midst of many different emotions at the moment: you may be feeling pain, frustration, fear, depression, or even hopelessness all at the same time. But from the moment you picked up this book and wanted to know how people in similar situations were able to transform their loss, you were demonstrating that you wanted to move on. You were suggesting that you wanted to put all your effort into continuing with the precious gift of life.

This book is only a means for providing you with some hope. It is like a rope suspended from a mountain to help you, little by little, climb the steep slope out of the pain and grief of your loss. With every step that you take, you will build self-confidence. Hope in the future will return, and the moment will arrive when you will be able to overcome the grieving stage. The time will come when you will find meaning and direction that will help you transform your loss.

I have found the work of the Psychologist Sameet M. Kumar very relevant to the topic of loss, since he has specialized in grief and works with cancer patients. Kumar applies Buddhist principles to deal with loss and the process of grief.[4] One principle that dominates this philosophy and can be very useful in dealing with loss and life transitions is that nothing is permanent, that everything is in a continually changing process. Kumar believes it is important to try to live a life of compassion and respect.

While we have the opportunity to work conscientiously on our grief, we will transform it into an opportunity for growth through self-compassion. If we can accept the notion of impermanence, we will realize that our affliction will undergo a process of change as it is not permanent or constant. To arrive at this belief and the ability to overcome the pain of loss is what will give us the necessary tools to take control of our lives and our suffering. Therefore, when undertaking the journey through our time of grief we have two options. The first is to deny our situation in every moment and make our life miserable, and the second is to take each loss as an opportunity to learn about our own existence and about what is really important in our lives.

Sometimes, it is after a loss that we realize our most important values and set our priorities. Let us keep in mind, that when faced with a loss, just wanting to recover does not work, especially if we have not taken the time to adapt to our new situation and accept within ourselves that something has changed. While it is true that with time the pain of our loss decreases, our life is marked by the loss, and what we must try to learn is to live with our new reality instead of pretending that every bit of our loss will disappear with the passing of time. That is why, as so well stated by the thanatologist Kenneth Doka, it is better to use the word "ameliorate" instead of "heal."[5] Although many mourners choose to use the word heal to describe their personal need, mourning a loss does not mean you are ill. Rather it means that life as you know it has changed and requires taking time out to reflect on your grief and to find your deepest inner strength, although you may not believe you have any at this time. It often becomes evident that we tap our spiritual strength only when we feel the need to face moments of pain and despair. So, first try to spend a few minutes reflecting on the following question:

> Have you ever taken the time to think about your life when everything is going tremendously well and you are in a constant state of joy?

If you have, I congratulate you, because you are one of the few people who has. Usually we take time to ponder our life and evaluate our immediate issues when something distresses us or shakes us to our foundation. It is then that we recognize that not everything in our life is wonderful and that we have had problems, injuries, and losses along the way. Facing a loss or a significant challenge tends to force us to refocus our priorities and goals. Keep in mind that these are all experiences that make us who we are and that it is necessary to re-direct our energy to continue our path with a new perspective and hope. The bottom line is to overcome the affliction that the loss creates and find hope and consolation.

In the next section I address affliction, the types of grief, and the manifestations that occur in this process.

I will introduce you to certain kinds of losses, as there are many, including intangible ones such as the loss of hope, trust or enthusiasm. But because it is impossible to dwell on all of them, I will limit them to the death of a loved one, loss from divorce, and loss of a job.

LOSS FROM THE DEATH OF A LOVED ONE

Love is eternal ... Death does not separate the one who loves from their loved one.

KAHLIL GIBRAN

We suffer the loss of a loved one when someone whom we love is no longer with us. When we need to talk to them or hug them, it grieves us deeply to realize they are not physically close by. But let's not forget that love is everlasting. Consider the beautiful words of Luisa, who recently lost her mother:

It is terribly painful to have someone die, but if we accept this law, it should not be so painful. It is very natural that we are often sad and tearful and that there are times when passion carries us and we shout out ugly words and confess doubt and atheism towards God....Recently my sadness increased on her birthday. I remembered, I cried, and in the end I knew that this was a natural reaction because love never dies, but she (my

mother) had her time and now is there, surrounded
by love.

As Luisa said, love is in our hearts and the memory of our
loved one will stay with us forever.

While the person is no longer with us physically, they will
remain emotionally and spiritually in our heart and soul.
Although I lost my father thirty-six years ago, his love, advice
and guidance remain in my soul. So do not think that by losing
your beloved one you will forget them at some point. You will
learn to live without their physical presence and you will learn
to move through life without them, but their memory and love
will always be present to you.

After a loss, our life is not the same; it is changed. We can
fall into an abyss and be immersed indefinitely in our pain and
anguish, or we can be reborn with a feeling of hope and
spiritual growth through the help of others and by our own
inner strength. As humans we are not exempt from the harsh
reality of loss, but through this guide, I hope to give you
encouragement and hope in your situation, and, at the same
time, enable you to understand that you are not alone in your
pain.

In this context we refer to the loss of someone dear. Then
we feel an immense emptiness inside. It is a hollow feeling
that nothing and no one can fill. I felt that emptiness after my
father died when I was only twelve, and I imagine you are
feeling this too. When we lose a loved one we feel that we
lose a part of ourselves, our family identity, albeit distant,
close, or friendly. But let us not forget that although our

beloved is not with us physically, they will continue to exist forever in our hearts. Despite the passing of so much time, I still keep a flame of love alight in my heart for my father, and I know that it will never go out. It is precisely this flame that has inspired the transformation of my life and has enabled me to accomplish many of my dreams, including the power to complete my studies and prepare myself to help others, who, like me, have had to cope with grief or loss. This was my first encounter with death, and I suddenly understood that our loved ones are not immortal or timeless, and therefore we must cherish and love them as long as we have them with us.

As the adage says, "Everything passes," but when referring to the loss of a loved one, I prefer to say "things gets better" because the memories always remain in our hearts.

As many of us know, death is often very difficult to deal with. One of the most painful experiences is the loss of a loved one by a violent or tragic death, either through suicide, a crime, or an airplane or car accident. Perhaps the worst is the death of a child.

As Laura, who lost her husband in a plane crash, tells us:

One of my close friends told me on one of those long days of waiting:

"I see you are upset, let's go out."

And against all expectations of how a widow should behave, I went with two of my friends for a drink at a small bar close to my house. There, I remember I told them:

"I feel as though this is cutting my heart with a razor blade, I have never felt such pain in my heart or in my soul..."

If we lose someone close, a spouse, a parent, or a work colleague, we become afraid; we do not know what to do. We are conditioned to think that we and our loved ones are immortal, that change does not exist and that life, as we know it, is always the same. What scares us is what we do not know. And yet what we do know will cause us even more pain. But this void, which is not entirely filled over time, gradually becomes more bearable. The grief caused by the death of a loved one is regarded as the greatest grief, and is an unavoidable and difficult process. Yet we all have to go through it at a certain point in our life. This process carries an adjustment period, which often involves acute periods of sadness, from which we think we cannot move forward. But although these moments are to be expected, we must try not to remain in our grief for an excessively long time, even though we understand that it is part of the mourning process. Little by little you will recover your energy and concentration. You will re-integrate your daily activities and you will resume your normal social activities. While this emptiness in your life from the death of you loved one may not be entirely filled over time, it gradually becomes more bearable. At least I hope that within these pages you will find the means to experience the peace and comfort that you need. But do not expect your pain to go away completely since that is highly unlikely. But be assured that the pain *will* decrease and transform.

The episodes of intense and deep pain from your loss will gradually go away, but don't think that the pain will disappear by itself. The more you try to ignore it, the more it will manifest itself. The way we experience life is inevitably a reflection of our nature. Remember that we live from the inside out. What we feel inside is what we project to the outside. When we suffer an injury, the wound heals from the inside out, and it closes and forms a scar. Although the wound of your loss may no longer be open, the scar is a reminder of the wound. Our scar will not hurt as much as when the wound was new, but our psyche is deeply wounded, and from time to time, as Silvia, a woman of sixty-five, who lost her daughter of twenty due to a cerebral aneurysm, has said:

> The scar no longer hurts like an open wound,
> but yes, occasionally when it is cold, it annoys us
> and it is sensitive....

In the same way, the loss that we think has healed will be felt again at certain times, such as on anniversaries and birthdays. But little by little, with time, it becomes more bearable. Losing a loved one usually makes us think of how much we miss them and how empty our life is without their presence, to such an extent that we might even forget the good times we shared with them. Why can't we remember the happy moments we had with that person instead? Let me suggest how. Take time to reflect on these occasions and write down what comes to mind.

A MOMENT OF REFLECTION

Remember one of the following occasions you shared with your loved one (writing them down is another way to preserve them):

A special birthday
A time that made you feel proud
An unforgettable holiday
A funny situation

Remember that you shared some wonderful moments with your loved one. Recollect them and see how your heart fills with wonderful feelings to know that you had these times with that person, and realize that these feelings and memories will live with you forever.

LOSS FROM A DIVORCE

When we split up because of a divorce, we separate from the loved one with whom we had hoped to share the rest of our life. When the relationship dies, one often feels lost or without direction. This is a death that many go through in life. The death of a marriage is very difficult for many to cope with because, generally, when you first contemplate marriage, you assume it is for life. Even if it lasted only a few years, a failed marriage is a source of disappointment and loss. Sure, there are cases where some can be happy having gotten divorced, as my friend Benjamin told me. He believes that divorce is not always synonymous with loss. And this is true.

In many cases it is not a devastating loss, but in most cases, all of a sudden finding oneself not being part of a couple hits us hard and sometimes we ask,

- How was I wrong?
- What mistake did I make?
- Could I have done something different?
- How did I not realize what was happening before?

To go through a divorce, you close a chapter in your life, but it does not end your life. In front of you is a path that you can walk down with strength and hope.

If you feel any bitterness in your soul, let it go. It is not healthy to keep negative feelings inside. If you think you are doing harm to your former spouse, you are wrong. The person you are doing harm to is really yourself. Therefore, forgive and go on with your life.

There are many challenges that many women face when confronted with a divorce. For example, perhaps you are a woman who while you were married was terrified to confront life, but now that you are divorced you will have to. At first, it seems impossible for you to make decisions or to carry out plans and projects on your own initiative. But if you commit yourself to doing them on your own, you can take small steps every day until you achieve certain goals. The pain and loneliness can instill fear and doubts about your ability to meet the future. This fear could make you use behaviors that do not help; it can endlessly distract you with things that ultimately leave you empty: alcohol, drugs, or unhealthy relationships that can confuse you or harm you even more.

You might be missing your ex-spouse, and his or her help to do certain household tasks or solve problems that perhaps for convenience or out of habit ended up being his or her responsibility. Indeed, you may have been completely dependent on your husband or wife.

Take the example of Carolina, who during her twelve years of marriage never took care of the household expenses. Her husband paid everything, from the electric bill to the property taxes. She did not even know how much their monthly home maintenance costs were. From the start, when the divorce had been finalized, she had to take care of her home, but she felt completely lost. Bills began to accumulate, and there came a time when she was unable to balance her budget between taking care of her children, her job, the divorce proceedings, school, and the household. But because she wanted to take control of her life and be a good example for her children, she took classes in organization and time management. She managed to change her situation and maintain a meaningful, productive life.

Maria, at seventy-eight, after fifty years of marriage, decided to get a divorce. Above all, one could ask, what was it that had prompted her to terminate a marriage after many so years? It was virtually a lifetime for Maria, but she was tired of suffering from both physical and emotional abuse, and leading a life without meaning. With her divorce, Maria felt liberated and re-born as she was released from a prolonged emotional burden.

At the age of seventy-two Maria attended a university to learn a profession that had always attracted her: teaching. She graduated with high honors and today is dedicated to providing classes to adults living alone.

I recommend that you not avoid facing your feelings when confronted with a divorce. You do not have to assume the role of a strong, tough person, or behave as if nothing has happened. If you feel anger or feel yourself holding a grudge, let it go. Ignoring these feelings will not help and will make them worse. Remember that some days will be better than others. The grieving process is like a roller coaster, with ups and downs. When facing a divorce, it is difficult to accept that it has happened. For example, you may realize that your partner was unfaithful. You might even pretend that it did not happen; it had to have been a mistake, but...do not fool yourself. If it happened, accept it. Take the necessary steps and move on. If you stay submerged in the pain and bitterness, the only person who will suffer is you.

Another common emotion in a divorce is fear of the future. As Carla confessed to me, she had depended financially on her husband for years because she had been exclusively devoted to caring for their children. So, after eight years of marriage and two young children, she faced seeking work and starting a new life as a single mother. She was afraid of not being able to find a job. What could she do?

I advised her to prepare herself, take some courses, and put her fear aside. It is normal to be afraid, but what we must not do is let it control us, or worse, freeze us up. We can channel this fear in a positive way, like an engine that drives us to act and take the loss as a challenge, to prove we are able to act positively and to rebuild our lives. By recognizing that we are facing the death of our marriage, we can answer the following questions:

- What do others think of me?
- What does my future hold?
- How will I meet someone worthwhile?
- How will the divorce affect our children?

Do not despair; it is normal to ask these questions. You will find the answers when you are able to create a new life, full of possibilities and opportunities. It is at the beginning when we face more challenges that we may be shaking. Take, for example, a woman who just got divorced and finds herself alone with responsibilities which, for convenience or comfort, she had not had to deal with before. Do you find yourself in that situation? Do you feel suddenly inept? It is likely that you can weather the insecurity and fear, especially if your ex-spouse constantly told you that you were incapable. On the other hand, if you start to regret the divorce, you may even start to fantasize about getting back with your husband or wife and that everything will be as before. Do not delude yourself; it is time to accept your new situation: you are a divorcee and must move forward. If you are a man who is facing life alone, it will be the same. Maybe you used to arrive at home and have the food prepared and everything in order. Seeing that all this has changed, you may yearn for the "good" old days and would like to see everything as it was before. This is natural. As the saying goes, "it is better to stay with what we know," even suffering, than embark on new ventures.

But please remember how much it took to reach your decision to get a divorce, and that it may have been beneficial in some way to one or both of you. Take action, accept your new situation, and move on. Remember, you have the power within you!

Loss of a Job

When we start a new job, it fills us with joy and excitement, because we think we have security for the present and hope for the future. We feel confident that when we are older we will be able to count on a retirement plan and benefits, which will help us to live comfortably in our old age. But...what if we lose this security? We are living in a time when a jobs not as secure as before. We don't have the same security that our parents or grandparents had. Now, in the blink of an eye, we can lose a job that we have worked at for years. What can we do about it? In addition to the material benefits, the tasks that we fulfill in our work are of great importance to our personal value and self-esteem. Therefore, such a loss can cause us a great deal of anxiety and stress. When we lose a job, we often go through a grieving process, seeing that what belonged to us and what we were proud of, no longer exists. The loss of a job has many implications; it can affect our financial security as well as our personal relationships.

Take for example Carlos, who after working for a food producing company for fifteen years, received two weeks' notice. This was because the company was going through a reorganization phase and they had to reduce their staff. What do you think Carlos' reaction was?

Initially he was total astonished and in denial. It was impossible for him, as he had always been such a good worker, and now, he was being dismissed from his job, without a valid reason. He thought of his pension, his plans for the future. Similarly, he admitted he was dumbfounded that he and his family would not have health insurance. Upon arriving home, he decided not to share his news with Roxana, his wife of ten years. He hoped that his boss would call him in to tell him his job was still waiting for him. Every day Carlos left the house pretending he was going to the office, and each night he took refuge in getting drunk to avoid having to confront Roxana.

After a month in this situation, and without the possibility of contributing money to the household, he finally accepted the reality that he was not going to be called back to work, and decided to confess to his wife. If he had shared his job loss with his wife from the beginning, he might have had her much-needed support. He could have saved himself many days of anguish and anxiety, as well as avoided the guilt of deceiving his wife and using alcohol to deal with his loss.

Or you may be going through what we call anticipated loss. This happens when you hear rumors that your company is downsizing or has internal problems, and you fear losing your job. Although there has been no loss yet, you could be experiencing anxiety and unease in advance of the possibility of a job loss. If so, do not be taken by surprise. Assess the situation and your options. If you recently lost your job and you feel devastated, accept your new situation, express your thoughts and feelings to your spouse and family, and decide on the appropriate action to take. Remember that how to deal with this transition is up to you. Evaluate other possibilities. A job loss can be traumatic, but less so if you seek support and help with processing this loss.

If you have lost your job, or are anticipating such a loss, remember that in the last part of this book I will present you with the necessary tools to transform your loss. Read each principle and apply it. You will see that what now appears to be a devastating loss can be an opportunity for personal growth and improvement. If you have already lost your job, I recommend that you evaluate your situation by doing the following exercise.

A MOMENT OF REFLECTION

- How long ago did you lose your job?
- What happened?
- What was your reaction?
- Did you share it with your family?
- What are your fears?

The period of confrontation of a loss is a time in our lives when we experience a lot of confusion and vulnerability. I especially recommend that you not take important decisions in the early days after your job loss, as you can act impulsively, and you may regret your decision. Give yourself a reasonable time and then re-evaluate to see if this decision is what you want.

Once our life has been touched by loss, it changes us. But within each of us lies the ability to transform this loss into something meaningful. Once you experience a metamorphosis of your pain and suffering over time, you will look back with the satisfaction of having weathered the loss and met the challenge at a difficult stage of your life.

WHAT IS GRIEF?

To spare oneself from grief at all cost can be achieved only at the price of total detachment, which excludes the ability to experience happiness.

ERICH FROMM

G rief is the natural reaction we experience when we suffer a significant loss in our lives. The term was introduced in his essay *Mourning and Melancholia* by psychoanalyst Sigmund Freud, who describes it as "(...) a reaction to the loss of a loved one or an abstraction that replaces them, such as our homeland, freedom, or an ideal."[6] According to this definition we can then apply it to different types of situations that cause us a sense of loss and therefore produce suffering. The time that one lives after a loss generally is known as a "time of mourning." When people suffer a loss they say they are "mourning" which expresses the suffering for something or someone that was lost or something that was not realized. But in terms of loss, mourning is necessary in this process, because it is when we really process the deep pain that afflicts us as we can paralyze ourselves if we do not live consciously.

The way to express grief differs between people, as each of us has our own story and way to process the grief. Therefore, it doesn't make sense to judge others by basing their grieving process on our own reality. Surely you have heard the following comments many times:

- *Is this the widow? But she is not even crying....You can tell she did not really love him.*
- *Although she said she was suffering through her divorce I see that she is constantly going out...*
- *He says he misses his homeland, but I never hear him talk about it...*

We all have heard comments like this over and over throughout our lives. Why? Because we are used to seeing life from our perspective, not from that of others. How can we know whether this widow when she arrives home does not collapse in sorrow? Does the newly divorced woman need to see a friendship as a point of support? What if the immigrant prefers not to talk about their country because they left their mother and suffer every time they think about her?

Therefore, let us not forget that each person's grief is individual and that our grief is our own and nobody else's and that furthermore, it can be experienced in different ways:

- Physically
- Spiritually
- Emotionally
- Socially

In our society we tend to think that we only show our grief emotionally, as we cry for a loved one who died or when we go through a divorce or another great loss. But what if we feel a pain in our chest from what we are experiencing? And how about that child who has just lost their pet and complains of terrible stomach pain but does not know what is causing it? This happens because sometimes the emotional pain is so strong that we manifest it somatically, and it reflects badly on our physical body, when, in fact, what is suffering is the soul. One of the best ways to prevent this from occurring is to communicate, share our feelings, not keep them inside.

We have to feel the freedom to express our sadness and the pain in our heart. At the end of the section we will visit each of these dimensions so that you have the opportunity to evaluate your own situation. The duration and intensity of grief is also individual, and each person processes it according to their personal situation, their history of loss, and the meaning of the loss in their life. For example, in the case of the loss of a loved one or a divorce, we have to take into account what our relationship was with that person who is no longer with us—if our relationship was loving or conflictive, if we had established a pattern of co-dependence, or if we were fully independent. These aspects of the relationship influence how we feel towards this loss and how we will work to recover from the grief. But for now I want to delve a little more into the grief process, and we will start with the death of a loved because it is particularly difficult to process, and I always like to give it the value it deserves. I do not want to say that other losses are not painful, but the process of grief during the loss of a loved one, including rituals, is necessarily different.

GRIEVING THE DEATH OF A LOVED ONE

Death, like any loss, makes us mourners and dumps us on the highway called grief. Grief spins us to and fro, but also invites us to claim our sorrow and share our stories and memories. We all follow our own pathways, hopefully with the care and support of others. And the journey begins, inch by inch, moment by moment, feeling after feeling as we transform from the sadness of loss to the comfort of remembering.

RICHARD GILBERT

The pain we feel when we experience the death of a loved one can be so devastating that it seems impossible to live without them. That is what I felt with the death of my father. It was as though my life was suddenly meaningless, that there was no reason to continue. I was without water standing in a desert, hopeless, completely lost. But my mother gave me strength and helped me find my bearings since, a month after losing her husband (my father), she lost her beloved mother. I cannot describe the pain of the losses she suffered in just one month, by losing two of her most beloved family members. But her faith and her commitment to carrying on the legacy of my father drove her to transform this loss into an opportunity for growth, both personally and spiritually. I do not deny that I saw her cry a lot, but within her was this willingness to immortalize the memory of my father...and she succeeded. Her example showed me that within us is the source of inspiration, the tenacity to continue, and the will that our life is too precious to let it go. That in the terrible times after a loss, we can tremble but not collapse, and that our life is so precious but only we have the chance to live it.

One of the questions that people ask over and over again is, "How am I going to experience the grief?"

And although one can form an idea of how to react, it is impossible to know with certainty. When we experience the loss of a loved one, we might respond by shouting, crying, or being silent. We can share it with someone or be silent. We can write our thoughts in a diary or turn to our religious beliefs. All these reactions are possible and necessary. Members of the same family can experience different types of reactions. Take for example the case of Susana, who lost her eight-year-old son in an automobile accident. Realizing the terrible accident, it was she who, in the midst of her grief, planned the religious service and the funeral. Juan, the father of the child, did not even attend the wake. He could not stop crying and feeling guilty for not having acted "as the man of the house."

We must be aware that as human beings we are different and, therefore, manifest grief in our own unique way. We cannot compare ourselves with others and vice versa. For example, we have René, who for a space of three years provided bedside care for his mother, who was suffering from Alzheimer's disease. René devoted his heart and soul to his mother, and when she died he found he had no comfort. Being "the man of the family," according to the rules of society, he did not expect to cry so much, because that is "something women do." But René expressed his grief by crying uncontrollably, while Sara, his little sister, was the one who took charge of the funeral arrangements, with calm precision.

In the previous example, we could see how two siblings expressed grief quite differently; one "intuitively" or "emotionally," a female attribute, and the other, instrumentally, or by "taking action," a male attribute. But in reality, it does not always happen this way, and this is one of the reasons why you should not presume to judge a person's reaction to loss or to how they will express their grief.[7]

BONDS OF CONTINUATION

In recent years much has been written about the bonds of continuation and the value they evoke in our loved ones. It used to be said that an object could represent a way of not letting go, but now that way of thinking has been reversed given that the same object has a sense of presence and company.

This reminds me precisely of a conversation I had with Gabriel. He told me that he still kept the last wallet that his uncle used, as well as his watches. He thought that his house was like a museum but, in reality, the objects represented memories of his loved one.

This is something beautiful, and it is a kind of legacy. But do not confuse this kind of memorabilia or significant objects with the obsessive need to have an object that belonged to someone else and then not be able to let go of it, thinking that the person will return or that the objects represent the deceased. This is different because it can develop into something compulsive. But we can keep an object such as a photo, a pendant, or something that belonged to the deceased only as a symbol or a way to maintain love and the memories alive in our hearts. Particularly through rituals these objects can be very meaningful. There will be more on rituals in the section on transformation.

HOW DO WE EXPERIENCE GRIEF?

What is grief exactly? Is it the same for everyone? When we suffer a loss it is normal that we ask a series of questions, because our reactions can be diverse and confusing. We might ask, "Why do I feel like a spear is penetrating my stomach, but it is impossible for me to cry? Is this normal?"

Carolina, a woman dominated by the sorrow of having lost her job, asked me,

"Why if the discomfort is in my heart do I feel a profound stomachache?"

"Well," I answered, "because grief can be manifested in several ways, from a physical ailment to emotional problems."

So I encouraged her to write a list of all the emotions she was experiencing. At first it was difficult for her to identify exactly what she was feeling and what she was thinking. But eventually, after writing the list, she realized that many of her ailments were caused by controlled or unexpressed emotions.

The following months she kept a journal in which she wrote about her feelings whenever someone asked her about work or when she was looking in the classified ads of a newspaper for a job. She came to realize that her predominant feeling was fear.

We did a series of visualization exercises to help her release her fear, and shortly afterwards she found a job that gave her great satisfaction. The important thing was that she connected with her inner self.

Grief is a process that is not stable or linear. It is like a roller coaster; it has its ups and downs, sometimes sharp, sometimes less so, but never constant. It is impossible to impose a time limit on our affliction, but most people faced with grief wonder how long it can last, and the truth is that it all depends on how much the person is willing to work on their grief (Baldwin, 2004).

However, even when one thinks that they have passed the most difficult stage, something can evoke the image of the missing person or events linked to them, and they can regress into suffering. Such situations are often triggered by anniversaries, birthdays, or special dates that can re-pierce the soul, and evoke the original pain. We permit our hearts to experience the feelings and we re-live them. We cannot suppress them. They are like a big wave. As when we see a tsunami, we can go with it, flee from it, or let ourselves be taken by it. Of the three possibilities, the appropriate one is to let the wave take us to the shore, go with it. It is the same with the pain, it is better to let it carry us with it, not to fight against it or try to confront it, much less escape from it. Let us feel the depth of the experience and go deeper into it and continue on our path.

Manuel, a twenty-one-year-old, remembers when he lost his grandfather. Upon learning that he had died, Manuel became very stressed due to the surging pain and the great emptiness he felt. But even so, he believes that people should not live in suffering for their loved ones, because they do not want to see us that way. When they are no longer with us, it is not that they disappear from our life altogether; we always have the memories, and sometimes it is these memories that inspire us to keep on going. I wish to clarify that we should always make this observation regarding our memories of a departed person. We cannot live through memories, but need to integrate them into our "new" daily lives. When we lose somebody or something, we have to adjust to our new world.

One of the essential steps for carrying out the transformation of our loss is to find out what sense it makes.

- What significance does your loss hold?
- What meaning do you find?
- What helped you the most to confront your loss?
- What helped you the least to confront your loss?
- What advice would you give to someone who is facing the same kind of loss?

We will return to the process of searching for meaning in your loss and rebuilding your life in the last section, where you will find *The Eleven Principles of Transformation*^{tm}.

In the following statements, what do you think does or does not help the most during the grieving process?

- To just keep going.
- Everything has its time.
- Time heals everything.
- They are with God.
- Such is life.
- Do not cry so much.
- It is time to feel better.
- You cannot talk only about this.

I suggest that you never compare yourself to others or listen to comments that people say, though they have the best of intentions of giving you encouragement.

The following expressions are examples of what we might hear when we are in mourning:

- But you are still young; you can re-marry (In the case of widows or divorcees).
- At least you enjoyed a long time with your mother (In the case of the death of an elderly mother).
- You are young, you can have another child! (In the case of the loss of a child).
- Maybe this is the opportunity you need to advance in your career (In the case of loss of your job).
- At least you were able to get out! (In the loss of a homeland).

- Why are you crying? It was only an animal! (In the loss of a pet).
- If you pray with fervor, God will cure you! (In the case of a disease).

The previous expressions tend to be said with good intentions. Often people do not know what to say and seek to encourage in the only way they know how, including, in most cases, these comments which come from the discomfort of the friend or relative when confronting the grieving person. If you feel that what they say bothers you, and you trust the person, you can let them know there is a better way to help.

GRIEF: TYPES AND MANIFESTATIONS

There are three types of grief: anticipated, sudden and complicated.

Is there any difference between a sudden loss and an anticipated loss? Let me analyze this below. Although both are losses, the manifestations of grief can sometimes be different.

ANTICIPATED GRIEF

Anticipated grief is produced when we are expecting something to happen that we know will hurt us badly. We are aware that we are going to suffer a loss. Although we think that a loss is always the same, it is not, especially when one is prepared for it, compared with when it happens suddenly. Helen Fitzgerald, a pioneer in thanatology, expressed in her book *The Mourning Handbook,* how she experienced anticipated grief when she learned that her husband was suffering from terminal brain cancer. Helen confessed that this situation helped her prepare for the inevitable situation she would have to live with. Similarly, this news gave her the chance to say goodbye to her husband. But this can only be beneficial if, as she says,

"You accept the Doctor's prognosis and internalize what is happening"[8].

Rosaura, who faced a divorce, told me that she was suffering from anticipated grief, because she knew beforehand that the situation would be difficult in the months ahead.

In the case of a job, we can experience grief when we receive a dismissal notice at work that will be carried out in the coming weeks, or when planning to leave our homeland to seek new horizons. We leave our homeland with enthusiasm, awaiting our new life, but at the same time we leave behind our family, friends and traditions. This can cause us great sorrow and produce a sense of anticipated mourning.

A MOMENT OF REFLECTION

- Are you confronting a possible loss?
- What kind of loss?
- What do you feel when thinking about this?
- How do you imagine life when facing this loss?
- How is your current behavior influenced?
- How do you imagine your life will be after going through the loss?
- Is there anything you can do about it?

SUDDEN GRIEF

This type of grief, because it occurs unexpectedly, causes us great pain. This is the case of a sudden death, loss of a home as a result of a natural disaster, a terrorist attack, or a dismissal from a job without notice. Many psychologists say that this kind of sudden loss can cause what is known as "complicated mourning" because the person has no time to process or absorb the loss over a period of time. It is worse when, in addition, the loss is a tragic one. Sudden death surprises us even though we know that an illness exists.

I present the case of José who suffered a tremendous shock when he realized that his best friend from childhood had died. José was aware that his friend was suffering from cancer and that he had difficult times in the hospital, but death occurred suddenly because his friend was supposedly in remission.

The reaction caused by a sudden death can manifest itself in different ways. I remember Carla who, just before making a presentation at work, received the news that her brother had died in a car accident. Her reaction was total shock. She flatly refused to accept the reality and continued with her presentation. It was not until a couple of hours later when her husband picked her up at work to take her to the funeral home that Carla internalized her brother's death, but even so she was unable to cry. In front of her brother's casket was when her childhood memories suddenly hit her and she realized that she would not see him anymore. After a stifled cry she collapsed, unconscious. After several months of counseling and attending support groups, Carla was able to return to her job, as during this difficult time she had identified her place of work as the source of pain and suffering.

A MOMENT OF REFLECTION

- Have you lost someone suddenly?
- What happened?
- How did you hear?

- Was there anything left unsaid?

In the following lines write what you would have liked to tell that person:

_____

_____

_____

_____

COMPLICATED GRIEF

Facing a very difficult loss, like the death of a loved one, always causes us tremendous shock. But there are situations in which the grieving process can be more complicated and severe. Although in all situations there are several variables, these are some of the causes of complicated grief:

- Sudden death from homicide, suicide, or trauma
- The death of a child
- A history of complicated loss
- A long and abusive divorce

According to the recognized thanatologist Theresa Rando, "in all forms of complicated grief, there is a desire to do several things: deny and suppress or eliminate the element of grief and understand the implications for the bereaved; or refusing to let the loved one go."[9]

Facing the loss can present us with serious problems in functioning in life, such as denying that anything has happened, remaining stagnant, or getting involved in destructive activities, such as alcohol abuse or the use of drugs. If this is your first experience of grief, I advise you to find help from your family, friends, and/or support groups. If you continue to maintain negative behavior, to the point of wanting to stop living, I advise you to find professional help, either from your doctor, a therapist, or your spiritual guide. It is imperative that you succeed in getting out of this cycle and continue with the grieving process. I suggest you respond to the following questions to evaluate what you are feeling. If you answer any of them positively, I suggest you look for help, and you will see that you can move forward in your grief and rebuild your life.

- Do you feel stuck in your grieving process?
- Do you deny having suffered a loss?
- Do you resort to alcohol or drugs to deal with your loss?
- Do you have self destructive thoughts?

MANIFESTATIONS OF GRIEF

A t the beginning of the chapter we saw that grief can be manifested in different ways. With each of these manifestations, let's evaluate how you have experienced your grief. If you take the time to see what you have felt, you can delve further into your process and understand how you have externalized it. We already said that the grieving process can manifest itself in different ways: physically, emotionally, socially, spiritually, and mentally. But how do we differentiate these types of manifestations?

We will begin with the physical. We sometimes feel that we have a headache or stomach ache, or we do not know why we feel incredibly tired, but simply we have internalized our grief, and we somatically reflect what we have lost. I suggest to you that at the end of this section, at the *Moment of Reflection*, you evaluate the type of symptoms or manifestations that you are going through in your grieving process.

On the other hand, let us not forget that the emotional side has a big influence on our physical condition. Emotions can come to dominate so much of our existence they could become our worst enemy. We, ourselves, can increase the negative feelings that harm us, and instead of moving forward, our own emotions can betray us. That is why it is important to be aware that this can happen, so as to identify the situation and take measures to counteract them.

At the end of the section, you will also find a list of emotions. I suggest that you examine them all and then express which of them you associate with. Write down why you feel these emotions; identify their origin and how you can transmute the negative emotion into an emotion that restores your life. We must live the pain, not suppress it. We must never assume that all is well. I remember a very popular book by Thomas A. Harris: *I'm Okay, You're Okay.* We could always ask ourselves whether we are really OK! We are so conditioned to not externalize our feelings (at least those which are not happy or positive) that we learn to conceal the pain, sorrow, anxiety, and anger. This does not imply that we should go around sharing our intimacies with everyone, but we should do it with the people who care and worry about us. We can share with them when we do not feel well and express what we anguish over internally.

This discussion reminds me of Juanita, a lady who cleans the building where my office is located. In recent days I asked her how she felt. She told me she was well, but on hearing some hesitation in her voice I asked her directly whether her family was okay. After looking me directly in the eyes, she told me,

"Well, the truth is, no, my dad is in hospital with a heart condition."

She then sat next to me to talk about the problem. It only took a couple of minutes, but what relief she felt as she expressed her feelings! I felt so glad that I had extended my hand to her and given her my full attention. This is a tangible example of what I was saying earlier. We automatically answer that we are fine. But when we are not, we should say so to those who care about our well-being and can lend us a helping hand.

Here I present different forms of manifestations. Take pen and paper and try to identify which of them you have experienced. This exercise will give you the chance to go deeper inside yourself.

A MOMENT OF REFLECTION: MANIFESTATIONS

Physical
- Headache
- Stomach ache
- Dizziness and nausea
- Back pain
- Heartache
- Lack of appetite
- Excessive eating
- Lack of sleep (insomnia)
- Too much sleep

Emotional
- Depression
- Anxiety
- Fear
- Hyperactivity
- Lethargy

- Mistrust
- Despair
- Shock
- Numbness

Social
- Isolation
- Poor communication
- Excessive going out
- Overwork
- Excessive shopping

Spiritual
- Lack of faith
- Inability to forgive
- Lack of hope
- Anger towards God
- Anger towards life

I hope you have taken the time to do these exercises and have been able to identify what you are feeling. You may have discovered that you are experiencing anger or shock, and you still cannot believe that a loss of this magnitude has happened to you. If it is the death of a loved one, you may even feel angry with the person or be unable to forgive them for having left. If the loss is a job, you can quickly develop a sense of incapacity or insecurity. Do not worry; all these feelings are normal.

Sometime ago, Claudia, a young widow who was filled with bewilderment, asked me, "Am I going crazy? All these thoughts assault me day and night, and I cannot forgive Luis. He left me when I needed him the most."

I replied that it is not easy to adjust to your new reality and that's why you must remember that grief is a process and that it is essential to be aware of your own reactions. We must be careful not to fall into the pattern of incessantly asking about different possibilities. For example, if you suffer from feelings of guilt, we can arrive at the following assumptions:

- If at least ...
- If only ...
- If anything ...
-

If we suffer from feelings of anger, we may think:

- How is it possible?
- What right...?
- I don't forgive you!

If we suffer from feelings of insecurity we may think:

- I am not able to...
- I do not have the power to...
- It is not possible for me...

It is not worth punishing ourselves for the loss that has occured. The pain we feel is simply a manifestation of our ability to love. If we do not love, we do not suffer at the loss of a loved one. If we do not feel our love for our pet or nation, we cannot be estranged from them. Let us not forget that we experience different forms of love. But the grief is caused by the suffering that we have when we lose someone or something that has produced a positive feeling in us.

Psychiatrist Victor Frankl, in his book *Man's Search for Meaning,*[10] in relating his own experience of being in a concentration camp, described how important it is to find meaning in pain and give value to life. Frankl believed that when a person finds meaning they achieve spiritual peace and personal transcendence.

Do not forget that:
- Grief is different for each person.
- Grief is like a roller coaster; there are ups and downs.

- Grief can last a long time.
- Grief is not eternal.

Similarly, Julio Beviones, author of the spiritual book *Living in the Zone,*[11] reminds us in his article "Suffering" that pain is part of life and that we should not ignore it:

When we suffer and experience pain, we should not avoid it, we should listen to it and use it to our advantage. We can recognize it and do any of the following:

1. Calm it in some way to decrease it.
2. Be thankful for it and get back on track.

The first option will make the pain go away momentarily, but it will surely re-appear because the message was not heeded.

The second is an invitation to pay attention to the pain and focus on getting back on track. This means re-connecting with spirituality and love.

Do not expect to process grief in the same way as other people. Your pain is unique and only you can know whether the period of acute suffering has passed. Living in a fast-paced society, we can worry and even feel guilty for delaying our grieving process. In a study conducted in 1992 by Psychologist Stroebe and other authors, they explained that due to the modernization that prevails in our society, the bereaved "(...) need to recover from their state of intense emotion and return to the normal and effective functioning as fast and efficiently as possible."

But the reality is that there is no stipulated time; we should not expect this to happen uniformly at all. The duration and intensity of grief is individual and each person processes it according to their personal situation, their history of losses, and the meaning of that loss in their life.

For example, in the case of loss of a loved one or a divorce, we have to take into account the nature of our relationship with the person who is no longer with us. That is, if our relationship was loving or conflicting, if we had established a pattern of co-dependency, or if we were totally independent. Anyway, relationship issues influence how we feel when faced by our loss, and how we will work on the grieving process.

I do not deny that for most people to work on grief requires a lot of effort. Maybe you are one of those people who think it is impossible that this book can work for you. But do not deny yourself the opportunity to transform and grow, because life is actually a gift, and we must appreciate everything it offers us. Do not let it pass you by. Don't focus only on grief.

Remember that life is full of happy and sad moments, but...it is your life!

> "When we grow we learn that the only person who is capable of disappointing us, probably will. You will surely feel that your heart is broken more than once and that each time it is increasingly more difficult....You cry because time passes quickly, and eventually you will lose someone you love.
>
> Therefore, take many photos, laugh a lot, and love as if you have never been hurt, because every sixty seconds you lose to anger, it is a minute of happiness that will never happen again. Do not worry that your life ends, fear that it never starts."
>
> Anonymous

A MOMENT OF REFLECTION

What do you think about the following statement?

"Pain is inevitable, suffering is temporary."

Do you agree or disagree? In the following lines write your opinion:

_____

_____

_____

_____

_____

_____

Now read what you wrote.

June Hunt wrote: *"No one can climb the mountain called maturity without going through the valley of the shadow of pain."*

Write your reaction to this:

_____

_____

_____

_____

_____

_____

PART TWO

PART TWO

SHARING OUR STORIES

SHARING OUR STORIES

INTRODUCTION

Many people have shared with me on a personal and professional level the fear they experience when facing a loss or making a transition to a new stage in life. Because these stories involved different kinds of loss, I decided to write a book that included these experiences. I wanted to integrate different life experiences to which we as human beings are exposed.

The stories shared here are testimonials of strength and hope. They show us our internal capacity which, after going through the necessary phase of grief, allows us to change our lives by transforming our losses.

The stories are grouped according to the type of loss suffered: the death of a loved one; loss of health; loss from a divorce, or other life transitions. The stories start with a series of testimonies about the greatest possible loss: that of a loved one. But first, here is a reflection that the writer Susanne Berger sent me. It is a message of hope and solace when thinking that our loved one has gone onto another life.

> I have looked for a situation of grief in my life, and actually, I could not find one, because I know that death does not exist. What exists is a bridge to another world, to another kind of existence.

It is our own selfishness, our uncertainties, and our fear about death which lead us to that level of suffering. Death is a word that fills us with doubt, because we do not know the truth (the human mind needs to constantly be tested). Here on Earth, everyone can hide their true soul...we are not free; we have to deal with our mind, which is connected to our body and its emotional reaction. Everyone has to go to the spiritual world, so why not feel happy for those that have managed to get to the true existence of light and love? We need to learn to see, feel and hear the deepest part of our bodies: our soul.

—S. Berger

Transform Your Loss: Your Guide to Strength and Hope offers different paths for each of us in our losses, as these stories illustrate. But you can choose your own path. In this section you will find the testimonies of many people who have walked different and sometimes difficult paths, but who have been able to move on from their loss. It is for this reason that the contributors share these stories in which you may find something of your own experience. Each story has been reported in the writer's own style, the "voice" that distinguishes it. This is what I wanted to convey, the essence of the original message. The stories begin with the loss of a loved one.

SHARING OUR STORIES

We cannot see what is inside of us physically; only we know our inner feelings and inner strength. But remember that you are the creator of your own destiny, as these stories show. No one can live your life for you. You are the one who decides how to transform your life after suffering a loss. So I ask you, once again, to open your heart and listen to these messages. These stories should be read with the eyes of your soul for the seed to be received in your heart. Some seeds will take root and flourish in your new life and you will feel the desire to move on, through a metamorphosis that will transform your loss and positively change your life.

After each story that follows is the contributor's "message of strength and hope."

LOSS OF A LOVED ONE

UNCERTAINTY AND RELIEF
Adriana
43 years old

This is about the loss of my best friend in 1999, when I was still single. It all began with his disappearance. It continued with the anguish of his family and friends, the uncertainty and speculation about his whereabouts and ended with the unusual and unexpected outcome of the way he chose to die. The sense of failure and frustration about not being unable to do anything was the first thing I had to overcome and it is why I wanted to share this story.

I met my best friend while studying for my psychology degree. He always showed an interest in me, but I never interpreted it as anything more than a friendship. I remember that after one of those breaks where one ceases to see friends, we resumed our friendship. By then I wanted to have a relationship, but it seemed that he did not because of my initial feelings on this. Difficult to understand.

The last conversation we had on the telephone was a clear signal of what was coming, but I did not see it. He told me that I had always been the love of his life.

The next thing I knew of my friend was when his brother, who I had met a couple of times before, started asking me if I knew what had happened to him. It seems that my friend had left home one day but had not returned. Then a journey of inquiry, searching, contacting all the people who knew him, began. Everybody was afraid of the reality that was so common in our country Colombia, kidnapping!

I personally did everything in my power to find him: I gave out his picture and a personal description; I talked to a public official who was responsible for contacting members of criminal organizations, and tried to negotiate the release of kidnapped people; I talked to mutual friends, who were of great support to me during those days. I even, met someone, who coincidentally, had seen him the day he disappeared. What he told me about my friend, made me realize that I had not known my friend at all. After more than twenty days, I received the news that my friend had been found dead. His body nearly decomposed and hung from a tree. He had committed suicide.

If I tried to describe what went through my mind and everything I felt, I would come up short. I realized the suffering that resulted because of the uncertainty of not knowing what had happened to a loved one was worse than actually knowing about their death. I remember that, upon learning the truth, my first physical reaction upon hearing the news was to sigh and relax. It was not to cry or be sad, but it was relief. Then other reactions developed I tried to understand all that had been discussed with friends and family. Sadness and frustration continued, because there were things I had not known about my friend. It was obvious there was a lot of suffering he had experienced for much of his life. Then there was my reaction towards him. When I considered his disappearance, I mentally talked to him to console him. I told him I would have liked to have known everything that was going through his mind. I would have liked to have given us a chance in an intimate sense as maybe that might have made him happier. I blamed myself for not having realized this, because as a psychologist, I normally see these things in others, and I thought that "nothing could escape me" in relationships with people I knew. It was obvious I had feelings of inadequacy.

Talking with another very good friend of his was the beginning of my spiritual reaction and it was now clear that I was not his best friend, which added to my loss. Now there was not so much sadness, but a greater understanding of what had happened. Without this, I would never have been able to control my feelings. I prayed a lot. In the messages of the Catholic religion that I internalized, I realized my friend judged himself negatively because of choosing this type of death. However, I found a most appropriate prayer for my friend, from a very special Catholic devotee, my mother, whose death was the last that I had experienced before this one. The prayer was so beautiful and full of meaning for this event that it gave me the strength to heal this very deep wound.

I continued with my life and moved countries that same year, but he was still in my thoughts. I took his picture with me...and the special prayer, along with others. My relationship continued spiritually with my friend, but best of all was that I had found how to give myself hope and to resolve the fact that we had not given "us" a chance. I mentally gave my friend the task to help me choose the one that would be my partner. I now understand the meaning I gave to his loss because my husband bears the same name as my friend, but that's not all. When I got married two years ago to my husband and went to visit relatives and friends in my home country, the first thing someone said to me was how much my husband resembled my friend and how much he reminded them of him....I had not realized this. What began with frustration and inadequacy now meant peace of mind and an absence of guilt.

A MESSAGE OF STRENGTH AND HOPE

It is of the utmost importance to know that there are things that cannot be controlled. Knowing the truth about any death is the best medicine. In my story, knowing the truth was the solution to the uncertainty. I learned that it was good to be honest with my feelings for my friend when initially I did not want any romantic relationship with him. This means that I can now be at peace with him and with myself.

I went through many stages, but that tells me that we can overcome any situation, as difficult as it maybe. I think if he regretted having committed suicide at any point, God understood, forgave him, and allowed him to help me choose a good partner with whom I am very happy. That happiness I will always dedicate to him, to my friend's soul.

DAD, YOU ARE ALWAYS IN MY HEART
Alice
47 years old

Six years ago I received the terrible news that my father had died. They called me on the phone to tell me the news, and it hurt a lot. I felt that a part of my heart died at that time. My best friend, although not present physically as she was in Santo Domingo, was on the phone to me all the time. At that moment, I felt that God had taken from me the person I loved the most, and I felt so bad that I stopped eating for several days and my superficial neuropathy began. I cried a lot on special occasions and I remember that just a few days before his death, on Father's Day, I had told him how much I loved him and that if one day he was reborn, I would ask that God grant me that he could be my parent again.

A Message of Strength and Hope

One must never allow time go by without expressing love for the people you love, because we can never recover lost time. Express your love to those around you who are still alive.

The Power of Prayer
Alicia
87 years old

At the age of fifty-two after twenty-nine years of marriage, I suffered the greatest of losses. I still remember the great grief when my husband came home from work with a sharp pain close to his gallbladder. When I saw how bad he felt, I immediately called the doctor, and after a lengthy consultation, they decided to transfer him to the hospital. When I heard this I was sad, very sad, and was filled with fear. At around five in the morning I was informed that we would have to go to Miami. At that time we lived in Managua,

Nicaragua, and his doctor suggested that we go to Miami because there was a colleague of his there who would make the necessary preparations to admit my husband to hospital. Upon learning this news I went to my mother, who lived with us, and informed her about my husband's situation. I could leave my elderly mother with a sister and her husband. My two daughters also stayed in Managua. After hugging them and telling them the news, they burst into tears.

We left for Miami with one of my daughters and my husband's son, who was very close to the family. We admitted my husband Julio to the Miami Heart Institute Hospital, and after a week, he was to be sent home, but he died of an aneurysm in his aorta on that last day.

I remember it like it was yesterday when we were informed that we were needed at the hospital immediately. That morning, my daughter and I were at the hotel getting ready to leave and to meet my husband, who was expected to be discharged. On arrival at the hospital we received the terrible news that he had died. I felt a deep pain inside my body, and the doctor had to give me something to calm me down, because I was beside myself.

They immediately made the arrangements to transfer us to Managua, but I was numb, unable to believe what was happening.

When boarding the plane that would take me back to my homeland, instead of my husband being next to me, I was accompanied by his casket containing his body.

When my husband was ill, I prayed constantly to our Lord and the Blessed Virgin Mary for him to get better.

On the return journey I found myself praying for his soul and that God himself would receive him in his glory. Prayer gave me peace because I felt that God and the Virgin Mary listened to me...

My husband had been a businessman, entrepreneur, and business owner, and I now saw the situation I faced of taking over this new role as president of the company. I discovered a side of myself that I did not even suspect existed. From housewife to business woman, determined to follow in the footsteps of my husband and to continue his legacy. There were difficult times, and I continually missed the words of Julio and his constant affection, but with love I managed to carry on his legacy, on his behalf. I was the president of the company for twenty-five years after his death.

A MESSAGE OF STRENGTH AND HOPE

Tackle your loss in peace, and with resignation, take God, our Lord Jesus Christ, and the Holy Virgin Mary into your heart. A loss can give us the opportunity to discover aspects of our personality that even we did not suspect we had.

THE ANGELS PROTECT ME
Alma
56 years old

I suffered a lot when twenty years ago my father had a sudden stroke while we were having breakfast. It was unexpected and provoked great anguish, and changed my life abruptly. I prayed to God a lot not to take him and in this way, he lived for nine more months. Although I felt very sad about his death, time has helped me a lot. I have been able to go on, and I am sure that the only thing that can offer us solace is God and the passing of time.

A MESSAGE OF STRENGTH AND HOPE

I recommend to anyone going through the grieving process to take refuge in prayer, as it provides peace and at the same time gives strength. In particular I feel that the angels protect us and help us when we are feeling down and without hope.

I LOVE YOU!
Arelis
51 years old

Twenty-eight years ago I lost my mother to cancer. Upon realizing my mother had died, I reacted very badly, even though my siblings and father were present. I reacted by losing faith in the Lord, but then I realized that He had a place especially for her. I felt very lonely and, though I always remember my mother, God gives me the strength to continue living, until the day when I return to be with her. I realized when I experienced this terrible loss that although the earth and sky come together, there is always an escape route to continue with the plan for your life, which God has written. I learned how important it is to get along with others and say "I love you" again and again.

A MESSAGE OF STRENGTH AND HOPE

We must realize that we need to get along with others and say, again and again, "I love you!"

LOSS AND GAIN
Carlos
20 years old

It was in the early hours of August 10th, when I was a boy of eight years of age that I opened the door of my bedroom and saw my whole family in there. When I saw this, I thought I was dreaming because there was no way that my whole family would be in my room at this hour, and I simply closed the door and went back to sleep.

Some minutes later my mom came in and woke me and my brother, her face solemn, looking as if she had been awake all night long. She informed us that my dad's flight had crashed into a mountain in El Salvador and that the chances that he had survived were remote. Immediately, Francisco and my mother started to cry profusely and began to say the Our Father prayer. Although I was only eight years old I still remember reciting the Our Father prayer in silence while questioning my Catholic faith, and my faith in God. I did not understand how the prayer was going to help my father, alive or otherwise. It was not a matter of praying at that time. In the next few days my house was filled with tears and people from all over paying their condolences.

I remember the first time that I actually cried was while I listened to a radio presenter who knew my father, announcing his death. I cried, screamed, and kicked.

Upon receiving his body at the airport, we went to the funeral home. My father's face was deformed and his body was swollen, his nose broken and hair completely burned off. My mother's words calmed me down, telling me that he had been asleep and did not suffer during the accident. I, an innocent child, believed her (but now I understand the truth).

The Mass and burial were difficult for me, but they were necessary to process what had happened.

In less than a week my brother and I went back to school and my mother went to work.

Despite the loss we suffered, I learned a lot from my mother. I learned that life goes on, and I did well at school. However, my life had changed, my mother cried all the time, especially on special occasions, and my brother dealt with the loss in his own way, and I in mine.

Although I saw some psychologists throughout elementary school, I did not really confront the death of my father until I reached adolescence. I do not remember mourning the death of my father much.

Life teaches us that we must never stop, that the world keeps turning, and does not wait for us to recover. So, I continued on with my life.

When I turned fifteen I was already drinking. Without a father to teach me how to grow up and interact with women, I learned from my brother and his friends. My life was all about excesses of alcohol, women, and fighting. It was then that my mom took me to a psychologist. I saw Conchita for several months and she showed me how angry I was at life. I took it out on my mother and made her suffer because I felt she was responsible for my father's death. I did not understand anything the psychologist was saying about my relationship with my mother, but I knew I was angry at the world. God never stopped existing in my mind, but I fought him. By continuing to drink, I expressed my anger toward both the world and towards God. The anger turned me into a monster.

The aggression made me do a lot things of which I regret. I expressed my anger to God for the life I had and for taking the life of my father, which was unfair.

I remember one night I broke my hand hitting it against a concrete column; this was what led my mother to take action to try to protect me, as any good mother would do. She took me to Alcoholics Anonymous. I attended AA for about two months where I met people who had lost their lives to alcohol.

I learned that my drinking was a disease and it doesn't discriminate between rich, poor, whites, blacks, young, old, men and women. I learned a lot about the philosophy of Alcoholics Anonymous, and I recognized that they are effective for some people, but not me. I needed more than a twelve-step program, I needed God.

At that time I was visiting a counselor who I really liked. A good friendship grew out of the weekly visits and I gained a lot of good advice.

In January 2005 I had the opportunity to travel to Guatemala with my Uncle Rodrigo.

With considerable time and preparation, I made sure to process again my grief for my father. The counselor helped me a lot with that. I got out old newspapers and photos from my childhood and I made peace with my father's death.

By then I had learned that my father had not died in his sleep as my mother had told me when I was eight, but he had, in fact, suffered significantly before he died.

When driving to Guatemala we passed the hill on which his plane had crashed, and we held a few minutes of silent remembrance.

That day I saw the world differently: I accepted the death of my father as part of life.

Two months later, in March 2005, I attended a spiritual retreat. The retreat was different because it was about following up on the past. It consisted of seven talks and seven activities, two of which surprised me. In one activity we had to write down on a piece of paper three things that we did not need and on another piece of paper three things we would give thanks to God for.

For the things I did not need, I remember writing down my car and two other material things. For the things I would give thanks to God, I wrote - my intelligence, my family and something else I don't remember. The piece of paper with the three things that we did not need was put in a pot and burned and the piece which contained the words "thanking God" was saved in another pot.

The next day we had to take a piece of paper from this pot, in which someone else had given thanks to the Lord; this was to inspire us to give thanks to God for the things in our own lives.

On the paper I picked out, the first thing that was written was "father and mother." I laughed. The activity had failed. I had never seen my father as a gift from God. What is more, I thought God had taken my father from me.

After a few moments of reflection, I realized that my father had in fact, been a gift from God and a great blessing in my life. My father, despite dying when I was only eight years old, was a great example for my life and had given me a lot of love and principles in my early years. At the same time I realized that God was trying to tell me something.

Not knowing what the activity had meant to me I went to see my friend Marcela and explained to her what had happened. She had no idea what this meant either and suggested I go to my spiritual guide.

Luis listened for half an hour in which I expressed a little of my life and I recounted the events of the exercises. Luis invited me to visit "Jesus in the Holy Sacrament of Adoration."

Upon entering the room with the Eucharist on display, I knelt in front of Jesus and was surrounded by people I did not know who spent days praying there.

Luis told me to say out loud to God what I was feeling. I closed my eyes and I prayed. That day I spoke to God, I said everything I had on my mind. I asked Him why He had left my father to die as he had been a good dad; I told Him that my mother cried a lot and I asked why He had given me a difficult life; mainly I questioned Him as to why He had taken my father.

From the prayers the people around me were saying, I started to hear a lady in the corner of the room "speaking in tongues." Despite this fact, I more or less understood her. The woman asked me why I had sinned; a sinner without reason, only excuses. I had no answers. Luis approached me and told me that I was speaking to the Virgin Mary and that I should respond, so I responded. Crying, I asked for forgiveness. Yet the voice that was speaking in tongues resonated in the room, and in the words of God; she showed me that He was my father and that although my earthly father had died, He would never leave me orphaned, and that He had always been with me and loved me very much.

At that moment I understood that God has a perfect plan for all of us, and what He wants is for us to be good sons and daughters and love one another. I must have spent nearly three hours in that room, three divine hours I will never forget as they marked the beginning of my search for God.

A MESSAGE OF STRENGTH AND HOPE

I have learned that nothing is worthwhile if one is not with God. I have made mistakes in my life of which only a few were mentioned in this text, but I trust in the Lord's mercy and I seek His love every day.

IN MEMORY OF A GREAT LADY
Fidel
23 years old

Losing my friend has been the greatest of my losses. Her daughters informed me that she died in her sleep, and although it was expected, the news left us all in a state of shock.

I was left speechless, perhaps because I did not believe or understand it. I could not move; I cried when I heard the news. I experienced a great feeling of sadness, desperation, and helplessness. I could not understand why this had happened because she had never committed any sin to receive such a punishment. But if God did this, it was for a reason, I just wanted to know why.

My sadness continues, but I think the important thing in situations like these is to overcome them. We should always attempt to show our "best face" to the world so people do not see our sadness.

When I am sad, I like to read alone, especially on the issue that is affecting me. Whilst I read, I may cry to let out my feelings. I will also talk to people about what has happened. I realize that since my friend died, I have become bad tempered and my tolerance level is much lower.

I only hope that time will heal me and I can then move on.

A Message of Strength and Hope

Express your grief the way it feels more natural to you, because if you keep those painful feelings inside you, they could harm yourself!

Two Big Losses
Isabel
46 years old

The two loved ones I have lost are my father and my brother Juan. My father died seven years ago and my brother only a few months ago.

The death of my father was calm and happy because we expected it. I found out while in the hospital where Jorge, my son, was having a medical exam. That morning my father was alone in his apartment, but was not answering the phone; we could not locate him. As I expected something like this was going to happen, I was psychologically preparing myself.

My sister called me and asked me to come immediately as she was in my father's apartment. I immediately imagined what had happened, but I could not tell anyone until I was with my mother.

On the way to his apartment I called my aunt, his younger sister, and left a message on her answering machine to tell her that I thought my dad was dead.

When I knew that my dad had died, I prayed for his soul and asked for strength and resignation from God.

The death of my brother was completely different, as it was a tragic death. He committed suicide!

When the phone rang at 5:30 a.m. and my husband answered, I asked him what had happened, but he could not talk. I started to ask him if Javier had committed suicide. He confirmed that it was true with a facial expression, and I was shocked that I had guessed what had happened. I felt a lot of anger at the news because I had only spoken to my brother at midnight. I had asked him to wait for me until I could go to his house the next day to see how I might be able to help him solve his problem.

I told my husband, "You will not shed a tear for this idiot!"

I took control, called my sister Nora and asked her to accompany me to get my brother's body because my husband was still in shock.

When I called my younger sister, it was pathetic because she has the tendency to exaggerate everything and she did not expect anything like this to happen. Therefore, she took it like a slap in the face.

I was extremely hurt by the death of my brother after having spoken with him on the eve of his suicide. I had prayed with the "Miraculous Medal" to help him find peace. I had prayed for a period of two hours. I could not get to sleep. I believe that God receive my brother because at the time he died I was praying. I feel that the Miraculous Medal gave me what I asked for.

Now I ask for things to improve. After his death I prayed a lot and still do. Sometimes I dedicate all my evening prayers to him.

When my father died, it was very hard for me because I took it as a punishment.

I remember, with sadness, that every time I was in Miami and he invited me to lunch, I never went, because I was always working. There are moments that one loses without knowing until it is too late. He always commented on how many times I told him, "Someday, but not today." I visited the cemetery every evening and kept mourning for five months. I cried incessantly, until one day I went to the cemetery and I told him this was going to be the last time I would visit. That afternoon I decided I was going to stop mourning and would let my pain go....And so it was!

With my brother I felt very sad. A few times I have felt a heartbreaking pain, but I remember that when I arrived at his wake and saw him, I let out a cry and fainted.

Those who saw me said it was shocking. I continue to feel that pain as it is not something that can be forgotten. Now while writing this I am crying. It is still painful for me to think he is dead and how he died. I am afflicted by many unanswered questions. I wonder why I had not invited him to my house more and why I did not try to protect him more.

When we spoke on the eve of his suicide, I was hard on him and challenged him to stand up and be a man and to face life, as I was not always going to be able solve his problems for him. Unfortunately, everything I told him just served as fuel to his intention to kill himself.

It is very difficult to even think about his death. It is a pain that manifests itself when I talk about him or when I think about him, but it is not something that depresses me.

By losing two loved ones, I have understood that pain does not make you stronger just because you suffer a loss, but that it is only a fact of life. While you love and have feelings, you will feel pain!

If I ever suffer another loss I would react in much the same way: first try to solve any problem and then mourn. Sometimes it would be more intense than others, but it will always be painful.

I do not want to change my way of being because I think when I feel pain and suffering, I have a chance to adapt to that loss over time.

A MESSAGE OF STRENGTH AND HOPE

To experience pain is part of human nature, but by living your pain you eventually learn to live with your loss.

AN UNEXPECTED SURPRISE
Carol
46 years old

The greatest loss I have experienced in my life is the death of my mother, twenty-seven years ago. She died due to health complications. My mother was taking a nap and lost consciousness. When she arrived at the hospital, she was already dead, but the doctors did not tell me, as I was in the emergency room with my father and my younger sister. When they finally told us the news, it took me completely by surprise and I felt terrible. I lost the strength in my legs and fell to the ground, and the doctors had to take me out of the room. I could not understand why God had decided to take her.

My mother, after giving birth to my sister and me, became very ill, but after each relapse she was capable of recovering to some extent. She had to go through many complicated surgeries but was able to recover from each of them.

When she died, I could not understand why God did not prevent her death. I was emotionally devastated, totally alone. I was so young—nineteen, and my sister was seventeen. Although we had our father, at that moment, when I learned of her death I thought that my sister and I were totally alone. I thought I would have to be strong to help my sister. I could not allow her to feel that she was alone. I had to be there for her!

I can never forget that when my mother died, virtually all of my family disappeared with her. I have not been able to forget or really heal in that aspect. Although now I am coping fairly well with the loss of my mother, there are many things in life that cannot be changed.

All this has made me into the strong woman that I am today. I am proud of how wonderfully I have turned out as a person.

I cannot forget what happened; it still hurts. I look back and see everything that my sister and I had to endure. This great loss has only given me blessings from both God and my mother. They take care of us from heaven.

The painful moments have made me stronger.

A MESSAGE OF STRENGTH AND HOPE

To confront painful moments caused by something or someone we must think that despite the fact that the tunnel is very dark, there is always light at the end. Pain teaches us to enjoy happiness and that all wounds heal with time. This experience made us grow up very quickly because there was only the two of us, and I realized I had to be strong for my sister.

SHOW YOUR LOVE
Carolina
60 years old

Nineteen years ago my father died of cancer one night in February 1987. I could not accept his death and I cried a lot. My husband was with me but I felt lost. I asked God for everything to be a mistake.

I felt a lot of pain and my stomach could not hold down food or liquids. I felt frustrated, desperate, and totally impotent, but I eventually got past the stage of pain. And now I am at peace when I think of my father.

A MESSAGE OF STRENGTH AND HOPE

We need to love and show that love. Do not have reservations in showing your love to your loved ones. That memory will fill you with peace when you do not have them at your side.

ALL IS NOT LOST
Diley
23 years old

My father died on September 19th, 2005. I remember that day, as upon returning from college, the phone rang.

Answering it, I heard a voice that I had not heard in almost ten years. My cousin had called to tell me that there had been a terrible accident and that my father had died upon impact. A vehicle had run over my father while he was crossing a street in the early hours of the morning.

I could not figure out how to react or what to feel. The thing was that I barely remembered my father's face; I only remembered him from photos. The last contact my sister and I had with him was when I was five years old and she was two and a half. Even so, I remember one event clearly. It was the next to last day that I went to see him, all those years ago. I only remember the lights of the police car and my father in handcuffs. He had been arrested because he had been drunk and had hit my mother.

According to her, that was the first and last time he had hit her. It was also the last time I would see him, but it was enough for that image to be ingrained in my mind.

I struggled with myself about whether to attend the funeral of a man who was absent for most of my life. He was never able to maintain a job, not even for his daughters' sake. I decided I would go to the funeral. My mother and my sister went with me me, and we offered each other mutual support.

My father's family, who I barely knew, attended the funeral as well. I was introduced to my godmother, a woman I did not recognize. I also met my father's brothers, sisters, cousins, and other family members. I did not really remember any of them, and what little I did remember was all bad, because like my father, they were never able to live a normal life without problems.

I have vivid memories of the hours prior to being informed of this disaster. I had a kind of vision. Although it may seem ridiculous, I feel it was a premonition.

I was at school waiting to start class, but I could not enter the classroom until the refugees from Hurricane Rita had left. Suddenly I had a vision of my father entering the room. It was him, in the flesh and the color of blood. At that moment I knew that something bad had happened.

My thoughts about him were very rare and sporadic. Believing that he was there gave me the certainty that something had happened, but I pushed the thought aside and entered the room. Predictably, he was not there.

Later, after hanging up the phone after knowing the terrible news, I told my mother about the vision. She told me that this was how my father communicated to me that he had died.

At the funeral I managed to finally let out the tears that had been repressed for a long time after watching him leave us with a smile. Unfortunately I have never really prayed to God and only used his name in vain. I denied myself the opportunity to meet my father and for him to be part of my life.

I have continued my life without believing in God, but somehow I maintain my belief in the spiritual world. Although it may seem strange, I studied many religions at college, but I have not maintained a strong belief in any of them.

I felt terribly tired and continually found support from my sister who, in turn, I supported whilst crying. I know I cried a lot. I cried more than I expected. I kept so much in for so long. I let it out all at the same time. I tried to be strong for my sister, but I feel I was not as strong as I should have been.

Over time I have learned to live with the pain, and now feel I am better, compared with what I originally was like.

The main reason I attended the funeral was to not have regrets later. I have always felt remorse, but I felt that it was a good step to take. I was not sorry when I saw the face of my father. Although it was very difficult, I had to do it. I felt released from a terrible weight. When I forgave him, a terrible pain in my chest disappeared, a pain that had resurfaced after so many years of questions without answers.

I have heard the phrase "with each death a new life is born."

I knew I couldn't take this phrase literally, but I hope that with the death of my father, a part of me has been reborn, perhaps even a greater sense of desire to live.

Hope for the future is a feeling I am missing.

A MESSAGE OF STRENGTH AND HOPE

Death always affects us. You can believe that your heart is made of stone, but it is not. We are all vulnerable to death. I hope that when you go through this experience you come back stronger and you become a better person, because there is always a chance to grow. I think I took the right decision at that time, without remorse, as we do not have a second chance. I hope you will also take the right decision…

I HAVE ALWAYS BEEN ALIVE!
Elgin
57 years old

On Wednesday, January 25th, 1989, my brother Freddy was meeting once again with all my family. My husband and our five children went to visit him at his house. We had a nice time, although he was in the final stage of a terminal cancer.

When we returned home, my son Álvaro José, aged 16, told his Dad and I that he wanted to go to my mother's ranch with his cousins the following Saturday, January 28th, to do some archery. His father granted him permission and Álvaro José took the opportunity to ask for the use of the truck because, if not, he could not go. His father agreed but only if he filled the trailer with soil to put on the lawn. Álvaro agreed.

Saturday the 28th arrived, and at 7 o'clock I was preparing for my usual trip to the market. Meanwhile, Álvaro José was preparing the shovels to collect the soil and placed them in the trailer.

Before leaving, he came in to say goodbye to me and hugged me from behind.

He said, "Mommy, today I am not going to accompany you to the market," which he did every Saturday, as he had got permission to go to the ranch. He said, "I will be back by one thirty at the latest with the soil, so that we can have the Lord's Supper together." (The Lord's Supper was an activity that we celebrated with our prayer group).

We left the house, each to their own activities. When I returned from the market, I saw that it was still early and I went to see my brother Freddy. I found him very uncomfortable and in pain, so I stayed for a while and went home very sad.

Upon my return, I sat down to lunch with my other four sons and served food to everyone, saving a portion for Álvaro José.

We finished lunch and everyone went to their rooms to rest. I was sad about my brother. Crying, I took my Bible and started reading it. Then the doorbell rang and I heard the servant going to open the door. I heard that another of my brothers had arrived.

I left my room and saw that my brother had come with my brother-in-law; both saw me with teary eyes and got scared. They asked what had happened, and I replied that I had gone to see Freddy and when I left I felt very sad. They asked where they could find Álvaro, my husband, so I told them, and they left. I continued reading my Bible.

Some thirty minutes later, my husband came into our room. I could see he had been crying. When he knelt, the first thing that occurred to me was that Freddy had died.

"What has happened? Has Freddy died?" I asked.

He bowed his head and said,

"No, our son Álvaro is dead!"

"What!"

I came running out, screaming around the house totally uncontrolled. I went into my children's rooms screaming and repeating, "Álvaro José is dead!"

"This is terrible!"

Totally out of control, I ran and screamed around the house. I went into my other son's bedroom screaming and repeating, "Álvaro José is dead" with much confusion and pain! Suddenly I stopped. I went into my room and closed the door and remained there in silence. Two invisible hands touched my shoulders and heat began to run through my head to my feet, and I was filled with peace and serenity.

I came out of my room, took the car keys, and told my children and my husband that we had to go to the house of my other brother Adolfo, where the body of our son lay. My brother and my brother-in-law asked me if I was going to drive. I said "yes" and we all went together.

We arrived at my brother's house and my husband, and I entered the room where my child was. I approached him and knelt beside him.

I started very slowly and gently to whisper in his ear, "Our Father, who art in heaven, hallowed be Thy name! Thy will be done on Earth, as it is in heaven!"

I got closer and continued, "Forgive us for our trespasses..."

I wanted Álvaro José to ask forgiveness for his sins, so that our Lord would receive him. At that moment I did not feel anyone, but I knew that his spirit was near me while I looked at him. I checked his body, saw his wounds. Everyone in the room prayed the Rosary while they took him away to the hospital to prepare his body, and then we all went back home. I thought, "He did come at 1:30 pm, only he was dead!"

A short while later they brought in the casket. The wake was held the next day and then we buried him.

A deep silence fell upon my house. My tears were silent in my soul. The pain was so deep! Total pain! It felt as though the pain was actually physical, as I felt like I had had a part of my soul amputated.

I now understood why the elderly Simeon had told our Mother, the Holy Mary [at the time of her son Jesus' death],

"A sword will pierce your heart." That was exactly what I felt; something had pierced my soul!

Sometime later, I dreamt about my dead son. He was sitting on my lap, a sweet little boy, not talking to me.

He approached me, kissed me on both cheeks. I remembered I lifted up my arms as if pushing him away saying, "Son, do not suffer. Go, as you are no longer of this world! Go away, go away...."

My husband woke me up wondering what had happened. I told him about my dream and then it all ended.

After a while my son came back to my dreams.

I saw him leaning on the door frame of my room, and I remember saying, "What! Here you are again!"

And he answered me, "Yes, I have just come to say goodbye because I'm leaving."

Seventeen years later I dreamt of him again.

He was lying in the street and I thought he was dead. Upon getting closer, I saw that his eyelids were moving. I approached and asked him, "Are you alive, son?"

Suddenly, smiling, he stood up, hugged me, and said, "Mom, but I have always been alive!"

And this is the reality, we leave this world but an eternal life!

A MESSAGE OF STRENGTH AND HOPE

During the sermon at Mass on November 17th, 2006, the priest said the following words:

"The Lord does not remove us from the cross (the problems), but he gives us strength to carry on."

As I promised to write about my pain, I associated the priest's words with the hands I felt on my shoulders and the heat that had traveled from my head to my feet and return to my head. That was precisely the strength he was conveying, which in turn, I transmitted to my children and husband.

A STORY
Francisco
22 years old

It was a cold night like no other. For a child of twelve it was a very boring night, but at the same time, the night was special. I was with my family heading to the airport to pick up my father, who was returning from a business trip to Guatemala. It was always very exciting for my brothers and sisters and me when our father was on his trips, because somehow he always managed to bring us gifts and make us feel special. It did not matter that they were small; they always made us feel happy.

What I remember is that it was almost seven in the evening when we arrived at the airport. We went with another family as my father had been on a trip with his boss, and we had decided to go together to pick them up. Upon arrival at the airport my brothers and sisters and I started to play with the other children. Occasionally, some of the group approached the airline desk to ask what time the plane would be arriving, as it had been scheduled to land in Nicaragua at 7:30 p.m. It was now 9:00 p.m. and the plane had not yet arrived. The airline hostess always gave us the same answer that due to rain the plane had to make a stop in El Salvador, and as soon as the weather improved it would take off again.

At 10:30 p.m. we children were very tired and restless, so our mothers took us to the house closest to the airport and left us there whilst they went back to the airport to await the arrival of their husbands.

When we were left at the house, I remember having fallen asleep around 11:30 p.m. For some reason all the children slept in the parents' room, and when our mothers returned, I just woke up to say goodbye to the other families, and I sleepily asked my mom about my dad. Her response was very similar to that of the airport hostess. Only this time she explained to me that he would probably spend that night in El Salvador and would be back in the early hours of the morning.

Therefore, I went to sleep hoping to see my father and wondering what he would say and what he would bring me.

It was five oclock in the morning when someone touched my shoulder. I woke up, and the first thing I saw was my mother sitting on my bed beside me, with a false smile and cheeks red as apples. For the first time I felt something was not right. I knew when my mom had been crying because her cheeks and nose became red. Gradually, I became aware of people outside my room and their familiar voices.

How strange! I thought.

Then my mother said something I will never forget, "The plane crashed, it crashed!"

At that point I turned to see the beds next to me, my brother, eight, and my sister, two, and I felt dizzy.

At first I thought that I had had a bad dream. I got up and left the room. Due to my state of mind, I found I did not remember very well who was in my home. All I did remember was my grandparents and the lady who lived in front of us. After that, came the worst days of my life.

Just so you know, my father's plane crashed on a mountain in El Salvador. Due to the altitude, it was not easy to get to the wreckage to rescue the people. I tried to believe that my father was strong enough to survive the accident.

He not only was my father, he was also my hero! I somehow knew that was alive; he was going to survive. Despite the news saying that the probability of survival was zero, I never lost faith.

A few days later the reality hit me really hard.

During all those days the house was always full of friends and family. One morning I was in my parents' room watching TV, trying to distract myself by watching one of the news channels—I do not remember which one—when I saw images of the accident. It was so graphic that it will remain etched on my mind forever. I did not see corpses, rather body parts in the trees, on the ground, and up on pieces of the plane. I started to scream at the top of my lungs. However, despite my efforts, I could not hear any sound coming out of my mouth. My mom came into the room, hugged me, and I began to cry. It was then that realized what had happened.

My dad was not going to come home!

For several years I was angry at God. I blamed God for what had happened to me. I could not understand why He had allowed this to happen to my dad, my family, and especially to me. Only years later I let go of my bitterness and finally understood that "bad things" happen in life but life continues.

I am not what you would call a very religious man, but I do believe in God, and I have a strong faith in Him, but I believe in Him in my own way. I do not go to church and if I do go, it is for some special occasion or to please my mom. I do not think that to talk to God, it is necessary to go to church. I talk to God constantly. But for a couple of years I was very angry with Him. It is funny; I never lost faith in the existence in God, as many people do. I just lost my faith in Him, but now I have matured.

It is really hard to lose a loved one. It is even harder to grow up in a home without a father.

I know many families that have only grown up without a father or a mother, but it is not the same if he or she just left, as it is to suddenly lose them.

Somehow I have learned to live with the death of my father, and although I have unresolved issues, I know that these will heal with time.

The death of my dad had a huge impact on my life and being the eldest son, I became my mother's right hand. When I grew up, I grew up quickly, maturing faster than other kids my age. I did many things and I learned to appreciate life. I went through a stage of life living as if there was no tomorrow. I participated in extreme sports, and my mom thought I did it because I was facing my personal issues, but it was because I liked the rush of adrenaline in my body.

Would I have done all these things in my life if I had not lost my father? I imagine that there is no way of knowing.

Eleven years have passed since the death of my father, and I still miss him and always will. But now I know he is always with me, taking care of me and my family. What inspires me in life is not wearing my father's shoes, but continuing the legacy he left behind.

One thing that I have not said is that I carry his name with pride, and although I am a different person than my father, I know that the apple does not fall far from the tree. He is still my hero, and when I am faced with a conflict, I wonder what he would do.

A Message of Strength and Hope

One's life can change from day to day without warning. No matter how hard or mild, change is a fact; and not only does one have to accept it, one must learn from and be strengthened by such change. That is how we achieve growth and become better people.

The Lord Gave Me Strength
Hector
23 years old

I will never forget the day I turned seventeen. I drove my father from one specialist to another, to see why he was bleeding so much and why he had strange test results.

At the end of the day, they told us that he had tumors in his chest and stomach. My dad constantly asked for forgiveness because he thought he had ruined my birthday; in reality the Lord allowed me to spend the whole day with my dad, which was precious time that was drifting away. He had cancer in his lungs and small intestine.

In January 2006, when the surgeons were removing these tumors, they found a mass in one of his kidneys. It was so small (like half the size of the big toenail), so they chose not to take it out, explaining that this mass would never grow and would dissolve on its own.

In May when he went for a check-up, the doctors found the mass had grown so rapidly that the cancer had already spread to his chest.

The pain was very intense, but I had to be strong in front of my mother, sister, brother, and niece. My father knew that I was crying inside. Like him, I knew that the family needs were beyond mine at the time.

The Lord gave me the strength and grace to be strong in such difficult times.

Until that moment I went to church only to "visit God." I had not given Him my heart. The first night of the wake, I had a long conversation with Him, and it was then that I understood his plan: to be my eternal Father. He always loved me as his child, but I never saw it. That night I made my peace with the situation, and I completely gave myself to the Lord Jesus Christ, God Almighty. Many believe that when my dad died I became the man of the house, but in reality the Lord took care of my family, and there is evidence of that still today.

I lost and gained weight; I ate when I could, after making sure that the others had eaten.

I missed my father a lot! There were so many things that I wanted to ask, so much advice that I needed. My dad was the man I wanted to be, and I know he would have been able to teach me many of the lessons I had to learn the hard way, although perhaps I had to learn these this way because I am stubborn. I still cry every once in a while, especially when I hear an old Cuban song. I cried when I saw the film *The Lost City*, with Andy García, because it reminded me of my dad.

There are times when I am going through something, and I know that if my dad was here things would not seem so bad. I think a lot about him when I am driving, and I look up at the sky. I imagine him watching me and smiling. If God wants me, one day I will ask if He is proud with what has become my life.

I continued on with my life and got married. I moved and everything continued.

I live one day at a time now, and I never forget that the Lord is good. With this great loss, I have learned to be the same kind of man my father had been: full of love, integrity, and honor for my family. I learn as much as I can to help my children and my brother. I am always available for my mom and sister, and show them how much I love them. Nobody is perfect and I never will be, but I try to make life for my loved ones better every day.

A MESSAGE OF STRENGTH AND HOPE

We have to be better with our loved ones, much more than with ourselves (even the Lord was sacrificed by those He loved). If you live with all your heart, this heart will give you eternal life.

GOD REWARDED ME WITH AN ANGEL
Ivette
43 years old

It was only one month before my son, the youngest of three, had his fourth birthday. Fernando was a happy and gifted child; he was extremely intelligent, and many say that he was brilliant. He was one of those people that, because of his extreme intelligence, could not remain long with people.

He did not really belong to this world. He was born with a serious congenital heart problem, one of the most rare and serious kinds. At six months he was operated on for the first time, and the diagnosis meant that it would be necessary for him to have at least five more operations during his early years. It would not be possible for him to be able to have any sort of normal life until adolescence.

In those days he was very tired. It was determined that he would need a surgical procedure to thin his blood. There was only one private hospital that could do this operation in Nicaragua, but there was no pediatric intensive care unit or the instrumentation needed. The only choice was the state-run children's hospital, which was impoverished and neglected by ten years of the Sandinista Government. I was horrified by the idea of taking my child to an intensive care unit where a bed had one or two more children in it, with no guarantee of sterilization, and horrifying cockroaches and mice. We decided to take him to Mexico to meet with the child cardiologist who had diagnosed my son and operated on him years ago, who was interned at a private child facility in Mexico. Fernando and I traveled on Saturday, June 6th, 1992, and to my surprise, the doctor informed me that my child had improved so much that no more than one operation would be needed to solve the problem definitively.

They gave us an appointment for the surgical procedure in the ICU for the following Friday on Monday. We left very happy, heading for the Chapultepec Zoo so that Fernando could see the elephants, one of his greatest wishes. My mother accompanied us. The child was tired a lot of the time, but this was normal due to his thickened blood, and the added altitude of Mexico City, both of which caused him a lot of fatigue.

But we could not see the elephants because the zoo was closed on Mondays.

That night I spoke with my husband in Nicaragua and gave him the good news. The process on Friday was a simple one. Fernando would be twenty-four hours in intensive care and then we could travel home. The final operation was scheduled for October of that year; four more months and the nightmare would end.

On Wednesday, June 10th I woke up early as Fernando was crying a lot. I did not want to be separated from him for even a second; even the idea of going to the zoo did not calm him down. At ten in the morning he suffered the first attack from stenosis (a lack of oxygen in the brain). I ran with him in my arms. I was more than an hour away from the hospital so I took a taxi. I remember the only thing I did was give him mouth-to-mouth resuscitation, and tell him that I loved him more than anything in the world, and I gave him my blessing.

When we arrived at the hospital, I ran to the cardiologist's office, and the people at the information desk were running behind me shouting at me, telling me that the ER was on the other side of the building and that I should go there. They knew it was something serious and that there was no time to lose.

But for me, the only important thing was handing him over to the cardiologist. When I asked for him, I was told he was with a patient, so I ran into the office with everyone behind me. I opened the door and put the child into the doctor's arms. He ran towards the ER.

I could not run anymore. They stopped there and I started to agonize.

At reception they handed me the clothes cut from my child. They were taking him to the ICU; they had drained some of his blood and his condition was very serious.

I had the money for the procedure scheduled for Friday, the 12th, but in these circumstances that money would only cover the first two hours in this hospital and the emergency procedures. I do not remember how my mother found out. I do not know if I called her from my aunt's house, where we were staying.

The money provided by my mother and my aunt barely covered the next procedures. I had to find and make a millionaire deposit as soon as possible because, otherwise, we would be moved to a public children's hospital.

I looked for a way to resolve the financial problem, and had the support of the cardiologist, who prevented any action on the part of the hospital, as Fernando was too ill to be moved. He could die at any time.

I spent all day going to and from the hospital and making phone calls to friends, as well as trying to call my husband long distance. He was on a cargo ship carrying shrimp, which had put to sea the previous day and would not return until that evening.

During all this time I could not be with my child, and that's the biggest regret I have.

All of my sisters-in-law sent money to cope with the hospital bills, but that money would take two days to arrive, and the hospital administration did not want to wait.

It was 7:00 p.m. They allowed me to see him so I could kiss him and cuddle him. I returned to give him my blessing, and he started having another attack. I was taken outside the room.

At 7:45 p.m. the doctors came out to inform me that Fernando had died.

I asked my mother to wait for his body and have it taken to the hospital chapel, while I went to make some phone calls.

I did not have the strength to hold him in my arms as I got scared; I do not know why I could not manage to hold him. I asked a friend to help me with the whole process of finding where to hold the wake.

First I had to pay the hospital, because they were practically holding his body hostage. I could not take the body if I failed to pay the bill. I realized that they were serious when they put a security guard at the entrance of the chapel, which was the only place we were allowed to be with the child.

All of us, including my mom, Fernando and I, had to spend that night in the hospital.

At 8:10 p.m. I called my sister-in-law in Guatemala; she was responsible for calling Nicaragua to break the news to everyone. At 9:00 p.m. I managed to talk to my husband and asked him to tell our other two sons.

Carlos needed to apply for a visa to travel to Mexico, so it was impossible to come before Friday.

The next morning, after a lengthy meeting with the hospital director, he agreed to sign a promissory note, with a maturity of one week, so that we could take my child to another place for the wake. We decided to cremate his body, thinking of our other children. I could not go home with their little brother in a box.

On Friday morning I received the money. I went to the hospital to pay. I had wanted to throw it in the faces of the director and the accountant of the hospital, but I did not have the strength; I was dying inside.

I went to the airport to wait for my husband, as we had waited for until he came to cremate the body.

At 5:00 p.m., Friday, June 12th, we were given a small urn with Fernando's ashes, and the "ashes of our hearts" were in the urn with the body of our son.

We still had to wait for his death certificate, due the funeral home bureaucracy, before we could go home to Nicaragua. So we went to a hotel to wait and to mourn.

On Sunday at noon, I received the document and on Monday, the 15th, we returned home. We buried the ashes of my son at the grave of his grandfather on June 16th, his father's birthday.

I cut off my relationship with God; it's not that I suddenly no longer believed in Him, but something worse. Amidst the most pain I had ever felt in my life, the only possibility of returning to trust in Him was if He returned me my son, if He resurrected him. Wasn't it His promise?

I challenged Him every day. Would He be able to do this miracle? No, of course not! Therefore, I was not interested in knowing anything more about Him. My faith was completely lost; it had vanished. I hated God with all my might.

Losing a child is the worst thing in the world; nothing compares with it; the pain is unbearable. It tears you up, literally speaking, the heart inside your body. You become short of breath; it is like a thousand stabs at the same time; it is simply indescribable.

I felt empty, alone, abandoned. I felt that suddenly I had removed all stimulation from my life. The four years of fighting for Fernando's life had finally beaten me.

This grieving process lasted for many years, but I think in my bitter process the only thing that helped me to survive were my two other children. If they had not existed, I am fully convinced that I would have gone crazy, or what would have been worse, committed suicide.

I felt a lot of things, guilt for not having done more for him, for failing to be able to save him, for taking the decisions that I took, and by not giving more, more, more! The sadness from not having him! The envy of seeing other parents around me with their healthy children!

Why my child and not that child or this one?

Every day of my life I blasphemed and died inside. The years passed, and the only thing I asked for was to find the faith I had lost. I only needed a bit of faith to be consoled.

I was also affected physically like the time when I was sick. I had gastritis all the time, so seriously that I spent two or three days in the hospital as my nervous system had been destroyed.

I visited a psychologist twice a week as the depressions were becoming more acute, and I was taking sleeping pills for my nerves, other pills for my gastritis, and so on.

One day I hit rock bottom, after weeks of waking up, opening my eyes only to find my medicine. It was a weekend, neither of my children or my husband was at home (I did not know much about their current lives and they were my loved ones.) I found all the anti-depressants, the sleeping pills, and everything else and threw them in the trash. I decided that from then on I would take control of my life, head on, and stop evading the reality. I would not return to the psychologist, as I found that this just served to depress me more. I embraced my emotions and faced the world. I also began my process of reconciliation with God. With time, I realized that the faith that I looked for outside, with so much disappointment and despair, the Jesus that I needed to deal with my pain, was actually within me, in my heart.

The wound caused by the death of a child is incurable; it never heals. One does not cease to suffer; one does not stop mourning, and certainly one does not forget. It hurts the first day, after two months, ten, fifteen, and even twenty years later. So, is there hope?

I think that time helps to confront the suffering, but the pain will remain there forever. It transforms and becomes more bearable, and one finds solace more easily in faith and relationships with other people who have suffered the same thing. Listening to the experience of other parents is one of the best medicines; only those who have gone through it are able to understand the ups and downs and know the process, and can find the right words of consolation.

God lent me a beautiful angel. I lulled him to sleep in my arms for a while; his beauty and splendor bewitched me. This is why I did not accept his departure. With the passing of time I have found peace; it was a long and very stormy journey. I still weep bitterly. I cannot help that my tears flow from the bottom of my heart as I type this, but I have the firm belief that Fernando is sitting at the Lord's table. He is one of the brightest angels singing his glory. I am infinitely grateful that he was given to me for a while, and, more importantly, I have countless evidence that he is acting as my family's guardian. I am sure that the day I die, I will see his face once more; feel his arms hug my neck, his cheek tight to mine and I will hear him say once again,

"Mom, I love you!"

A MESSAGE OF STRENGTH AND HOPE

Love is eternal, and if you have faith in God, He also gives you the strength you need to deal with the loss of a loved one.

YOU ARE NOT ALONE IF GOD IS WITH YOU
Joaquina
81 years old

The biggest loss that I have suffered is the death of my husband, which occurred four years ago.

We lived in New Jersey and he began to suffer from Alzheimer's disease. Before being diagnosed, Nico, my husband, realized that he was not right. The doctor attended Nico with great care, and he was prescribed medication, but the doctor did not tell Nico that he had this disease. When we went to Miami, my husband became anxious at night.

He became restless. He kept saying, "I cannot sleep."

So we went to a pharmacist and got the medicine that the doctor had prescribed. The pharmacist told us he had Alzheimer's disease, because these were pills that were for Alzheimer's. Nico wanted medicine for his anxiety, but they refused the drugs, arguing that they created a habit. Finally, another doctor saw him and gave him medication for the anxiety. After this he was officially diagnosed with Alzheimer's, and as Nico was suffering from anemia, they had to do a colonoscopy.

He had the exam and the result showed he did not have colon cancer, but he had a high probability of having leukemia. As a result of the laxative they gave him for the colonoscopy, they upset his balance of potassium and other minerals in the body. This in turn caused some heart problems. The doctor sent my husband to another hospital to give him electric shock treatment to relieve the heart problems. But before he got to the hospital, he had more complications with his heart. They put in a catheter and ran more tests. Nico was now not fully conscious. He received a transfusion because of the blood loss. They did a test on his hip, and the result was that he had leukemia.

He complained, but I told him quietly, that I would move his pillow and he went quiet again for a while. They finally administered morphine for the pain.

At the time of his death, my children were present. I remember the last time I spoke to him before going home.

"My beauty!" he whispered in my ear.

Just before he died, he received final communion and was able to take the offering. Then, shaking my two sons by the hand, he died.

My son Reinaldo came to the house looking for me to give me the news. I was very calm and without crying I left with him.

When I saw my husband, I kissed his forehead and feet, and then I returned home. When my husband died, I didn't want to go to the funeral home. My son Reinaldo told me, "It will be done as you wish." On the other hand, I wanted to see my husband, so they took me to see him.

All the people who came to my house said how special my husband had been. Still those were very difficult moments. I believe that my faith in God helped me a lot to cope with the pain. I adored my husband and he adored me. We dated for a year and then enjoyed sixty years of love and peace.

As Nico was a member of the Masons, we were not married by the Church for ten years. In my heart I have some wonderful memories because he was very good to me and we were extremely happy. My parents loved him as their own son.

During my life I suffered two major depressions from which I miraculously recovered; people prayed for me to get better. My depressions were profound, even to the point of not wanting to answer the phone. I remember that after the death of Nico I had no depression. Renaldo helped me with everything as people drove me crazy.

"Sell the house." "Don't sell the house," they would say.

Everyone had an opinion about what I should do next. I felt confused, so one night I asked God to enlighten me as to whether I should sell the house or not. I decided to stay in my house, and I understood I was not alone. God was with me!

A MESSAGE OF STRENGTH AND HOPE

Hold on to God with both hands. If you have God and you feel like I do, you won't miss anything.

THE RED BUTTERFLY
Karyl (mother of Arlyn who died at age 18)
59 years old

Shortly after midday, I went to my daughter Arlyn's room to get some items. I had to drive approximately three miles into the countryside to Woodhaven Road. Standing in the middle of her room, I looked around for a few minutes. It was full of Arlyn's things, but it seemed so empty. I picked up a folder with some of the poems she had written; her words, thoughts and feelings. I put it under my arm while looking for some more stuff: a Cabbage Patch doll, the dress she was baptized in, and the blue ribbon she had won by baking a cake when she was ten. All these things meant something to my daughter, but I just left them where they were.

As I moved my hands over her dressing table, I knocked over a small photo frame. It fell face up; it was a photo of Arlyn with bright red hair and a happy expression on her face.

She was three years old when I made her the Raggedy Ann costume, using a mop for a wig. For many days she practiced walking like Raggedy Ann. I smiled as I remembered this; I took the picture with me. That was everything I needed.

I got into the car, making sure a garden chair was in the boot. Slowly, I drove the three miles to "that place" on Woodhaven Road that attracted me with a horrific force, but at the same time an irresistible one.

Minutes later, I parked beside a stream. I looked at the time. It was early. The tatty wooden bridge crossing the creek seemed to get lost between the trees and the weeds surrounding it. There was no other man-made structure around.

My eyes tried to follow several yellow butterflies that were fluttering around this picture postcard scene that would otherwise be static. I placed the garden chair on the narrow dirt path a few feet from the two wooden crosses that told the world that this was a place where a death had occurred. (The original cross had been stolen and two crosses were made by two different people as a replacement.) I grabbed the small picture and the folder that contained her writings and sat down on the garden chair. I realized, suddenly, I had placed the chair in the very place where my daughter's body had fallen. For a moment I became stiff and thought about moving, but I did not. A morbid need to connect with her made me stay there. I opened the folder and I took out a sheet of paper with Arlyn's handwriting and read:

"...the smell of death surrounds me, and I was overwhelmed by its beauty."

I shook my head. I could not understand.

It was terribly hot, like the day that Arlyn died. I sat in silence, wondering what she would have thought during those last moments I wondered if I had been around....I looked down and read on. I felt a strong pain in my chest. Her hand had written the words I was reading, but her heart had felt those words.

After a while, I looked up, my mind open watching the yellow butterflies. Then I looked at my watch and saw that it was almost that time. If Arlyn's spirit was coming, it would be now. I began to talk. Initially, I spoke casually:

"Arlyn, how are you doing? Tell me how it is up there? Are you with Mammaw, Grandfather and Lori? Have you played the guitar for them?"

I waited, but Arlyn did not respond.

I felt that my anxiety was growing, so I started to ask stronger questions, waiting for a response to each one.

"Arlyn, do you miss us? When you pulled the trigger did you have any idea how much you were going to hurt your Dad and me? Did you know how much we loved you?"

Then, I asked her if she had seen her cousin Adán, who had been killed the previous day, and I asked her to take Adán under her wing.

Again, I closed my eyes and waited. And waited....

Nothing happened. I felt so sad. Finally I decided that I had to try again, to persuade Arlyn to answer. I asked for a sign to let me know that she was there. She had been gone for four years. I had waited long enough. I opened my eyes and looked around me. While looking for a sign, I thought I would not know what would be a sign.

How did one recognize a sign?

Would it perhaps be a flashing light, a roar of thunder, an image in the clouds? What would it look like?

Then I saw two yellow butterflies in the forest, behind the crosses. At this time of year this kind of butterfly is common in southern Georgia. They appear only in yellow. I looked at the picture of Raggedy Ann. I was smiling. The mop of the red wig looked almost like wings around her face. I smiled and talking to trees in a loud voice said,

"Arlyn, if you hear me, I need a sign! Would you send a sign so I know that you are all right? You know how much I love you and how much I miss you. Could you send me a red butterfly? A red butterfly, Arlyn, please!"

By then, the tears were running down my cheeks, making their own small streams. I closed my eyes. I felt the stillness, until a cool breeze came and I started to shiver.

When I opened my eyes, I saw the two crosses still in front of me. The difference was that in the forest, the yellow butterflies had left. I sighed as I was so disappointed to spend another very important date without a sign from Arlyn. I felt like I was drowning.

I was a persistent traveler on this road. Sometimes it seemed to be very difficult to move forward. Sometimes I wanted to give in and leave to join her, I missed her so much!

A moment later, I saw something out of the corner of my eye, which was flashing red. I turned and I saw a big red butterfly below the bridge. It flew slowly towards me, fluttering up and down as if it were in a sea of soft and undulating waters. As the butterfly moved closer I held my breath. The trees behind it faded, creating a misty background, accentuating the brilliance of its scarlet wings. To my amazement, it fluttered close to me. Then it flew around the crosses that carried Arlyn's name, not once but twice. Twice the red butterfly circled the crosses while, I, spellbound, stayed seated. I was so close that I could have touched it. It remained still for a moment before heading into the forest and out of sight.

Was it a coincidence that the red butterfly flew by at the time that I was waiting for Arlyn's sign? Was it really a sign from her? If it was a sign, what did it mean?

I do not know if it was a coincidence or not. I had visited this place on Woodhaven Road many times in the past four years. The only butterflies that I remember seeing before were yellow.

A sign is something that can suggest the presence of someone missing. For me, the butterfly was a sign of Arlyn, because otherwise there is no rational explanation for its appearance.

So, what did it mean?

I think it was a sign that the spirit lives after death and that the soul of my precious Arlyn is at peace. I think the red butterfly was the sign, through which Arlyn let me know, that she knows how deep my love is for her, and she understands my sadness. I also believe she sent me this sign to let me know that she is always with me.

Knowing this does not erase the fact that I miss her, but it helps me move forward. I now feel an internal calm that I had previously needed. I think I have a mission that I must accomplish while I'm here, and now I understand that the spirit of my little girl is going to provide the wings I need to get up.

A MESSAGE OF STRENGTH AND HOPE

Love is eternal. The red butterfly proves it. One does not die when the body dies. The hearts and souls that are bound on earth are united forever.

PELU, MY SPIRITUAL FRIEND
Ligia
47 years old

With my heart overwhelmed with grief, I write this story in honor of my friend Fernando, known as Pelu. Although I call him my friend, he was actually the best friend of my husband Mario, since their childhood. When I met Pelu, we got on really well and he became a close friend.

I remember the day I met Fernando, known as Pelu. As a visitor from Venezuela, his native country where he lived, my husband Mario brought him home and we talked for a long while. I was impressed by his sensitivity and simplicity. He captivated me with his sense of humor and his contagious laughter. Upon entering into more profound subjects like life and death, he shared his story and his fight against lymphatic cancer. We commented on the procedures and treatments he had been subjected to and what he had learned about life, due to this process. One of the things that struck me most was that he managed to transform his life and suffering through his spirituality. Pelu constantly referred to God and his faith.

Pelu was a *pilates* instructor and loved people. He and I shared a passion. Like me, he loved working with senior citizens. He felt a special connection with them, and among his clients were many elderly people. As Pelu was so sweet and affectionate, it did not surprise me that he captivated them too.

The three of us went out for sushi, as it was one of his favorite meals. It was an unforgettable evening. The night was short because we discussed so many issues and how we shared so much. In those three hours I met his pure, white soul.

Pelu returned to Venezuela with the intention of traveling to Miami again in the near future. Mario and Pelu continued to communicate by phone and email. My husband mentioned my book project and that I was collecting stories about losses. Pelu and I spoke on the phone and talked for some time about the book.

He was moved by the idea of the project and told me that he would send me his story. He told me that he was not sure how extensive it would be, because he had just completed a series of treatments, but that it would arrive.

Pelu died on December 25th 2006, in Caracas, Venezuela. Two weeks, before his death, I received an email from him on December 9th 2006.

I want to share with you, dear reader, this posthumous message from Pelu:

> Hi Ligia, I took a little longer to write this because this week I did not feel in good health. I

will recount my experience that I think you may find interesting.

Until May 9th, 2006, the idea of losing a family member terrified me. However, the same day, when I went for my routine checkup to control a melanoma, they did a biopsy on a scar from the first operation to remove a malignant mole. Well, I had another operation and thanks to God, everything went well. However, a final MRI of my skull resulted in the presence of some lesions, like small cysts, and that same day I was given sessions of radiotherapy and a treatment of pills.

What had always worried me before suddenly became a totally different scene. I lost the tranquil healthy feeling, but I won the union with myself, I grew spiritually!

A MESSAGE OF STRENGTH AND HOPE

Facing the end of life, either our own or that of a loved one, we need to embrace our spirituality in order to grow and transform our loss. Always remember to express the affection you feel for your loved ones when they are alive. Do not assume that they will be around tomorrow. Share with your family and your friends! Continuously tell them how much you love them and how important they are in your life. This will give you a sense of peace when they are no longer at your side.

A COMFORTING END
Linda
51 years old

Hester had many years of experience in nursing homes and so she was asked to look after a Mrs. Mercer at home, who was ninety-two. Mrs. Mercer had no children and her husband had died eight years before. Hester's own husband had also died recently, so the opportunity to care for Mrs. Mercer was a welcome distraction. At the time, Hester could not imagine that in the next three years she would experience the deaths of her brother, her son-in-law, and her new-found friend, Mrs. Mercer.

The nephew of Mrs. Mercer recruited Hester. He told her that Mrs. Mercer had had a wonderful romantic marriage. After retiring, they had moved into a district where they did not know anyone. There they bought their retirement home and lived a private life for the next twenty-five years.

For Mrs. Mercer, the death of her husband had been a great disruption in her lifestyle.

When Hester arrived, Mrs. Mercer was still mobile, but shortly afterwards she began to fall when she tried to move on her own. She was provided with a walker which helped for a while. Hester reported that like many other people, Mrs. Mercer had thought, before her husband died, that she was immortal. She never thought about her own death. Mrs. Mercer became more limited and impotent due to her immobility. She became more discouraged about the future.

Finally, the lack of mobility meant that Mrs. Mercer had to be placed in a nursing home. Hester faithfully visited her three to five times a week, and when she could not, she called. Mrs.

Mercer's nephew had asked Hester to do this, but in reality Hester did it because she was fond of the old lady. Hester said that nobody shares more than two years together without love growing in their heart.

Mrs. Mercer's body continued to weaken, but not her mind. She suffered terribly when she tried to eat. The doctors said it was due to a muscle wasting problem of her esophagus. Hester commented that Mrs. Mercer hated the texture of liquidized food, but she hated the idea of drowning more. In Hester's voice there was a certain disdain when referring to the arguments as to why the doctor did not perform corrective surgery.

"The surgery is not a consideration when you are so old. Doctors think these older people will die soon anyway," said Hester.

Hester said that most of the personnel working in the nursing homes see physical deterioration as something common and even expected. Few residents who come to a nursing home later return home. Hester recalled Mrs. Mercer's animated words during her first visits; she said she would improve and return home. However, according to Hester, people go into a nursing home to die.

During one of her visits, Hester saw that Mrs. Mercer could barely speak; she expressed herself in whispers. After sitting with her for a while, Hester told her she would soon be leaving.

Hester said, "I knew Mrs. Mercer was dying because her gaze told me not to go; her eyes were begging me to stay. So I told her I was going to the bathroom at the end of the hall, and I would return immediately. I went to the nurses' station and asked one of them to check on Mrs. Mercer because I knew that the prognosis was not good. The nurse said they would be there right away. I went back to the room and I did not want to leave her again. I held her hand until she died and then I went to call the nurse."

The nurse verified that Mrs. Mercer was dead and tried to contact her nephew. Hester had trouble being heard because she was not a member of the family. She had to convince the resident staff that prior arrangements had been made with a local funeral home. Once they had been convinced, the body was moved discreetly to the appropriate place. Hester chose the clothes in which Mrs. Mercer would be buried and attended the funeral. Hester remarked that Mrs. Mercer had a really nice funeral, but only about fifteen people attended. When one is so old, one tends to survive everyone else.

I asked Hester if, in her experience, she felt that the death of Mrs. Mercer's friends and her own family members had taken their toll.

Hester said they seem to know that their time is coming soon. Hester believed that Mrs. Mercer had resigned herself to die a month earlier.

Hester said, "This does happen, as I saw my siblings behave in this way. It seems that only this interests them." Hester said that one of her brothers was the type of person who liked to take care of his garden. However, the day before he died, Hester asked whether he wanted his grandson to cut the garden, and his response was that he did not care. It was suddenly not important. Those things become very common in someone who is already resigned to die. Hester continued, "Death gives you a real concept of what life is and that it is ending. Why collect things when one leaves empty-handed?"

Hester recounted the problems Mrs. Mercer's nephew had with the inheritance.

"When you have many things there are many technical problems after you die. One thing is to live comfortably, but most people who have many material goods have them because they have really been stingy in their lives. These people do not get their things in order before they die."

I asked Hester if there was a difference between the loss she felt for Mrs. Mercer and that of her siblings.

"People who are in your life hold a place in your heart that cannot be filled by anything or anyone."

Thus, although the loss of her siblings hurt and created a large void in Hester's heart, the absence of Mrs. Mercer also hurt her and left a void. Hester still missed them all. I could hear the tone in her voice when she said, "I have seen more deaths in the last three years than in the rest of my life."

When I asked if that made her think of her own death, she told me, "I do hope that everything is ready, not just material things, but also my relationship with God."

She said that there were times she became so busy with her daily duties that she focused only on the present day, forgetting about tomorrow. Other times, when her obligations were lighter, she could relax and plan ahead. She asked God to take her before having to go into a nursing home or to avoid death in a hospital. She thought that life on the other side would be nice, and she wanted to live her life here in such a way as to lead to that nice place on the other side. From time to time Hester still has lunch with the nephew of Mrs. Mercer. They no longer speak about his aunt, but they share memories of their own lives. Through the death of this ninety-five-year old lady, there has grown a friendship between Hester and a distant relative, between him and the "stranger" who consoled Mrs. Mercer in the final stages of her life. Together, they continue giving meaning to a life that no longer exists.

Hester is my mother. She was delighted to learn that I took classes about death and the processes of dying. She was very impressed that they provide this education, as she felt the need for this in nursing home care. During my interview of my mother, she made several comments about the sense that death gives to life and its fragility. Her response to the presence of so much death in her life during the past three years was what helped her to aspire to live in the best possible way and to prepare to die in the best possible way. Others' deaths did not make her consider her own, but her life!

The comment she made about life's trivial things when a person is resigned to die made me think that it is impossible to accept mortality and still be capable of operating in the world of the living. Perhaps the illusion of immortality is required to want to continue living. This could explain the relevance of faith in life and why almost all religions offer a belief in the immortality of the soul or some kind of life after death.

I accept that death is an integral part of life. I think our identity includes those we love, those we admire, and even those we do not like. The loss of life that is within our sense of identity is a part of our life. The grief allows us an introspective time to adjust our own identities. Hester said that the void left after caring for someone can never be filled, but I think that while grieving, if we rebuild the pieces on the basis of faith, our heart may remain strong. Through the years I have watched my mother go through many situations associated with death and the dying process, but she always remained strong in her heart.

I conducted the previous interview with my mother while completing my first postgraduate year in 2000. I did not know that the same year my mother would be diagnosed with breast cancer and would refuse treatment. She failed to tell us, her five children, until two years later. She died in 2004, after "putting all her stuff in order." The family lands were prepared and given to each one of us a year before she died. She chose her own coffin and made her own funeral arrangements well in advance. She did not waste a second of her last four years in a doctor's office or in the hospital. She suffered no invasive treatments that left her weak and fatigued. She traveled and preached in a sister church two months before she died. She lived her life the best she could, just as she had planned. During those four years, she saw her grandchildren grow and her children succeed. She was able to read my master's thesis. She traveled with me to Wisconsin to see her grandson graduate, and her last trip was with my sister to give what would be her farewell sermon in a church that she often visited.

She spent quality time with each of us. As she approached the end, her health deteriorated rapidly. In a period of two months she went from using a cane to a walker, to a wheelchair to being stuck in bed. In her last month, her granddaughter, a nurse, moved in with her to take care of her. When the cancer reached her liver, the pain was very severe and the hospice service provided palliative care. Therefore, her prayers were heard. She died in her sleep at home instead of waiting to die in a nursing home or in a hospital. She left a great emptiness but a foundation of strength in the hearts of her children.

A MESSAGE OF STRENGTH AND HOPE

My mother had a very strong heart and left us all the legacy of that strength. My hope is that I can pass this legacy on to others. When I teach my ethics class, I tell about my mother when we discuss bio-ethics and the right to choose to refuse treatment. I hope to show my students that sometimes they are not choosing to die, but how one is going to live until death.

YOUR EYES NOT WILL NOT SEE THE SUN
Lua Zial
48 years old

The biggest loss that I have suffered is the death of my mother, on November 16th, 2006. I was told over the phone, and upon hearing the news, my eyes filled with tears. I then felt a great emptiness, but I thought that God took her so that she would suffer no more. Her death is very recent and there are moments when it is very difficult to believe the harsh reality, but it helps me to think that she is not alone and that her loved ones are with her.

With the loss of my mother I learned to be more tolerant and love my fellow man. It is important to understand that a mother is the most beautiful thing that God has given us. She gave us life and gave us her best years.

My mother went slowly, but has left in all who loved her, a big void. But I know that she is not alone, and it is a great comfort to know that all her suffering has ended. I am sure she is very happy wherever she is. We are the ones who must ask for the peace she has now.

Mom, you are always in everything I do, in everything you did for me. I am eternally grateful to you! I love you, Mom!

A Message of Strength and Hope

I know it is very difficult to say certain things because, as is commonly said, "It is very easy to say, but it is not so easy do." But we must not think that we are the only ones who have suffered a loss. In a world so large with millions of souls, every time we sigh one flies to the house of the Creator.

We cry and the pain is so intense that we believe we will not overcome it. But we will. Just as He gives life, He also takes it and gives us the strength to get past it.

I wish that the loss of a loved one were not painful, that you remember them with joy and do not forget those moments which you had. Think that their time on earth was happy and even more if you were given everything you asked for.

With Love, The Memory
Luz
56 years old

My mother died of a heart attack while we were talking, sixteen years ago. It was horrible; I was desperate. Next to me were my younger sister and two nephews. I had to take her to the hospital and make arrangements for the burial. I asked God to give me strength, because my dad had passed away and I was alone. I felt very bad because it was a very strong impact, but I sought refuge in God, who has always been my support and strength to succeed in my life.

Despite the fact that time is a very important factor and everyday life dissipates grief, when I remember my mother I feel a lot of sadness, but despite all the pain I learned to face life alone.

A MESSAGE OF STRENGTH AND HOPE

Life has to continue, and only the memories of our loved ones remain. Let's look at these memories with love and not to further fuel the sadness you feel for the loss of a loved one.

RESTING IN GOD
Maigualida
48 years old

In the past fifteen years I have suffered the greatest loss, that of my father. He had an accident at work. He was an aircraft mechanic, and it happened during maintenance to an aircraft. He had no physical injury, but he fainted, lost consciousness for a long time (I never knew how long). When he regained consciousness (in nursing care at his work), he received no medical attention and was not transferred to hospital. When he recovered, like every day, he went home. But each day he became worse, his brain was affected; he lost motor ability, he dramatically lost weight on a daily basis, and had to be hospitalized. In less than a month and without leaving the hospital, he was dead.

When this happened, someone went to the house and alerted the family, because at the time of his death we were not at the hospital. However, we knew this would happen because he had been in the ICU in a coma for a few days.

I cried a lot. I was worried about my mom. I don't remember who was present, but probably my mother and my sisters (we were four sisters of fifteen, thirteen and six years, and one month). I cried a lot. I got used to accepting words of sympathy and saw more than one person fainting or a close relative having a crisis, but I did not help. I did not want to be noticed; it seemed as if I were watching from a distance.

After the funeral we had to go back to normal life. I felt deeply empty, but there was something very strong which made me think and analyze what was going to happen thereafter. I did not decide to think about the future; the concern seemed to be there already, and a determination that changes had to happen. A month later I had already decided to move with my maternal family to another city to study for a career that would allow me to work and earn a decent salary to support my family. My mom had never worked or had a profession. She was left with four daughters all of different ages and had only given birth to her last daughter a month ago. All girls. I felt empty, incomplete. I had a lot of questions but did not talk to anyone about them. I got used to the look of pity in people's eyes. We became known as the widow with four orphan daughters. I remember that for the first anniversary of the death of my father I wrote a beautiful poem, emphasizing the emptiness of our home, his last moments with us, his wife and daughters. It ended with a dialogue between my father and me, in which, incidentally, he did not reply. My mother helped me a lot to deal with the loss of my father. For being a devout and exemplary Christian, I thought that my dad had gone to heaven and that my mom would be very happy, because they would find each other again someday. Not only did I believe it, but I knew it to be true. My mom was a

Protestant and she spoke of the Gospel of Jesus Christ and the promise of eternal life in Heaven if my dad converted to her religion, which he did. So I knew that my mom was going to be happy.

With these values and memories and admiration for my father, I could begin to travel the road without him. I initiated a new stage in my life away from home, which I did by obligation; away from the memories and sadness of the rest of my family. I think without this loss, much of who I am, where I have been, and what I have done would not have happened.

First, my father was a protective and chauvinistic father. We did not learn to ride a bicycle because he feared that we might fall and hurt ourselves. As toddlers (my sister and I, being the oldest) never walked barefoot for fear that we could become ill. He never accepted that my mom should go to work because she had to stay in the house, looking after the children, but furthermore, he was a good provider, therefore why go to work?

Why work?

So to think that I was going to leave home at an early age to try to get professional education would not have been accepted. Of course with him there, the economic situation would not have been a problem. With time all is healed. I remember my father with much love, and I am very proud to be, out of his four daughters, the one that most resembles him in character, fortitude, and determination. My father was my idol, my role model.

A MESSAGE OF STRENGTH AND HOPE

We must live life intensely sharing with those dear to us. We need to express what we feel now, and we must prepare ourselves to be independent. We also must love and accept ourselves as we are. Furthermore, we must always try to contribute something positive in life to those around us. And above all, trust in God. There is nothing more powerful than Him. The courage, confidence, resignation, and everything that involves a loss is more tolerable if we rest it on God. Death is inevitable! I think we should prepare ourselves and comprehend it as something that is sure to happen and be prepared. It is very important that we try to be useful and give something positive to those around us and to our family. I think it's a very nice way to transcend.

THERE WILL ALWAYS BE LIGHT
Margarita
60 years old

What permanently marked my life was the suicide of my mother. It occurred in Cuba on April 22nd 1984. I was getting ready to go to church with my children as it was Easter Sunday. At that time, I lived with my mother, my husband, and our two youngest children. Our eldest, then seventeen, was not living with us. He was born with a lesion in his left temporal lobe; this did not affect his intelligence, but he was prone to the influence of undesirable individuals. At fourteen years of age, he left home with a group of "antisocial elements." My mother adored this son of mine; she loved all of them, but she replaced the love she felt for my father, with this first grandson. When my parents got divorced (curiously I was also fourteen), my mother suffered an irreversible impact, and was never again a "normal" person. Quite simply, when my son left, she could not accept the "flight" of her love for a second time.

That day, my mother had already taken her terrible decision. As usual, she went to the food market. She bought some alcohol and gasoline and concealed the bottles in a room that we hardly ever used in the house. At mid-morning, some people came to tell me that she had tried to throw herself in front of their car. They had managed to stop her just in time, but were certain that she had planned to do it beforehand. I told my mother,

"I do not want to think you've done this on purpose. We will go to the doctor to get you treated, and you'll see that you feel better soon."

At that time, I thought it would be more appropriate to hospitalize her because I feared for her, living alone in those conditions. My mother was silent, almost catatonic. In recent months she had experienced many ups and downs, both physical and emotional. I suspected that she found no reason to continue living, although she helped me in every way she could so that I could study and work. But in her family history there were five cases of suicide, so I decided not to risk it. My husband had taken the kids to the zoo, so thank God they did not witness the tragedy. I noticed that my mother seemed calm and asked her to get dressed, while I washed before going to the doctor before the others returned. She waited for me to get into the bath and then she did it.

Suddenly, I heard terrible screams, which for a few seconds I thought were coming from a horrendous radio program that the neighbors listened to. But realizing that the screams were going on too long, I ran down the stairs to the basement and broke open the door of the room, which had been locked. What I saw froze the blood of my veins. The flames were going out on her body. My voice was refusing to leave my throat to ask for help. I just about managed to get her to the shower and extinguish the remaining flames. In an instant, she slipped out of my hands, ran up to the second floor, took out a kitchen knife tried to stab herself in the abdomen. In desperation, I put my hand between her and the knife; my thumb received the first impact. Everything in the house became covered with blood: the floor, the furniture, and the walls.

My cries for help were heard by the neighbor, who called the police, as well as other people on the block. They took my mother, wrapped in a blanket to the burns unit at the nearest hospital, and I did not see her again. Her injuries covered more than 60% of the body. They did not admit visitors for reasons of asepsis. She survived for exactly one week, which was a long time, if one considers her bad heart condition. These were the worst seven days my life.

During the course of that week several psychiatrists came to interview me. They told me that my mother had regained lucidity and she sent them to tell me she did not know what had come over her to react so drastic, but we should not worry because she would recover and return home. This message moved me and gave me some peace. A few days before, I had asked one of the hospital staff to give my mother a note saying how much we loved her, and I promised my eldest son would return soon. It was a vain attempt to force a miracle. I do not even know if it was delivered, but I did what my heart told me to do. From a very early age I have suffered from intense bouts of depression.

The consequences of a suicidal act accompany those left behind. However, I decided to break the chain that was being passed from generation to generation. To do this I used various methods. The first was faith. That Easter Sunday I had organized part of the festival to be held in the church after Mass, a choir of children and youth, plus a small play. The religious community, who are also nurses, gave me their full spiritual support. The following Sunday, at the precise time we were praying for my mother she died.

The fact that I worked in a psychiatric hospital was also a great help to my recovery process. I did not take anti-depressants; every time I felt very distraught, I talked for a bit with some of my fellow psychologists. Although I've never been able to rid myself all of these Dantean images, I have understood that this action was not my fault, as I used to think at the beginning. We never imagine that a loved one may be "so bad" but rather say and do ridiculous things to attract attention. They are not exactly a clear warning.

My son is no longer absent. He has been re-habilitated and has a fruitful life. As for me, I have made peace with my conscience and my mother. I acknowledge that I was wrong and I have asked for forgiveness. I have written countless poems, but only one to my mother, I hope that redeems any shadow. It is called "Letter to Margot."

A MESSAGE OF STRENGTH AND HOPE

To those who have had the courage and patience to read this story, I say to them that it is worth living in this world of miracles because the caterpillar becomes a butterfly; the yolk transforms into a bird; the seed becomes lighter and flies until it becomes a flower; the immemorial step of the slug; the capricious air, rude and soft; the sky, that at the same time, is key and door, the water that bathes me and resting; the earth, goddess and mother, table and bed; the fire burning in my chest, the altar where my love to Love consecrates....What doubts are there now? Everything is clear. Lying before the Mystery I finally declare: Life, therefore, is nothing more than a great miracle.

As if it Were the Last Day
Mary M.
49 years old

The two great losses that I have suffered were the deaths of my two beloved siblings. My older sister Ana, who died seven years ago in a car accident, and my younger brother who died five years ago when he was attacked on New Year's Eve.

When I learned that Ana had died, my whole body was paralyzed, and I felt a great emptiness. I had almost the same reaction when I learned of the death of Rolando. But with Ana I felt guilty because that night she had visited me, and I had wondered why had she to come to see me. Why me? Why to me?

With the loss of my siblings I felt very depressed and suffered from muscle aches and headaches. I was shocked having lost both of them. Now when I receive a long distance call, I become scared because I fear bad news.

What has helped me through these losses is prayer. I have prayed and have learned a lot about how important it is give all of oneself.

A MESSAGE OF STRENGTH AND HOPE

Do not worry about insignificant things if they have a solution. Give all of yourself and live each day as if it were your last. Love yourself so you can learn to love your neighbor, and above all, give thanks to God for each new day.

WE GO TO ANOTHER DIMENSION
Marily
58 years old

During a period of three months I suffered the greatest losses of my life: the death of my parents. My mother died on May 16th 2006 and my father on August 1st. My mother died in her sleep and she just seemed to be still asleep. I wanted her to wake up, open her eyes and look at me. My father died while we were taking him to the hospital.

I am grateful to learn that both had a good quality of life, and I thank God for so many years with them, but I miss them tremendously. Mami was ninety-seven, and during the last few months could no longer walk, but she always knew who we were.

Less than six years before we—my parents, my husband and I—were strolling through Canary Islands.

One could say Papi, "died of love." He did not want to live without Mami. He was not sick, but he left two months later. I think it was because he wanted to be with her.

I saw them both on Sunday afternoon, and they died on Tuesday morning. Both suffered cardiac arrest. I gave thanks to God for listening, because in both cases I had been traveling; when Mami was sick I was in the Canary Islands, Spain, and when Papi died I was in Mexico. I had always asked God not to take them when I was away, and he granted me this petition, so much so that my father asked my son Alexis to ask me to come back because he was about to die but would wait for my return.

When my parents died I felt internally destroyed but controlled, as I do not believe in screaming. But tears are not something that can be controlled.

I still have a tremendous desire to go to see them, kiss them, hug them, and spoil them; to be with them. How sad it is when I have to admit that they are not here.

What has helped me a lot with the loss of my parents has been, besides asking God for his help, to honor them by sharing their legacy. Recently at Florida International University, I held a musical show with their favorite songs, which they danced to together. I also included two poems written by Mami, and I brought mariachis, as I took them to her last birthday. Producing this show helped me to harden my soul with the repetition of things and memories. I have also written poems for them and I have another project to write something more in their honor.

A Message of Strength and Hope

With these losses I have learned that without a doubt there is another dimension to where we are going. Everything does not end here, because I feel that my parents come to visit, both in dreams and in other forms, and that is a wonderful feeling. I feel they give me the love as if they themselves as being human, could not express, but now in spirit they transmit it in a way that words cannot explain. This can only be experienced and I have felt it .... There are no doubt the Spirit and God exists, and I am sure that there is another dimension and that everything does not end here.

THE FUTURE IS TODAY
Miriam
60 years old

I suffered my biggest loss twenty years ago when my youngest uncle of thirty-eight died suddenly. He was driving to work when he suffered his first heart attack. He was able to park, but he suffered a second heart attack while being attended to, which was the massive attack that killed him. I only learned of his death when I called the hospital to ask about his condition and they reported the news. Upon hearing the news, I reacted violently. I threw the phone to the floor and lost all notion of time. I was told later that a neighbor, on hearing the screams came round, but I do not recall this. I was angry with God and I cursed Him because of the death of my uncle.

This loss was very big for me because he was my favorite uncle. He was only eight years older than I was and so he was more like a brother. I was depressed a lot by his death. It was hard to stop crying, and I dreamed a lot about him. It hurts a lot not having been able to say goodbye, to listen to his last words, and know his last wishes.

What helped me to overcome this loss was my faith in the afterlife and dreaming about it. I felt that we could talk as if he were alive, and this led to a farewell between the two of us, until the last dream I had where I said I was clearly no longer going to dream with him because I already had told him everything that was inside me and he knew that I could live without him. We would see each other the day that I died and that he would be waiting for me, and that he was going into the light. I feel that this opportunity to dream with him was for me confirmation that he knew how I felt and that he wanted to give me the opportunity of saying goodbye.

Though much time has passed I still feel great emptiness, but it consoles me to know we will see each other again. When going through this loss, I realized how important it is to do good, to help each other and live life without doing harm to anyone, because life is too short. I have learned to see life differently. Do not take things to heart, and try to live and enjoy the present.

A MESSAGE OF STRENGTH AND HOPE

It is vital to keep in mind that the past has gone and that the future is today. It is the moment to live and to have fun, because you never know when it will be our last. I think we must always strive to be good, to believe in God, and, above all, love a lot and live "today."

LIVE WITH LOSS
Pilar
43 years old

On July 26[th,] 2001, I suffered my greatest loss: the death of my mother. I was visiting Nicaragua, as I lived in Paris and had gone out to eat with my sister Ann and my husband.

My nephew called us, and when we got home, we found out my mother had had a brain aneurysm. Two days later she died in the hospital.

Immediately after the accident I began to vomit. Normally these things do not happen to me. When she died, all my siblings were present. I became short of breath and was about to hyperventilate.

My spiritual reaction from the moment she became ill was to ask God that if she was not going to recover, it was better she died. After that, as always, I became closer to God, neither more nor less.

After her death, for many days I was not hungry and lost about ten pounds. My way of reacting emotionally was to fix things around the house and to distribute her things among the siblings. Then, upon returning to my routine in Paris, everything lost value; the thing that made me get up every day were my kids and taking them to school.

Since then, although I have had many moments of happiness, I always have a feeling of emptiness. Sometimes I want to talk to her and I do so in my mind.

Since the death of my mother I feel that there are still parts of me that cannot be filled, no books, no trips, no experiences....There is just a void.

The love of my family has helped me with the loss. I think my children, my family, and my sister Ana who are a source of great joy. I tend to be positive, so I tried to find the good things in everyday life one day at a time. I think the best way to face a loss is to accept what works or doesn't. For some people it's easier if you put your grief in the freezer; other people get wrapped up in their grief, as they live it and suffer it. But I am sure we should tell the people we love everyday we love them; I feel it makes you give true value to things.

I also tried to transform my life when, around two years later, I had the opportunity to go back to work, because I had a void in my life or lack of meaning. I feared the absence of my mother, and when my children went to the University (now ten and fourteen), my life would be meaningless.

A MESSAGE OF STRENGTH AND HOPE

You have to be honest with yourself and find out what works for you. Personally what has worked best was having a work plan for each day, something that made me get up and to some extent occupy my time. Over times one learns to live with the loss and understand that the loss is not going away; we simply learn to live with it every day.

WITH LOVE BUT NOT NOSTALGIA
Regina Maria
43 years old

My father died on February 17th 1982. He was a very strong and healthy man. He never smoked or drank. At the end of 1981 he began to have stomach pains. My mother took him to the doctor, and he was diagnosed with cancer. He underwent surgery, but the doctor told my mother that the cancer was already well under way and that they could not do anything. Two months of suffering began for the whole family, especially for my mother, who spent the majority of her time in the hospital chapel. The priest told us to have faith. The diagnosis was bad; the cancer had metastasized. My father died at the age of forty-two, and no one told him that he had cancer, although he was aware of what was happening and realized that he was dying.

On February 17th 1982, I perceived it was the end. At midday my dad began to expel some internal organs, and at half past 2 p.m. closed his eyes forever. At that time I was nineteen years old and was surrounded by friends and expected some improvement in my father, who was critical. At dawn on the 17th I wanted to enter his room, but I was afraid. Away from my friends, I sat in the yard of my house. I wanted to be alone with the nice memories of my father. At 2:20 p.m. I was called to my father's room. My brother was there with my mother. I sat on my dad's bed and I touched his frozen feet. I tried to pass the heat of my hands to him, but everything was useless, and ten minutes later my dad died leaving a huge void.

At my age I did not understand the true meaning of loss, but felt a very big emptiness. I cried and hugged my mother when she told me we had lost my father. We both were alone. I, for one, felt afraid to face the wake, the funeral and the Mass on the seventh day. The memories remained and that sense of emptiness that is part of my life.

I regret that I never told my father that I loved him. He knew that I loved him very much, but I never showed it with a kiss. I still miss him a lot. With the death of my father, I learned that life is very short. We lose many hours with trivial things and resolve them badly. The way we are educated also exerts great influence on our attitudes and the expression of our feelings.

A MESSAGE OF STRENGTH AND HOPE

Never be afraid to show your feelings for your parents. If you really love them, show them the affection that they deserve, regardless of anything else. Do not expect them to do something for you. If they do, great! That would be the ideal. Do not become nostalgic after they are no longer with you. When I close my eyes in prayer, I imagine my father in a very nice place and I hug him a lot. If you have them at your side, do it now; it's beautiful. It's beautiful to not be ashamed to express a feeling as beautiful as love.

ENJOY YOUR LIFE
Sandra
47 years old

Twenty years ago I had the great pain of losing my twin sister. When I got the news I felt like something had been cut out of my body. She died in an air accident. At that time I lived in Ecuador and life was hard, because my husband abused me. My mom was the one who gave me the news that Andreína had died along with her boyfriend. My sister and I were very close before her death, and I had had a premonition. Six weeks before her death she came to visit me.

I was living in Guayaquil and she came to meet my eight-month-old baby.

I am afraid of a slow death and my sister suddenly asked me, "Would you, if you could, avoid a long death from cancer?" and I added, "Who is thinking about dying?"

We hugged, laughed, and cried. Something in my heart told me I might not see her again.

A MESSAGE OF STRENGTH AND HOPE

Enjoy your life and do not expect that things will come by themselves. Do things you like and do not leave for tomorrow what you want to do today. Do your best to have quality of life and enjoy it.

WHERE DIANA WILL LIVE
Silvia*
51 years old

My daughter Diana was, until ten years old, a normal and captivating girl, happy, alert, and relentless. She enjoyed all the fruits of family love. Diana knew friendship, joy, games, and contentment, and discovered her beauty with surprise. Everything in her was a harmonious reality and a promise of the future until the day that the inconceivable happened. A malignant brain tumor, the collapse of life.

She is the protagonist of the book I wrote after her death, which tells the story of her relationship with the disease, her life in sickness and death.

I wrote the book for my own survival, to not die of loneliness. I wrote it to perpetuate what my memory does not want or is not able to forget. The pain made it possible for me to find the true place of Diana. What I wrote in *Living Without Diana* is like having her there in those pages. She lives forever, despite her absence. It is a well-deserved tribute to the courage and strength with which she faced her illness, and her ability to overcome the painful circumstances she had to get through. In short, it is a true example of life. *sappel@arnet.com.ar

The life of Diana made possible the realization of the book about her death. Over time, it became necessary. I found no solace in writing the book; it is just a shadow of my own intimate self, a mirror in which to see myself. Maybe other parents, who have lost a son, can find themselves in my story.

One of the purposes of sharing my testimony was to show a path, a way of passing through the pain and to continue living. Letting my feelings and my experiences out brought me, paradoxically, much satisfaction, soothing my soul, and the gratitude of many people who recognized that my experience and testimony helped them. For some years I walked the path of learning to live with the absence of my daughter and with the pain and the void left behind.

I try to be a better person: to help, to understand, to have empathy, to put myself in the place of another. I consider myself a person wounded for life, and every day I try to help others also wounded by life. This world that I brought Diana into, since she fell ill, is the world I will belong to forever.

I try to transform pain into creativity, I do not attempt to mask my pain; rather, I simply try to encompass it with sense, to create a space that is beyond death, to talk about meanings of life and its mysteries.

I chose the path to accompany the suffering, with all my dignity, with all my sensibility, with a wisdom that is the result of my experience and my professional background. I learned, over time, to live with what cannot be changed, with a latent pain, with an everlasting memory. I try to find, beside the tears, laughter; to have next to the sadness, happiness; a happiness that will never be complete. It will be like a sun that does not dazzle, but gives enough light to find a way, to continue living with the memory of my beloved daughter.

To go through this sad experience and to live with this immense pain I refined my personality, Allowing me to show a great need to give generously, without the need of receiving anything back, only feelings of well-being and inner peace.

It's a hard life; at times it is unbearable, and at the same time more spiritual, more thoughtful, with solidarity and compassion; with time to help and time to remember. It's my time, my life, my memories, my real and unconditional motherly love.

In the words of Denis Vass, "Love is, ultimately, what leads us to live, it makes us truly be born and die."

A MESSAGE OF STRENGTH AND HOPE

People who go through the painful experience of losing a child develop a sense of solidarity and sensitivity that makes us better people. We learn to live with that which cannot be changed, looking for intimacy and a profound spiritual growth, trying to find, over time, a sense of life.

EXPRESSING FEELINGS
Thomas
46 years old

I have had three big losses in my life: the first was my sister, twenty-four years old in an airplane crash. I was twenty-three; she lived in Caracas, and during a holiday left with several friends in a small plane; it lacked the required power and dropped a minute after taking off. That was actually the first loss that shocked me.

At the moment it happened I was playing golf with a friend. My parents called the golf club, and I was picked up, but nobody told me anything; they told me nothing. When I got home I called my mom and asked what had happened. I thought that something had happened to my father. I never imagined it had been my sister, so I called, and my mom told me that something very bad had happened to my sister. It had happened early in the morning, and it was already the early afternoon. Hours had passed, and in Venezuela there is a newspaper that comes out in the afternoon, and they were already selling the newspaper with photos of the accident. Well, I had had a presentiment, but I did not believe it.

A friend was driving the car and I sat in silence; I did not know what to say and I did not want to talk. I did not believe it. When we arrived at my friend's house, I got in my car and went home. When I got home, I saw some friends of my parents, and they were talking to my mom. She told them what had happened. My parents were at a club when a friend of my sister gave them the news. They had to call our dentist to go and analyze Andreína's body to be absolutely sure of her identity.

My parents were traumatized. There was much tension in the house. There was not much communication with my parents. My mother is German, my father English. It was a very good family, very united, but we never spoke of problems at home. I did not open up; neither did they. My mom gave me the news. We were all in shock. There was no hugging or sobbing. We all just endured it a little. I went upstairs. I bathed and, of course, there I cried. I did not know what to do.

I went downstairs and I sat in my Dad's study, trying to digest what had happened. Listening to a little of the telephone conversations; watching my sister's and my parents' friends arriving, and their reactions really touched me. I think I closed up and I took it all as something bad, but was not fully aware that I had lost my sister.

We went to the wake at a funeral home. Perhaps because of the people that went and the constant reminder of what had happened, I started to open a little and there, with friends, I cried a bit, but I still felt that at this moment I did not open fully….It was my first time at a wake of someone I knew.

It was like a dream, as if it were not happening, and I think it's part of my way of being. I tend to isolate problems and not deal with them in my own way. I do not like confrontation or conflict, and I prefer that things calm down and disappear by themselves, rather than facing them alone. I did not want to face the death of my sister. I wanted to see it as something that happened and let it heal over time.

When we went to the cemetery, I was a bit stronger. I saw the urn and how they buried it; one assumes it is the body and soul of the person. When they buried it, my parents suffered a lot in those moments. I feel that my dad blamed himself (He never forgave himself for having allowed the trip.). After the funeral, I began to work right away; in my office I cried alone. Then I met Gabi, my wife, because she was impacted by the story. I calmly talked about it with her. I know that I lost my sister, and I know I did not cry enough. I felt that this was an outstanding event, but I put it out of my mind like something lost.

The following losses were my parents, who never recovered from the death of my sister. We were a perfect family, but in a period of ten years, it disappeared completely, beginning with the death of my parents and sister, along with the divorce of my other sister, the twin of the one who died.

A MESSAGE OF STRENGTH AND HOPE

One has to react to their deepest feelings and open up from the first moment. Do not try to deny something, or fear the kind of suffering that happened to me. I do not like people to see me suffer, and I do not like to make people suffer. If I could go back and react to my sister's death again, I would hug my parents and cry, and try to open up everyone in the family, instead of each hiding their feelings. People should not have to fear opening up; one must express what they feel at that moment.

THE NEED TO BELIEVE
Umilda
80 years old

I have had big losses in my life. That of my parents, and recently that of my husband four years ago. I spent a lot of time with my parents because I did not have children. My father died in Cuba in an accident. He was traveling on foot and a train hit him. Afterwards my mother died, as she had very delicate health. When this happened, some friends called me by phone and let me know. It was devastating. I felt great pain. At that time I was alone, and I felt hopeless. Later my husband came home, and bit by bit, so did my nine siblings.

I am very Catholic. I take refuge in my religion to cope with pain. I cried a lot, but I never actually suffered depression. At night, if I suffered from insomnia, I prayed and read the Bible.

Over the years, and now after losing my husband, I became very lonely and sometimes had little desire to live, but I take refuge in God and that gives me confidence and at the same time comfort. I realized it is necessary to believe in God and have faith.

A MESSAGE OF STRENGTH AND HOPE

For people going through a loss the only thing I can advise is that you shelter in God and put your suffering in His hands.

EVERYTHING CHANGES
Vicky
59 years old

My father died in 1986. After spending five days in the hospital he died unexpectedly of colon cancer. I was at his side, along with my mother and brother. It was something horrible, but at the same time incredible.

I felt at the moment he died it was as if his soul moved to an invisible portal at the foot of his bed. I immediately felt that the body lying there was not was my father, but only his "shell." I was certain that he had been freed and was in a better place.

But even so I felt the pain. I had pain in my chest for many days. I was emotionally destroyed. No one expected him to die so suddenly. From the time the symptoms began until he died was less than two months. He went to the hospital, and after running several tests they decided to operate. In the middle of the operation they called me by phone from the operating room to tell me that they could not do anything because the cancer had grown so much. I was alone with my mom, and I had to prepare her for the news before they came out. It was a tremendous blow!

The most difficult thing was that my mother was already beginning to show symptoms of dementia, and my father was the one who always took care of her. After the operation, my father lived for three days, and as he was conscious, I asked him what to do with Mom.

Emotionally, the loss of my father forced me to deal with a lot of responsibility and forced me to be stronger and more determined. At that moment I realized that when you lose a loved one and you feel this sorrow, this pain, you are not crying for them but for yourself.

My mother died in the year 2000, after suffering from Alzheimer's for fifteen years. I divorced in the same year, after thirty-four years of marriage. I bought my own house and I had three jobs and two job losses in the course of all this. They were difficult years. For three years now I have been in a big company and earning good money. I am independent, and I have a romantic relationship with a good man. Despite that and all the years that have passed, every time I think of my parents I become sad. Sometimes I would like to go back to being that little girl protected and loved by her parents, and not have so much responsibility.

But even so, at this time and thanks to God, I am calm. My spirituality definitely increased greatly after the death of my father and my mother's illness. I feel calm, and I try to help others who have had similar losses.

Currently I am working as a director of a senior center and can help many people during the day. It is a job that requires all of my time and energy, but it has many spiritual rewards.

A MESSAGE OF STRENGTH AND HOPE

Nothing in life is stable. Everything is changing daily, and we have to be prepared and stay positive to be able to cope with these situations. It must be remembered that life in this world is not eternal and that we must take advantage of all the beautiful moments that we are offered. One must not waste time in fights and discussion. We have to enjoy everything that surrounds us, especially our family and our friends.

FAITH AND PEACE, FACED WITH ADVERSITY
William
61 years old

The biggest loss that I have had in life was the death of our daughter, María Alejandra. This happened six years ago, on April 25th, 2000, at 12:30 a.m.

At age 25, María Alejandra died in an accident when the vehicle she was traveling in as a passenger was hit by another that did not obey the traffic signs. My wife and I were notified at home by two members of the police in Coral Gables, at approximately 4:30 a.m. Upon learning the news, I collapsed on a sofa in pain. My wife Olga was present; I think she tried to assist me.

Initially, I questioned why God allowed the death of Alejandra, but with help from my wife, I focused on our faith and accepted His will, as my wife had already done. I had a questioning reaction but at the time resignation.

During the first days I lost my appetite and I felt disoriented. I lost interest in everything that was happening around me. Over the years, although I feel pain, I have come to accept that God allowed the untimely death of Alejandra for a reason that while not completely understood, I have full confidence is part of His plan in our lives. I feel that what helped us to cope with this great loss was our faith in God and the belief that our terrestrial lives are only temporary.

Our family's and friends' support also helped us, particularly members of our prayer group. However, the anger I felt for the other driver did not help, nor does the fact that for work-related reasons, I was physically separated from my family for much of the time.

To this day I ask God constantly for rest for Alejandra's soul. I take flowers to her niche weekly; she loved flowers. I relive many of the happiest memories of the twenty-five years Alejandra had with us, and that allows her to continue living in my mind and in my heart.

I have learned that life is fragile and that we must seize the moments we can to enjoy the love and the company of our loved ones while we can.

My priority is no longer success or money, but the good we can do while we are in this world, and in our preparation for eternal life.

A MESSAGE OF STRENGTH AND HOPE

The only thing that can sustain and help us move forward from what might seem the biggest and most inexplicable loss is our faith in God and the certainty of His promise for a better life, after our temporary transit in this world.

ALWAYS IN MY HEART
Yenny
48 years old

Fourteen years ago I had the greatest loss: the death of my father. He was living in a nursing home when they told us that he had suffered a respiratory arrest and had died.

I felt a strong pain, and above all I felt guilty for not having been able to be with him at the time of his death. When I was told, I was with my siblings and my partner. I felt great disappointment knowing that my father was gone, and I asked God for his eternal rest.

I felt very worn down inside. I felt as if a part of me was gone, and I became very depressed. I have never forgiven myself that on the previous day to his death, because for work-related reasons, I could not see him.

Although I have gotten over the loss of my father, I will not be able to forget him. He will always be in my heart.

A MESSAGE OF STRENGTH AND HOPE

Love people in your life. And remember the sage who stated, "Nobody knows what they have till they lose it." Today I apply all the advice my father gave me that I did not appreciate when I was young.

DAD, IN YOUR MEMORY
Ligia
48 years old

In my life I have felt moments of immense joy because I feel that I have served as a guide more due to the appreciation of friends than from my own doing. But if my advice helps my friends, how much I hope it is useful to my beloved daughters. Yes, and remember that you are my greatest treasure, next to that great lady who is your adored mother.
—Julio C. A. Martínez

On November 11th, 1971, the sun was shining in all its splendor, It was a perfect winter's day in my home country of Nicaragua. But...that day became the saddest day of my life. At the age of twelve, I realized that my father had died. I still remember the fear I experienced thirty-six years ago when sitting in my classroom. I could see, through the window, two of my relatives walking down one of the aisles of my school. My heart started beating very fast, because I knew that something terrible had happened to my dad, who was in a hospital in Miami, Florida, recovering from an illness.

"What could have happened?" I wondered.

One of the Sisters took me to the college chapel very quietly to pray for my dad, even though I had not yet learned that my dad had died from an aneurysm in his aorta. The bearer of this terrible news was the Mother Superior, who in an effort to console me told me that God had taken my father.

I felt an immense pain because I felt that God had not answered my prayers. I could not understand it. God was my refuge every night when I kneeled praying for the recovery of my father, and now I was faced with the reality of his death. I felt great sadness and confusion amid the tears. The Mother Superior took me home to participate as a member of my family in the rituals of my own Hispanic culture.

According to the customs, I had to change my brightly colored clothing for mourning dress and prepare for the longest night of my life. Getting closer to my house, I saw the streets were full of cars. My house was completely full of friends and relatives who had already learned of the death of my father and had come to give us their condolences and to join us in our mourning. I remember that my older sister came to greet me at the door, and upon entering my house, I hugged her. I heard a comment referring to myself that I managed never to forget: "Poor thing, she is so young!"

Those words were like daggers in my heart and only served to aggravate my pain even more. That night we held the wake at my house without the body present, as my dad's remains were still abroad. My closest friends accompanied me, and I remember with special care two teachers who did not leave me during the whole evening. They gave me all the support and affection that I so much needed. I remember that I could not stop crying, but I also had uncontrollable attacks of laughter, possibly a mixture of hysteria and nostalgia. I spent the night like this until exhaustion rendered me asleep, and I fell into the arms of my Aunt Anita, one of my father's sisters, whom I loved a lot.

The next morning, I woke up and I realized that it had not been a nightmare, that my dad had died and that my house, decorated with black ribbons representing our mourning, had lost its characteristic joy. My house, instead of being a home filled with light, was turned into a bleak and desolate place.

It was a rushed morning because we had to go to the airport to receive the body of my father. My mother, my sister, and my brother came to accompany my father to his final resting place. I remember that when I arrived at the airport dressed in black I saw my mom come out of the plane. At that time they still used stairs, and seeing her face marked with pain, I realized that my mother was a widow and that I was a girl without a father.

My mother took me in her arms and we cried for a long time, sharing the same sense of pain and astonishment at such a misfortune. The airport was completely full, because my father was a public figure of great virtue and was loved by many. The very fact that so many people had continually come to us with condolences and to express their distress was touching. I had only wished to leave and run and hide, not to confront my new reality. When my eyes returned to the runway and I saw the casket containing the body of my father, I felt as though my world had just ended. I just remembered that my dad, at the beginning of his trip to Miami, a couple of weeks ago, had promised to return. And now he had, but lifeless. In my child's mind I wondered what had happened. Had I done something wrong? Had I misbehaved? Was this my fault? With all these unknowns, a mixture of guilt and fear, I sought refuge in my mother, who gave me the calm that I needed. With only her hug, I felt comforted and loved.

We went to the house where we held a wake with the body present. I remember that I did not leave the head of my father. I could feel his stiff cold face in my hands, and although my tears covered his face, I was unable to warm it. I was there for a long time, in a state of total bewilderment. I looked around and amid all the flowers that surrounded the casket, one arrangement stuck out; it represented a golf course with a white ball in the center. The flower arrangement had a banner across it with the following words, "The Wednesday Group." As my father was a golfer, he met every Wednesday with a group of friends to play golf. This same group was present at his funeral, accompanying him with camaraderie and care.

After the wake we went to the funeral Mass, where the priest gave us words of consolation and hope, but by no means did my girl's heart understand what was happening. I wanted desperately to awaken from this nightmare, but the pain increased even more when we went to the cemetery. There were endless moments during which I thought I would lose consciousness or that I would go crazy with so much pain and distress. But it was not so. I managed to survive the first month without my father, feeling I was living in another dimension. I seemed to see him in every corner of the house and heard his whistle the way he had fondly called me when he got home. I thought that the world was capable of restoring my illusion, but it was not so. Little by little I regained my desire to live and to succeed in school.

I learned to live without the physical presence of my dad, but with his memory ever-present in my life. It is this memory that motivated and drove me to build my life so that I could help others find meaning in theirs. My father was a great motivator. He had great faith in humanity and thought that we all have the opportunity to grow in spite of misfortunes, and this is precisely the message that I want to transmit; I feel it is my mission in life. The death of my father has been the greatest pain I've experienced, but at the same time, it has been a source of inspiration to carry out my purpose in this life. His love and advice will always be with me.

A MESSAGE OF STRENGTH AND HOPE

The greatest loss that every human being can face is the death of a loved one, and if you have experienced it, you are not alone. Early in my life I realized that our loved ones are not immortal. That although one thinks that parents are eternal, the reality is quite different. Our loved ones are not invulnerable to death, and the more we are aware of this, the more we will appreciate them in life. That is why I decided to share my story with you, to let you know that I have been there and that this experience marked my soul for life. At times I thought I could no longer live, that I did not want to. But then I realized that, despite the fact that we feel weak faced with pain, we really possess a great inner strength that manifests itself when we least expect it, and that helps us to move forward and to turn our loss into a source of inspiration and spiritual growth.

LOSS OF HEALTH

OPEN THAT DOOR OF HOPE
Alba
43 years old

It happened about four years ago. At that time I was busy doing a lot of things. I worked a lot in the community, participating in programs for people on low incomes. I wanted to work with underprivileged children, but in a proactive way (not for reasons of pity), to give them training, since one should do something for the bigger picture. I was in this organization with several people where many women were collaborating in this program. It was a lot of work, and I think I got in over my head. I think that there is enough time in life for everything, to do and to give. In those days I was very busy, and this was a huge amount of work. On top of all these commitments, I also took care of daily life. I also felt that in the organization I was alone. People who worked with me needed to raise money, but it was just me, really, who was dedicated to it. When one is starting up and has no salary, one has to implement mechanisms to raise funds.

What happened at that time was that it was not the right group or the appropriate time.

Amid all this coming and going, I remember a night in which I was sitting at home with my husband, watching television. I felt calm and suddenly I disconnected from everything. I thought I was relaxed when suddenly I stopped watching television and went dizzy, and when I woke up I was in the hospital and a doctor was asking me, "Lady, lady, are you okay? Are you okay?"

I felt as if the words came from afar. They were talking to me, but I could not speak. I heard them saying, "Wake up, wake up!"

Then the doctor told me that I had had an onset of a stroke. I had never been ill, not even a cold. I felt everything collapsing around me. I could not speak, could not move. They asked, "Do you feel your left arm ...? No... Your leg...? No... "

I understood, but since I could not talk I answered in my mind.

At that time, I remember seeing my kids, and thought,

"Is it worth it what I'm doing? How tired I get! Where am I going? Is it worth it? "

Seeing my mother and my husband and listening to them saying, "You are going to lose your coordination."

I said to myself, "Get up out of bed!"

I realized then how important faith is. Independent of what you believe, but have faith. And I knew I had the strength to keep going.

They gave me some medication that knocked me out completely. I remember one morning my husband took the children and returned at three in the afternoon and found me asleep. And communicating through gestures I told him that I could not continue like this. I would not continue like taking the drugs. I stopped, always thinking that I would recover, because seeing me in bed, without moving, watching them do everything - brush your hair, bathe you, it makes you feel awful. When people start looking at you with pity in their eyes, it is terrible. I said, "No, I do not want pity or to be looked after by anyone; it was not easy!"

Then one morning when I was alone the miracle happened. My husband had gone to work, my mother too, and my children were at school. I said to God, "I know you are going to give me a miracle."

Having faith is very powerful. I feel I have not fit the usual diagnoses. I felt very powerful and I said to myself, "I'm going to get up because there is a lot to do in life."

Attitude in life is so important! You can say that everything will come down around you, but if you have the inner strength and conviction to move on, you can! Then, suddenly, lying on the bed, without hesitation I stood up and walked. It was an unbelievable feeling! I felt that I wanted to have a bath and take a shower. I spoke out loud and I realized I could speak.

After my bath and without calling anyone, I left the hospital and went to an English academy, because I told myself I would learn to speak English. So I went to the school and sailed through the different levels. My teacher could not believe it.

The day I got up and went to the school, I told my teacher I had just got out of bed after three months without being able to speak and that I had come to learn English. People stared at me in a strange manner. I told them I spent three months without being able to speak, unable to walk and now look: I could move my hands, feet, waist, and hips.

I know that this is because I believe we all have a mission in life. Sometimes things happen for some reason at the wrong time because you do not have a crystal ball, but I believe that things happen for a reason and one connects with a higher being and one allows it...

Miracles do happen!

When my husband came home and saw me standing, he hugged me happily. My children and my mother did the same. They always gave me so much love and affection.

In life one must always leave a door open to hope and another for faith, and the only way the two doors shut is from a great miracle from God.

Having gone through this experience, I definitely think that my life has changed for the better. I have seen people who have passed through similar problems to which I say, "You know what? You can get up!" I think everyone has a great power within their mind, but we barely use it. If we did, we would be walking towards perfection.

I realized that it was necessary to focus on my life to carry out my mission, while distributing my time and my priorities. I continue to help those I can and who God allows me to. I think especially about today. Not about the time I have left, but how to live today fully and with meaning. What I should give to myself and what I should give to the world. I do not focus on what the world will give me. I have a lot to give through love, compassion, and a desire to serve. Let us realize that with every step that we take in our lives, we sow a future.

A MESSAGE OF STRENGTH AND HOPE

Let us not forget that life can change in the blink of an eye. We have no control. So we must live it fully, and you alone have the power to get up. Sometimes, not physically but spiritually, because there is nothing in the world that can stop you once you feel your inner strength. So open that door of hope and allow the higher power: Buddha, Allah, God, or whatever you call it, guide your life.

GOD DOES NOT ABANDON US
Alvaro
62 years old

I was born in Nicaragua, and now I am a citizen of Costa Rica.

Descendant of a marriage in which differences in age and character were abysmal and antagonistic: for more than twenty years, one of my parents was full of sweetness and the other, all courage; therefore, there was no relationship between my parents, either romantic or comprehensive. This "cultural adverse baggage" negatively impacted my personal development. So much so, I came to be a young, self-conscious, engrossed (daydreaming), fearful person with a complex. I socialized with no one.

I moved to Costa Rica due to the many upsets with my father. For the first few months I went hungry and thirsty. Later, when I started college and lived in an apartment, in addition to academics, alcohol and fun also became part of my life.

The first time I tried alcohol, a shot was enough to get me drunk, and two to vomit. However I got to the point of drinking sixteen beers. But the biggest "achievement" was when I drank two litres of Guaro [a very strong alcoholic beverage] and a few beers in one night.

The time went by. Initially, I only drank on Fridays (after work). Later, I drank a few days during the week. But (in my case), I started to continue drinking at home. I fell into a vicious cycle: on weekends I bought at least two six packs and two bottles of vodka; at midnight on Sunday I was still drinking. Of course on Monday, I woke with a large hangover. To reduce it, I went for a thirty-minute run, but before doing so, I had a double shot of "hair of the dog" and later, when I returned, repeated the dose with a lot of lemon, which masked the smell of liquor. I also discovered that chewing gum neutralized the smell fairly well. So I spent all day at work, chewing like a ruminant.

On Monday I did not go to lunch with my co-workers. I escaped to a bar-restaurant where the chef, who knew me, was preparing a good onionized steak with French fries and a good green salad. In the meantime, I had two doubles and during lunch repeated the dose. And waited to finish work to go and take refuge at home and continue drinking as though I had been dying of thirst in a desert! And so, I "sat on the wagon" every day from Tuesday to Thursday in a "soft way" so that there was no interference with my work.

There came the moment that this whole "process" was worsening to the point that I no longer had the strength to stop. Then, the unexplainable happened: one night while I was at home with a drink in hand, I felt that everything was collapsing, and I sat in a corner of my bed and began to cry uncontrollably. I cried out as a helpless creature before my Creator, that only He, with his infinite mercy could help me out of this ordeal. With such deep, profound faith, as if by magic, I instantly stopped drinking; it was miraculous. It has been more than ten years that I have not drunk alcohol. I do not need liquor to hide my weaknesses anymore; I can confront them with my own strength and with that which I received from the Creator.

I have had some retrospective thoughts and questions that made me think that God never abandons us, that He always loves us, and He in one way or another has a way to change our approach. How is it that in my work as an economist, working in an institution as serious as a central bank, no one was aware of my alcoholism?

The smell of liquor, hangovers, and the smell oozing through the skin, and you feel uncomfortable with everything.

It is significant that although I had many traffic accidents they were never serious. The worst was when I crashed into a tree: I had wounds on my face, two broken ribs and a banged up leg.

From abstinence, and in other ways, I received many benefits, above all, my mother's joy and the rest of my family, who congratulated me for such action. I would no longer bother them with most of my drunken attitudes. The reaction of my colleagues and co-workers was also positive.

I managed to stabilize my body and my soul. I could wake up without a hangover, taste and smell the food, and appreciate the beauty of life. In other words: be me and see things as they really are.

In addition, I managed to eliminate my "drinking buddies," and I found those who really appreciated me.

According to my experience and respecting other's opinions, you must keep in mind that to solve the problem mentioned, among many others that occur in our lives, the following rules should be applied, with some exceptions:

1. We must form and foster "homes" where love prevails, the ethical principles and "socialization" between parents and children. The practice of these values will strengthen the group to overcome any problems that are present and will prevent any family members from falling into vices. Consequently, we create a positive multiplier effect on the younger generations and thus help build an increasingly better society.

2. When we have a problem like the one I set out for example and we want to get out of it, we must apply the aphorism, "Beg on your hands and knees." That is to say, we must implore God's help with faith, and at the same time, summon our inner strength that we almost never use, to solve our obstacles. In most cases, we also need the help of specialists. We should get into the habit of communicating daily with our Creator.

3. Once our decision to "rise up" is taken, we must not give in, in any way, shape, or form in moments of weakness. We must say, "I love myself, God gives me health and I must not destroy it. I am fine how I am."

Be self-critical and "see" that the resolution taken gives profit and that if we do otherwise, we sink back into the problem we are trying to solve.

4. Change our attitude on life. Let us be better people in every way. Also, try to create happiness through the daily practice of eradicating negative thoughts (hatred, envy, etc.) and be fed by the positive (philanthropy, solidarity, etc.). Thus, notwithstanding the setbacks that we face, we will try to remain happy.

5. We must pat ourselves on the back and love ourselves by eating well and exercising the body, mind, and spirit.

6. Finally, we must practice regular self-control of our actions. We must always exercise restraint, so that things never become future vices.

A MESSAGE OF STRENGTH AND HOPE

I sincerely hope that my story gives hope, support, and guidance for anyone who wants to get out of a vice (kleptomania, nicotine, alcohol, gambling, drugs, etc.) or problems of the soul (bad character, pessimism, inhibition, etc.) and any obstacle that affects them.

REMEMBERING MY MOTHER
Gema
46 years old

One of the greatest losses that I have confronted has been the loss of my mother to Alzheimer's. I realized she was suffering from the disease about two years ago, but in reality it happened gradually. I began to notice that she repeated the same story over and over, and continually kept talking about her childhood. Gradually she lost her short-term memory. So, on one of our visits to the doctor I mentioned my mother's symptoms, but the doctor simply ignored me until, finally, my mother was diagnosed when I decided to change doctors.

When I received the diagnosis, I kept calm because I knew the truth beforehand. My father was with me when we were given the news.

Although checking that my mother was suffering from Alzheimer's disease was difficult, I thanked God for the time that I had been with her, and I realized that the time I had left with her would be beautiful. I said that I would take care of her and be at her side at all times. I do not deny that I felt very sad to realize that my mother, although she was with me physically, little by little would deteriorate mentally.

I have realized that it has helped me by being very patient with her. She can still communicate with me, but I have noticed that this ability has declined in recent months. Keeping my patience with her, I have managed to find out what she wants at her end. I feel much better having achieved this communication.

I have learned to accept that these situations are part of life. What we must do is see what we can get out of a bad situation. I am very pleased to have the opportunity to offer her the same care that she gave me—although I am sure that I will never be able to match the care she gave me.

Usually I feel calm, but there are days in which I feel very tired because she needs my constant attention. But this experience has helped me appreciate the good times of our lives and to be able to live without remorse. I understand how fragile life is, and because of that, I am more careful now. I continuously listen to my inner voice to guide me.

A MESSAGE OF STRENGTH AND HOPE

Remember that, although sometimes life seems to be very difficult, those moments pass. Much depends on us, if we take this as a way to grow spiritually and emotionally. This attitude will help us to overcome any obstacle that we are presented.

LOVE BREAKS DOWN ALL BARRIERS
Liliana
60 years old

The greatest loss that I suffered is the consequence of living with a bipolar mental disorder suffered by my husband. It started when we had been married for twelve years.

I decided to stay with my husband, but from that moment on, our married life would not be the same again, because he never again was the man I married. There were very large and destructive changes caused by his medications, but despite this, our love is so deep that it unites us beyond everything.

It's not easy being married to a man who, instead of being a companion to me in our marriage, cannot, given his limitations. And, moreover, it isolates him, leaving me alone at social events.

He asked me to continue with my activities, unconditionally supporting me his own way, and sometimes I feel conditioned to do things. It was learning to live differently, to be able to assist and protect him and at the same time protect myself.

It costs me a lot to keep my mental health; I have had some depressions due to the conditions at home. Sometimes I see other married couples who go everywhere together, and I am amazed because they can do so. Perhaps they go through other problems, like everyone, but being together I guess would be easier.

Only those who have lived with a psychiatric patient can understand their depressions and mood swings.

With the onset of illness occurring in a single minute and, unfortunately, after thirty years of being an active man in the prime of his life, my husband became a person without prudence, sick for the rest of his life. His discussion with a very close family member, followed by the suicide of this person, destroyed my husband mentally. And so, in no time at all, everything changed and we lost our normal way of life.

I had never known what a depression or suicide was, or what it was like to blame another.

I read a lot; in tears, I looked for material in books, and I could see that suicides leave messages to destroy the lives of those who live.

Some relatives and friends sensed what was going to happen; they said, "Be careful with your husband!"

And I ignorantly did not imagine the terrible deeds and decisions that I would be taking from then on, or the harsh trials that I would have to face.

Even if one thinks in God, faith in the end is undermined. You start thinking about miracle cures; super pills that for others, perhaps, worked well; in spells to which perhaps we had been subjected, wanting to grasp at salvation in a way that no religion has found. We just wanted to get a bit of inner peace and balance.

At first, inserted into this terrible vortex I did not know what to do. Then I realized that despair and anguish were factors acting against us, since they created more setbacks in my husband, who thought he was destroying my life. And he wanted me get away from him, to continue with my studio and my work as if nothing had happened.

Years later, faced with so much spiritual anarchy, my body screamed with breast cancer, and we had to deal with many relatives and friends helping me.

My husband now felt that he was no longer the only sick person in the house; we were two diseased persons, both suffering. I despaired at the obvious: doctors, medication, hospitals, nursing, the sums of money that we did not really have. I had to keep working in order to sustain the job and the realities at home.

Now, after ten years, my husband is much better, although not fully recovered, because this is a recurring disease. I am still alone in the many things he cannot share.

Among the positive things of his personality, I can say that he has never been selfish. On the contrary, he asked me to go out and take a break; he could stay alone and sleep while on his medication.

Some of our friends disappeared because of the bitterness and uncertainty. Each continued on with their lives, as it is very easy to understand a physical disease, such as a broken leg or a flu, but generally, people are afraid and will not come close to someone who has a mental illness because they do not know how to cope. My decision was to stay by his side, to not abandon him, and that is what I do and will always do, lovingly, steadfast and loyal, although sometimes it is very difficult to bear.

To tolerate this situation, I relied on my endurance and my way of being helped. What did not help at that time was that those who were close to me saw that I was going to a reunion, wedding or a birthday alone, or sometimes I did not go at all, and what I received was their silence filled with their pity and many times cruel people asked,

"Is your husband not going to come?" or "Why do we not go out all four of us?"

Simple, normal questions, but they hurt, because I could not go with my husband and I dared not go alone. We lost many couple friends and gained many real friends, who understood the situation and that there are diseases, especially psychiatric ones, which are for a lifetime.

In order to sustain this whole situation, I try to adapt and be positive. But my anxiety is overwhelming when I am faced by my inability to change my reality, and I want to accept how I am supposed to live and that way to be able to keep on going.

I chose this path. I chose to stay at his side. It might have been easier to separate, to step to the side and go, but now, after many years, we can enjoy happiness, the occasional happy times. These are wonderful, extremely intensive moments.

These years have been a great learning experience. With this loss, I've learned that love can surpass all barriers, and I have met many friends who have supported me. Still…it is not easy.

Everything was very hard because, I had been a pampered girl who didn't have to deal with something unknown until it happened.

It was and is very tough, and I have lost my best years. I did many things on a professional level, but few participating with my partner; generally I do them alone or with a friend. Sometimes it is difficult because my husband stays at home, waiting for me.

I believe that, despite everything, if I were to go back to those times and go through the same situation, I would make the same decision.

A MESSAGE OF STRENGTH AND HOPE

Accept and fight for a better quality of life with your loved ones is a daily and arduous task that only love and daily life can forge.

WITH GOD AND ONE'S FELLOW MAN
Rey
59 years old

On September 21st, 1993, I had a HISPA (an association of Latinos who worked for AT&T) meeting, and on September 23rd was going to participate in another meeting, both in New Jersey. I decided to take three vacation days from September 21st to 23rd to address the issues of HISPA and spend the 22nd with my parents and sister who were living in New Jersey.

I had been feeling depressed for several weeks due to a combination of personal and work factors. On September 3rd I had requested help from a psychiatrist who worked in Ohio, who previously had helped me through two episodes of depression, triggered by my divorce and a number of pressures at work.

He prescribed antidepressants that had previously worked in ten or twelve days. However, on September 20th I was quite bad from the combination of depression and the side effects of the medicine, insomnia and anxiety, which always disappeared once the benefits of the medicine began to take effect. At the end of the day September 21st I was worse and on the morning of the 22nd I could not even read a verse from the Bible as I always do.

With the help of my family (the depression affected my ability to make decisions), we realized that it would be impossible to attend the HISPA meeting on the 23rd.

I had agreed to pick up two members of HISPA at Newark Airport and then go to the hotel to prepare for the presentation of the next day. My sister took me to the airport where I explained the situation to the first of two colleagues, Danny Simonsohn, that I was in the midst of a strong depression and anxiety attack. Danny immediately took charge of the situation, rented a car, took my notes, and promised to pick up the others and take my seat at the meeting.

I also contacted Gina Guerra, a member of the HISPA board. I explained the situation and asked her to do the right thing with HISPA and to coordinate the activities of the organization in my absence, as the president was abroad and I was the first vice president and president-elect. Gina immediately took the lead and did a magnificent job, bringing together the efforts of individuals and offering me appropriate assistance, help, understanding, prayers and unconditional friendship.

Thank you, Gina! I will never forget your kindness!

Meanwhile, I called my doctor in Ohio, and we agreed that I should see a doctor in New Jersey. I contacted the eminent psychiatrist Sergio Estrada of Fair Oaks Psychiatric Hospital, in Summit, New Jersey. He recommended a stay in the hospital and I was admitted on September 26th.

They did a careful and thorough review, and examined all the evidence of my previous attacks of depression, my family history, and many other aspects. Then they changed the prescription, and on Tuesday the 28th I began to improve.

I continued to improve thanks to the care of hospital staff and the prayers of friends and even people I did not know. I was discharged on October 7th and stayed with my parents until the 16th, when I returned to Ohio. Every day I felt better and I can truly say that within weeks I felt I could again enjoy things and admire the beauty of autumn and feel happy to be alive. These are feelings that I was missing for some time. In my best moments over the previous few months, before hospitalization, I simply felt "more or less" well.

Although it may seem strange, I consider the events that occurred to have been a blessing. In my previous episodes of depression, I recovered while working; I simply put all my energies into surviving. This time I had the opportunity to reflect and learn about my illness. I learned that the way I suffer from depression is similar to diabetes or high blood pressure. It is a physiological phenomenon; the "propensity" is inherited and can be triggered by emotional causes and can be treated with medication and kept in remission. One difference is that in many cases (and I still do not know how to differentiate them at their onset) the depression is cured after about eighteen months of drug treatment; just as diabetes and high blood pressure cannot be cured, they are only kept at bay with medicines.

It is also clear to me that God guided the events to make the most of this episode. There were too many "coincidences" to attribute it to anything else. To all those who prayed for me, thank you!

To all those who are experiencing symptoms of depression that I detail later in this document, or who know someone who has them, seek professional help and stay in treatment!

The statistics say that at some stage, 15% of the U.S. population suffers from depression. Only a handful seek professional help because of the stigma, but are still unfortunately tied to it. Of the many who seek help, some stop the treatment because unfortunately it can take up to eight weeks for the depression to improve, while the side effects, some of which may well be unpleasant, start the day that one begins to take the medicines.

Partly because of the social stigma that some still attach to depression, I decided to share my story in detail. I held the post of Head of Department at AT&T while I fought several episodes of depression. During this time I had four supervisors who reported to me and each of them, in turn had fifteen or twenty engineers below them. Each and every one of them gave me great support. After an episode sufficiently serious enough to require hospitalization, I still have the same level of management. While I decided to which job I was returning to, four vice presidents, and Ernie, my vice president, offered me jobs. And indeed I ended up getting the job that had been my dream for some time.

In the next seven years after this episode, I was head of Market Management for AT&T throughout Latin America and, when it split and became Lucent Technologies, I was chosen by the executive general manager to design and implement a workshop for new managers from different countries.

This is a testament and tribute to the people at AT&T/Lucent Technologies and an appreciation for the values of the company. If I had suffered from high blood pressure or a diabetic coma, there is no doubt that I would have kept my job. They reacted in the same way, at least at AT&T, for an attack of depression.

A MESSAGE OF STRENGTH AND HOPE

Even in the darkest moments caused by depression, God was always with me and let me know through several unexplained miracles, "coincidences." Also in difficult times generosity was demonstrated through the support and love of family, friends and colleagues. Cultivate the relationship with God and with others because that will provide you with a lot when you need it.

WHERE THERE IS A WILL THERE IS A WAY
Silvia
66 years old

In 1964 I left Cuba via Spain, following my husband with my two sons, ages two and one. We waited three months for our residency, and finally arrived in the United States with my two children. I was also four months pregnant at the time.

Those were tough times as on leaving my homeland I lost my roots. I lived in Miami for nine years and then, following my husband once again, went to Panama in search of a better future. Again I was being uprooted, because I was leaving behind my mother, my sister, my grandparents in Miami, and my recently acquired life.

When I arrived in Panama, I felt isolated from everyone in a country I did not know. I was accustomed to the American way of life, and this was a big change. I had to get used to the new lifestyle. I sacrificed everything for my husband so he could establish a new business and give my children the education they deserved. They learned the Latin American culture and I am grateful for this education. However, I started to feel anxious and wondered what I was doing there. When I had a social life, at first it was marvellous. I played cards with my friends, we went out at night; it was extremely active and entertaining. The parties...

When I first arrived in Panama, I hardly drank at all. But by entering into this party regimen, which lasted until four in the morning, I realized that I could keep up if I drank four glasses of wine. I danced and laughed at everything; it was perfect, but when my eldest child left for Miami and I was left alone with my daughter, the scenario changed. She had a boyfriend, a life, and I found myself alone. I sought refuge in alcohol as a form of escapism. Everyone knows that drink is a depressant.

One morning I cried because I felt guilty for what I had done. My daughter had arrived home and found me drunk.

I drank alone because my husband was always out with friends. So I was alone in the house, drinking. At six in the afternoon I listened to romantic music which made me melancholic. In the darkness I used to escape my life. I did not want to realize that I wished to escape and numb everything. It was as though I was asleep....I did not want to feel anything.

Then I realized that my husband had a friend, his secretary. I did not want to admit what was going on. Even though my husband was always out, I never thought that he was betraying me, and this was precisely what hurt me most and why I started to take drugs.

In the morning I took antidepressants, so I slept all day and then at six in the evening I started drinking. That is what I did all day. I spent all day in my bedroom, even when eating. I did this for seven or eight years. My husband tried to help but very little.

He had no patience to see what was happening to me. I could no longer go out because I started to suffer from panic attacks. I was afraid of everything; I suffered from phobias, especially agoraphobia. I did everything at home; I even had my hair done at home. I did not know what was happening to me, until I realized that I was suffering from anxiety and panic attacks.

At that time my daughter decided to go to Miami because she wanted to go to university. My other children lived in a house that we had in Miami, and circumstantially I also went back.

I felt very bad when I was sober because I thought I had done something improper, that things were not how they should be. I tried to hide it. When Friday arrived it was worse and I invented something, under the pretext of a party in the house for my children and their friends, for example. Weekends were great, all of us drinking together.

After a year in Miami, my daughter died of a brain aneurysm. At the time I was under the influence of tranquilizers. I looked around, but I could not feel anything, even though it sounds horrible to say. If I had been well I might have seen that my only daughter, my companion, my friend, was deteriorating day by day. She became like a monster, because her brain had swollen. She also had seizures. It was very painful because she was only twenty years old and was in the hospital one month and nine days.

I remember that two days before she died I no longer had the courage to see her, not even on four to six pills a day. I could not see her without feeling a terrible pain, remembering that pretty girl with blue eyes and long hair which as a result of the incision in her brain had been shaved off.

About a year after my daughter passed away, I nearly died from the effects of the medication and alcohol. I was sent away to rehabilitation where I learnt a lot, and I believe that God prepared me while I was recovering to start giving to others. I started to give catechism classes. I began to feel the satisfaction of being useful.

That first Christmas when the children of the catechism classes arrived with chocolate, I returned home as if I had received the most beautiful diamond in this world. It was the satisfaction of feeling that these children loved me, and I started to feel good.

I realized that my life and my marriage were not working and that if I was tied to a marriage that did not work, I would end it. So I bravely took a one-month trip to Mexico. There, when I was alone in the city, I realized that I could function by myself.

I had become dependent because I had left a protective family only to fall into a protective marriage. But now I felt able to face life by myself. I think that rather than loving my husband I became dependent on him.

The trip to Mexico gave me strength, and when I returned, I confronted him and told him that it was necessary to separate.

In order to keep everything clean you have to be selfish "me first," "me second," and "me third." When a person has an addiction to alcohol or drugs, they can relapse very easily when there is a problem, for a few hours. But unfortunately the problem is still there, and when the effects of the drugs wear off, everything is worse.

With my divorce, I suffered a second loss.

Survival means to learn to live with the loss, without the loved one, although one never forgets them.

I became very close to God to be able to carry on, but not necessarily to the dogmas of the Church. I sought the God of love, not God the punisher. In Alcoholics Anonymous I learned to understand the God of love.

With reference to the loss of my daughter, I have received various signs. I remember it happened after Hurricane Andrew hit Miami, Florida. I was in my room praying with the rosary. I asked my daughter to come and find me because I felt that in this world there was nothing left for me. I cried for my daughter, and suddenly I saw the crucifix from her casket that was hanging on the wall begin to move. I threw myself to my knees and asked forgiveness from God, and I understood that I was getting a reply, and that this was happening for a reason. From then on, my life began to take on new meaning. This is when I met César, my current husband, who has been with me for the past ten years.

These signs came to me, unexpectedly, at parties or anniversaries. I remember one Mother's Day I was at Mass and I found a pink rosary and understood that it was a present for Mother's Day. On one of my daughter's birthdays, I went to the cemetery and upon leaving I saw something shining on the floor. It was a silver bracelet with some Barbie doll shoes. My daughter always played with Barbies, and I took this as a message that she was okay, not on the physical level but in the spiritual sense because the connection between mother and daughter never ends. It goes beyond this physical plane.

A MESSAGE OF STRENGTH AND HOPE

It is very important to be positive and be sure that one is going to rebuild their lives. I say to myself, "I know I'm going to rebuild my life, I am going to cope with my life." And so I did, but at the same time I learned to communicate my feelings and, above all, to give myself time.

God's time is not our time, especially when we are suffering from immense pain from losing a loved one, and they tell us that everything is going to be okay, but you do not believe it. You cannot assimilate it; you cannot understand it. Only time, faith in God, prayer, and the belief that our loved ones are with us is what helps us move forward. But one must give it time. The wounds of the heart take time to heal. The healing comes in due course.

NINTH LETTER*
Xiomara
58 years old

For Sandra,
My sick daughter

Dear Sandrita,

I listen to the radio and watch television, and I read in the newspaper about the case of a little three-year-old boy that he was mistreated by his mother and left lying dead in the street.

Two days ago a baby died without a brain or skull and his parents want to donate its organs, but the law did not allow it.

The press named the first "Lollypop Baby" and the second "Baby Theresa."

These cases have made me think of you. When you were born, they brought you to me in diapers and a blanket, and I, like most mothers, counted your fingers and toes. I saw you were whole, and I felt happy because you were "normal."

At two months you smiled wonderfully and made baby noises. I recorded your happy baby sounds on a tape recorder. I loved to tickle you and talk to you. At nine months you smiled and waved your hand. At a year, you said two or three monosyllables. You developed normally so we did not suspect anything was wrong with you. At one year and three months you were in the children's hospital for a week. After many tests and medical examinations, we still did not know what was happening to you. After five years, my long-awaited baby, did not walk or talk. You were mentally retarded with many incurable physical disabilities. You were losing, little by little, the few skills you had; you became rigid. The doctors did not know what to say and I was terrified. There were those who told me that everything was okay and that I only needed patience, but I could not believe that everything was wrong right from the beginning. Sandra, you were diagnosed by your father and then by the doctors, with RETT syndrome. This rare disease occurs only in girls. It is a brain disorder, and although initially the girls develop normally, between six and eighteen months they begin to fall behind in their development, which leads to a condition of profound mental retardation and physical incapacitation. There is no known cause, treatment or cure. So far only about three or four thousand cases are known in the world.

Today, almost twelve years old, my beautiful baby, you cannot speak or eat alone. You wear diapers. You cannot walk or run. You take medication to control your epileptic seizures, and your curved spine barely lets you breathe correctly or sit up right. You are prone to urinary infections and pneumonia; this is why many girls with RETT have died already. We do not know how long you will live among us, or how you are going to die. Every phone call I get from your grandmothers or the nanny who cares for you or even the therapists, or doctors with a simple question, makes my heart jump, thinking that something has happened to you.

I read a study about your illness which said, "It has a complicated medical definition," but this is not about medical words, but about girls. Of little girls...girls whose lives are affected by this severe disease, RETT. Girls who have to use wheels instead of legs, who feel the raindrops fall, but do not understand rain. They like to eat, but they cannot do it alone. Who want to give a hug, but whose arms do not extend, who listen to music and love it, but cannot sing...girls whose parents seek to renew hopes each day. Minds trapped inside bodies that will never allow them to communicate or understand what the rest of us have and do not know how to appreciate it.

What is in the Lollypop Babies' minds?

What does the mother of a Lollypop Baby think or feel...?

Would she ever appreciate what God gave her...?

What does the mom and dad of a Baby Theresa feel?

The pain of having lost their baby and thanking God for having taken the child and for having given them a mission to be fulfilled, with only days of her life! The law has to consider situations like these. And I, Sandra, I do still thank God for your life, for the great mission that you bring with you, but sometimes I wish He would take you. The pain that I sometimes feel is great and profound. Some believe that I have done a lot for you. I cannot do anything, only accept you and love you. Some people think I am used to your illness. A mother, a true mother, never gets used to seeing their child getting sick and dying.

But even so, I thank God for you. A rose is beautiful, but the thorns prick us!

Once again I say to you, I love you always,

Your Mommy

*From my book *Mi Cruz Llena de Rosas from Xiomara Pagés*. Miami, Ediciones Universal, 1996. You can also see: www.xiomarapages.com

A MESSAGE OF STRENGTH AND HOPE

A mother never gets used to the suffering of a child. She can only accept and love them and give thanks to God. Roses are beautiful even with thorns.

A HISTORY OF PATIENCE, ACCEPTANCE AND A LOT OF LOVE
Ivonne
43 years old

Sometimes I feel sad but I know that I am not alone. I was living in New Jersey with my husband when we had Steven, our first son, now seventeen. When Jason, my second son, was born, Steven was twenty months old. I was thirty and I had

had a normal pregnancy, but as time went by, we noticed that Jason was not developing as a baby should as he did not move.

At eleven months old Jason suffered the first seizure.

I had told the doctors that I felt that something was wrong with Jason but they denied it. They said his weight was correct and he was sociable.

After the first seizure, they finally decided to check him more thoroughly. He was suffering from a degeneration of the nervous system and was most likely going to get worse. A year later they diagnosed him with "a delay in his development."

When the doctors did an MRI, they said that there was something wrong with Jason's brain but did not know what disease he actually had. At three he could crawl, but he stopped, and has never walked again.

I worked a lot with him. A voluntary service unit came to help me see if he would walk, but nothing changed.

The seizures continued to occur every two or three days.

When Jason was three years old we moved to Miami. New Jersey was too cold for Jason.

We gave him medicine and a special diet to control the seizures.

I was seeing a counselor and started to participate in a support group with other mothers where we all spent a lot of the group time crying. I feel that this helped me share something that we were all dealing with.

There was no prognosis for Jason, and this created a lot of anguish because he did not have a disease that I could read about.

"What is it?" I would ask.

"Well, he's slow" was the answer I received.

"Yes, but how long will this go on? Will there come a time when he will be like other children?"

The doctors told me to go home, love him, and save my money.

One doctor once told me, if he was not talking by the age of two, he would never speak, and if he was not walking by five, he would never walk.

Jason has never been able to talk much, about only ten basic words; however, he has always been able to understand. He communicates with facial gestures, he points with a look: to go the bathroom, he looks at the bathroom; he looks at the door or some shoes if he wants to go out.

I established a system of communication with him, through sounds and certain words.

At first he could grasp things with his hands, but he no longer has the strength to now.

Another thing that has helped me is the fact that I worked in an orthopedic hospital.

My mom worked there as well and she invited us to the homes of other children, and this helped me see that there were children who were in the same situation, even some in wheelchairs.

It was very hard when at nine years old Jason had to be given a wheelchair.

The doctor said to me, "When you're ready...." I felt that hope had just run out. I thought that at least I had done everything I could for him. I had tried hard to get him to walk.

I have had a lot of support from my husband and my eldest son Steven, although he was almost the same age. He would tell me that he wanted his brother to talk even if he never walked. I felt bad for him. I hoped Steven would have a real brother.

I got used to it and accept it, but it always bothered me because I did not want to see Jason in a class with so many sick children. I wanted him to be surrounded by healthy people and that Jason could demonstrate that he could love like a regular boy.

Jason was the king of his school; he was always playing with friends who helped him.

When he finished at the school, they gave him a medal for teaching others to communicate without words.

When Jason was ten years old, I told my husband that I wanted another child. I always wanted to have four children so that Steven would not be so alone. We talked to Steven (twelve at the time) and told him the risks.

"No, you know how it is, if it happens again you know what will happen," he replied.

At five months pregnant, I had the amniocentesis test and although I was told that everything was normal, I was very scared. I decided that if it happened again, I would not try to fix it.

After seven months into the pregnancy, Emily was born weighing four and a half pounds and had the same problem as Jason; the story was repeating itself. The doctors told me that being born prematurely was normal.

At one month old I took her home and started to get scared, as I saw that she was not moving a lot and I thought that I would have to start all over again. With the same problems as Jason, I had to take her to the pediatrician!

They did not understand and said I was imagining things. The doctor told me there was something in her nervous system. With that my head started thinking, "just like Jason." I became very frustrated.

They did not believe me until the first seizure. They only saw the child for a minute, while I was with her all day, as I was not working.

The story was repeated at eleven months when Emily had the first seizure. Five months after her checkup I was told that she was slow, just what they said about Jason.

"Here we go!" I thought.

The MRI confirmed that it was the same thing that Jason has. The brain had not developed enough for a one-year-old. Comparing both MRIs, I saw that they were the same.

What was I going to do now?

Most importantly I could not waste time suffering in the same way I did with Jason. We had a nurse who came to see Jason, and I told her that Emily had the same thing.

The nurse asked me how long I was going to worry. She told me that I had to get past this, as the first time I had spent three years trying to figure it out. Now I knew what I had to do, just accept it. But, now I had two children with this problem, not just one!

I sent Emily to school, but what really hurt me was that I dreamed of taking my little girl to things like ballet lessons but I couldn't. That was the greatest pain.

Only a short time passed between finding out and accepting the reality. I would not spend time thinking about what might have been!

The doctor told me she was the same as Jason, "no reflexes." I had moments of discomfort, feeling bad, and sometimes I wondered why it had happened again. I had not done anything wrong. People told me that God had chosen me because he knew I was capable of dealing with it and that helped me.

A counselor asked me what bothered me the most and I answered, "When I see other kids running about and I know that my children never will."

"You need to know they are like angels, they have chosen you to watch over them....You need to find someone to help you so you may help them and move forward," the counselor responded.

My supporter, Lili, said to me, "Ivonne, there is a three-day retreat and I want you to come." I said that I could not go as I was not used to being without my children. But she insisted.

"You have to come...."

Throughout the weekend I cried, looking for strength. Lili told me that I was not the only one; many other people also had problems, and little by little, I would accept my children as they were.

I decided to work as a substitute teacher to help other children. As the school authorities knew that I had disabled children, they placed me with special children, and I began working with all these children.

I forgot my pain and started to help others. I soon saw that there are so many people that you cannot fix, but at least you can try to give them a better life. It is the only thing you can do!

After awhile Jason's social worker offered me a job as a support coordinator, to help mothers of special children.

Jason taught Emily to crawl. They now have a very special bond. Emily is always at his side and they play together.

I had thought it was going to help Steven being Jason's friend, but Emily is actually Jason's friend.

When Steven had his first girlfriend, she told me that she knew Jason and they lunched together outside with his friends. She told me she thought that Jason was *cool*. It was as if God gave us these things along the way.

I always try to do things with Steven. We also always go on holiday together as a family.

My husband has supported me a lot. When he sees me down he says, "Don't be like that, because otherwise I'm also going to get like it." So I try to feel better and draw in strength.

We knew that when we got married it was for better or worse, and we are lucky as we have a lot of love.

There are many people in worse positions. The most important thing to know is that if something is not perfect that one can continue on.

I always want people to learn from my children, that they see them happy, because it makes me feel good. For example, Jason is in a class where they take him for a walk, which he likes. He is so charismatic and cheerful that everybody has to sympathize with him.

A MESSAGE OF STRENGTH AND HOPE

God sent me this situation. It has strengthened me and taught me to accept that nothing is perfect. I want other families to include our children because they also want to enjoy life. It is important to say everyday, "I have to live....I have to continue living to be here for them because they need my care and, above all, my love."

LOSS FROM A DIVORCE

BEYOND THE MISCALCULATIONS AND ARMOR
Ana
47 years old

Although I sit to write this now, I have thought about it for several months. When my friend Ligia suggested I share my feelings about grief, her proposal served as an exercise to think and reflect on aspects that I had not seen before.

When Ligia asked me to speak about loss, at first I thought I would write about the grief caused by the death of my father (twenty-five years ago) and my mother (five years ago). They were sudden deaths, "small blows of life" that left me with no direction in life.

I am forty-eight years old now, and although it is assumed that a person's parents will die first, I found myself at forty-three with no mother or father, and this seemed very unfair.

But Ligia asked me to write about another kind of grief, and I began the task of writing about my divorce. What I found surprising was that, although this grief was of a different nature, both processes had some similarities, which I will try to point out at the end.

I did not marry young; I got married at twenty-seven, but I was still fairly innocent. I was married for ten years and had two children who were five and ten years old at the time of the divorce, and today they are sixteen and twenty-one.

After the divorce (which was the end of a bad relationship full of infidelities and irresponsibility on the part of my partner), my children and I did not continue to have any relationship with him, as he is only their biological father.

The story has a happy ending though because my children are great, and I would like to think, very good people too. The divorce and the total absence of their father has not left them without doubts, maybe with some consequences. But I think between the three of us, we have turned out well.

My divorce came suddenly, because Mario, the father of my children, left suddenly. But it was only "a chronicle of a death foretold," partly because he had cheated several times and left us for another woman, which made the separation very public and embarrassing for me at that time. In the divorce process, there were many legal disputes, including lawsuits about the ownership of the house, which is mine, and thankfully I did not lose it. I also received a debt Mario had inherited through his mismanagement.

I said that my divorce was a "chronicle of a death foretold" because, in addition to his recurring infidelities, absences, and irresponsibility towards his family, Mario and I were married without knowing each other very well, having come from very different social and economic worlds.

The most profound feeling of this experience for me was shame, the sense of public rejection. He made me suffer because, even though I knew I had a bad marriage, I stayed married because of the shame a divorce would be for me.

So now I think that this grief, rather than being a grief from the loss of a marriage, was a grief from a failure.

I think that in this kind of loss (not the loss of a loved one) one faces one's own defeat, due to a certain arrogance in not accepting that one was mistaken.

When one loses a loved one, the sensation of pain should transform into the acceptance of reality: the loved one is no longer there.

In the case of a divorce, you must put aside your pride and accept your humanity, and know that you are not infallible, and that you are mistaken.

In the case of the death of a loved one, the relationship or the love for the loved one continues. We say that these loved ones are still with us.

In the case of a divorce, as I lived it, nothing can be rescued from a relationship with a person who has left a trail of destruction and betrayal. So the question is why one relied on a person of that sort, and it is a very hard question to answer. I, for example, was very embarrassed for my children because of the father I had given them.

The pain was for having made a mistake with the most personal of "companions" in life, marriage, and children.

Another element I can distinguish in my divorce is fear: fear that he could harm me legally or economically, or offend me, but above all, the shame.

Today, more than ten years on, there is nothing left. It is like an episode of my life that happened so that my children could be born, and to whom I was both father and mother, and to whom I feel intimately connected. I have a feeling of having gone to a war in which I learned a lot, above all, humility, that I can be wrong but that I can get up and move on.

I would say that there are different feelings and phases of grief which can include denial, anger, shame, acceptance, growth, and inner peace.

A Message of Strength and Hope

Through loss we grow, we become more humble, we see our humanity and that we are not infallible, and I believe that feeling brings you closer to God, a supreme being who goes beyond all human miscalculations and armor.

Pain Always Happens
Francisco
25 years old

A little over a year ago I lost my wife and my adopted child, because my wife simply stopped loving me. I realized this due to her change in attitude. When I realized this, I fell into an intense depression. The help of my family was important because I stopped eating and sleeping. I did not want to bathe or shave. I started drinking and smoking too much. I wanted to die, and I stopped believing that God loves us like everyone says.

Although times were very hard, I grappled with my loss, and I now feel totally healed, because my family helped me tremendously, and I met an "angel" to pull me out of my hole. I learned a lot from this loss because I am a much better man than before.

A MESSAGE OF STRENGTH AND HOPE

There is no evil that lasts a hundred years. Resist the pain. It passes over time. Sometimes it takes a long time, but it always passes.

WHILE I GROW
María
48 years old

In June 2006 I went to the beautiful fifteenth year party of my niece Analucía, which made me remember her birth, at the same time my marriage ended, after nearly ten years.

Then my world collapsed. This could not be happening to my life. A marriage is forever and divorce was something that I only heard about. I never imagined that I would live it.

A psychologist said that this separation would affect my children. Josefina was eight and Alejandro was seven. At that point Alejandro was very close to his father. He was learning about gender roles, but my children stood with me by way of rebellion and blackmail games.

Another psychologist said my self-esteem would decrease in such circumstances, but that I should not underestimate myself.

There were several reasons for this, but I believe I can sum them up, philosophically speaking, in that love, admiration, and respect had flown away.

That infinite pain and final acceptance now let me see life from another perspective.

From Catherine's life, as described in the book *Many Lives, Many Masters*, by Brian Weiss, to the personal legend of

Paulo Coelho in *The Alchemist*, and from other lessons of life and love, I can conclude that what one must live is in effect, o reap lessons of the past to pass the tests in the school of life.

This rite of passage, in bad times gives meaning so I may grow through, moments in life, when pain can seem endless, but we always find solace and remedy in time, as I would like inscribe this deep in Alsacia's heart, a college friend who is experiencing great sorrow from the loss of her son.

My niece's birthday always reminds me of that relationship, because each year adds one more year to my being alone, as in the song *¡Cómo duele!* (*How much it hurts.*) It is a chauvinistic song by the great singer-songwriter Armando Manzanero, but fits well here.) It says, "If I ever played to love in this life / if by that time in my unconscious years / someone was hurt / if there was a love that gave me everything without reservation/ and I ignored it / it is already settled, I am paying it."

I know that in life at difficult times I lose baggage. It is said that laughter teaches nothing; however, pain adds feathers to our wings.

I can only thank God for my life, my children, and everything that surrounds me.

A Message of Strength and Hope

I hope I have conveyed to anyone reading these words that pain passes and teaches us many lessons, but at the moment that we live them we seem to doubt the future that leads to greater achievements. Look at the past as an opportunity rather than as a heavy burden on our shoulders. This is how I, María, see it in the heart of America.

A Life-Changing Event
Gwen
68 years old

Life is too short to remain in an unhappy relationship. After a hard work week at St. Clair Travel in O'Fallon, Illinois, I returned home on a Friday night to an empty house, which was a common event. My husband Charlie, an Air Force pilot, was away again on a flight. I fixed myself a martini and started working on materials for a travel program I was to give to the St. Louis Ski Club about a new resort in Utah called Snowbird. The phone rang. I heard distress in Mom's voice, and instantly knew something terrible had happened. Mom was calling from Wisconsin. The news I was about to hear would change my life.

Mom told me to sit down. The Army called regarding my brother David, who was an Army sergeant stationed in Stuttgart, Germany. David had a German wife, Karla, and a seven-year-old son, Ronnie. I feared that something had happened to David. My Mom tried to explain what was told to her. Karla and little Ronnie were traveling in a car with friends, planning to surprise David by attending his graduation ceremony at an NCO school. The car was going at a high rate of speed at night on the German autobahn. It crashed through a barricade, then hit an oncoming car head-on. Seven people died, including Karla and little Ronnie.

My Mom and Dad asked me to fly to Germany to be with my brother, and to help make funeral arrangements. The funeral was to take place in Berlin, Karla's family home. My husband put me on an airplane late that night, and I was off to a nightmare.

My brother Dave, who had not been aware that Karla and Ronnie were traveling to his ceremony, was unable to deal with the news of their deaths. He insisted on seeing Karla and Ronnie in the morgue. When he saw them, he went out of his mind.

Most of what happened after I arrived in Germany was foggy in my memory back then, as it is now. I do remember that my brother and I made it through the funeral on sedatives. After a short stay in Berlin, I helped my brother vacate their apartment and find a new place to live. The stress and bone-chilling weather left me with a miserable cold. Cigarettes and alcohol didn't help. This trauma left me unable to even think about going back to my husband and our dysfunctional marriage. I returned to Wisconsin to be with my parents, to share in their grief.

But I could not put off the inevitable. I finally returned home to my husband; I was still very sick. It took the loss of loved ones for me to realize how short life can be, and to decide that I had to make new plans for my future. Our marriage was finally over. I had not been enjoying life and I had not been happy for a very long time.

I had to do the hardest thing in my life to that point. I had to start over, find a new place to call home, and find a new life. I needed the support of my mom and dad back in Wisconsin. I gained strength staying with them near the shore of Lake Michigan, but there were many days I felt like giving up and just driving into the lake. However, with great determination and the support of family and friends, I began the journey of my new life, not knowing my destination, yet having no regrets about embarking on the journey.

A MESSAGE OF STRENGTH AND HOPE

Life is too short to stay in an unhappy relationship, and it is never too late to start a new life.

WHAT WAS AND WAS NOT
Xonio
58 years old

One gets married thinking people come together because love unites them and because of religion. I loved the thought of marriage, family, and having a home. At my church I worked to help others.

My marriage had many problems from the beginning. Yet I have no bad feelings about my divorce because my main desire is to learn from the situation. Initially, I had problems with my ex-husband's character, but even so I think I did love him more than he loved me. I am not saying that he did not love me, but he loved me in his own way. Unfortunately, it was not a healthy type of love; his love was too dominating and he wanted everything for himself. When I became a writer, publishing books and speaking publicly, he began to feel insecure and was professionally jealousy of me, even though he was a doctor. I met him when he was studying, so I helped him finish his training, for the good of our children and family life, or at least that is what I thought. From the beginning I tried to change my character as we came from different backgrounds.

According to the society in which I was educated, I was taught that women had to be good, decent, and virgins when they married. He also grew up with the same values, but he wanted me to be an invisible woman who would support him and nothing more, but I am not the invisible type! I have character! The first thing he told to me once we were married was that I could not have any friends. My mother-in-law also said I had to stay away from friends. But I did not want to live in a fishbowl. I got along very well with my father-in-law as he was a quiet man. My husband's mother was over-protective, and he had a love-hate relationship with her, which he projected onto all women. I, on the other hand, grew up in a very healthy atmosphere full of love and good communication.

My husband could not communicate, and he hid his feelings, so our married life was not the way I was accustomed to living. But I mistakenly thought that if I loved him, I could change the negative things in the relationship. I made many personal sacrifices, and at the same time, I wondered what was going wrong. During this period we had three sons and a daughter who was sick. I decide to get involved in the church. I cannot say that we did not try to make our marriage work because we even went to marriage counseling. But my husband was absent a lot of the time, which I thought was because of his work, until I realized this was not the case. I always felt that I gave without receiving, until I decided that I also wanted to receive. I was always a daughter, wife, and mother first. To celebrate our twenty-fifth wedding anniversary, I suggested to my husband that we have a party at home. But he not only said "no," he forbade me to even invite my two best friends. Today I still wonder why I let him get away with it. The truth is I avoided conflict at all costs.

We asked several priests to hold a silver anniversary ceremony for us, but none of them wanted to because they felt that our relationship did not warrant one. I was the one who did everything, even though I was not a strict practitioner. It was I who got the family together for church events. When I realized that what I was doing was just a charade, I said to my husband one day, "We are living a lie." While he helped others, at home my husband did nothing at all. He was verbally abusive and violent towards me, and I still have the scars. If I had lowered my guard for a second, I think he would have hit me. On one occasion I was so verbally assaulted, the words pushed me against the wall. I felt terrible because I do not like violence.

My goal in life is to have inner peace. People talk about world peace, but if you do not start with inner peace, how can you bring peace to somewhere else? So that day we had a horrific shouting match. He became violent at the slightest thing, and I was worried about the children hearing what was going on. I did not know what to do. I told to him to control himself and to stop shouting, as I was worn out.

After all this, we did reach a divorce situation, because on the day we had been married for twenty-five years and were having a family get-together, I found myself alone opening the gifts. He was sleeping and my children had gone out.

I thought,

"I am alone on my twenty-fifth anniversary, opening gifts for a couple." And I began to cry to myself. I will never forget that I played Jose Luis Perales' "Now that everyone has gone to sleep I see that I have nothing."

Although he says in the song,

"(...) I have nothing but I have you."

I replied, "But I have nothing, I have given so much, I have done so much, yet sit here alone."

This led me to question. I wrote a letter to my husband after twenty-five years of marriage, which said, "I do not know how much you have paid for being by my side, but I do know that I have paid a very heavy price for being at yours."

I gave it to my husband, but I am sure that he never read it.

The following month we went to Europe with the children to celebrate our twenty-five years together. It was so nice because we shared it with the children, but being in Paris something inside told me,

"I am in Paris, in the city of lovers, but with the wrong company."

After this I sat down to talk to him and asked him, "Do you know that I no longer I love you?"

I am a loving person and to say that I stopped loving is saying a lot. I continued, "I have already given you all the warnings and I stay with you, but I am telling you I no longer love you ... there is no going back."

He looked at me and his first reaction was to say, "Fatty, this cannot be!"

I replied, "Let's not talk about sex as that was always very bad. You can go four or five months without touching even my shoulder. You never say, "Well done! I'm proud of you."

With this divorce, I learned how not to be insignificant. When I told my husband that I no longer loved him, he said, "You have found another man."

That was in July 1999. From July 1999 to May 2002, when the divorce was finalized, everything was worse—the violence, the challenging, the confrontation. It went on longer than usual. He was not interested in whether he lost money by selling the house, just as long as it hurt me. He threatened to fight for custody of my sick daughter. He hired a private investigator. He did so many things, but I do not even hold a grudge. I pray every day that God will help my ex-husband, "Lord, bring peace to his soul because you see the mistakes he has made, not so that he might ask my forgiveness, as I am not interested in that."

But I recognize that I really loved him, that I was dedicated to him and gave him a lot, even though I do not think that he values any of it.

Almost three years have passed since I first told him all of this and the lawyers handed me the document saying "Dissolution of Marriage." At court, when I left the mediation room, my lawyer asked me if I was okay. I said I was.

But when my ex left in his car, I realized: I am divorced! A divorced woman is something I never thought I would be. My original plans were to sit in an armchair, kissing and holding hands with the old man who accompanied me through life, playing with our grandchildren....Maybe this was silly, but it was my dream, and I fought with all my heart for it to become a reality, but now I will never have it...That was my loss...not his, but I gained many things as I bear no grudges, but I do not forget.

But I had to learn what I now know to be where I am now. I do not want anymore garbage in my life! When I see my sister with her family, I think of all the things I would have liked to have had and never will...

I got married for life, not to tire of the man I loved. During the divorce my husband told me, "Do you know that you are the woman I will always love?"

And I thought, "How can you love a person and yet do them so much harm?"

I was helped by an aunt who had gotten divorced. I remember that I heard her sobbing when I was fourteen, and when I asked her why she was crying, she replied, "Because we are getting a divorce," she said (and I will never forget). "I chose this man, but not all are equal."

This helped me through my divorce. We should not take pity. One must ask, why not me? I have friends who are not married and will not have an old man next to them. I also realize I have a lot to be thankful for: I do not have cancer, I have resources, and sometimes, when I feel bad, I write down all the things for which I have to give thanks: for my children, my intelligence, and my resources, and for the faith I have in spite of everything. I see the good things around me; for example, I see my closet and think, "All this is mine! I have gained it for myself, and nobody is going to tell me what to do in my house! It is my home"...and I see these advantages. I would like to have a person who accompanies me on my walks, a partner with whom I can share and talk to, on my level without hiding anything, in a mature way. Rather than being married to whom I was married to, I prefer to be alone! I have started to see what I have gained. I do not mind other people's opinions. I am tired of being the last on the list; I choose to be the first. I realized that nobody is going to make me happy. One of the tips that I give to people who are suffering is that nobody makes you happy. You have to learn to be happy for yourself. Even with a sick little girl, being divorced, and sometimes being tight for money, I say, "I'm happy!"

I get up in the morning and maybe sometimes I cry because I miss my mother Mima, but there is always someone I can call and say that I am hurting. Maybe I can find a person who can help and understand me. Maybe they might say something that I do not want to hear, but later it makes me re-think my reasons for getting divorced.

I remember when we were going through the divorce, my husband asked me what I was going to do, so I put on the song *Too Wounded* by Paloma San Basilio, because I needed to go through this important phase of grieving: first despair, then crying, then denial, then remorse when I asked myself, "Was there something else I could have done?" But I have no remorse.

A MESSAGE OF STRENGTH AND HOPE

I advise anyone who has gone through a divorce to cry and then create a new life. Many people say that we should not cry, but I think that it is a process we have to go through, but just not for too long. Another thing that helped me was knowing that there were people who loved me. Bear in mind that at the end of the tunnel...there is always a light.

MY REBIRTH
Margarita
45 years old

It all began after two years of marriage. My husband Juan was traveling to the Dominican Republic, supposedly for business, although I was on vacation, and he did not even ask me to accompany him. While Juan was away, I went to the cinema with my brother. My brother asked me if I thought it strange that my husband had not asked me to join him. I responded by bursting into tears upon hearing someone else put my thoughts into words. My ex-husband and I had had communication problems whilst we were married. When my husband returned, I picked him up at the airport and asked, "How's the girlfriend?"

He pretended there was no one else. That night I could not sleep. I was restless and so I got up. I found his wallet on the kitchen table. I opened it and found the hotel receipt. I phoned the hotel, pretending I had been a guest there and had left something behind.

The hotel confirmed that Juan had been there with a woman, but had not found anything left in the room. While I was on the phone my husband had woken up and heard the phone conversation. I had confirmed that he had lied to me. When I hung up, I confronted him and we got into a huge row. He realized that I had discovered the truth. That night was very hard. I did not sleep and he left.

I went to my parents' house, but soon returned to see if I could find out any more of my husband's lies. Eventually I found some photos dedicated to Juan from a woman. I also found some other bits and pieces. A week and a half later I spoke with Juan, and he told me he had made a mistake and that he would never do it again. We got back together, but I made the mistake of of turning the other cheek. We did not speak of it again. I wanted to leave it behind us and continue our life together. Not fixing the problems or finding out what had happened weakened my position, and so he kept on doing what he had done and I kept finding out.

This all happened in the July, and by the following February I found another suspicious receipt. He had sent me some flowers, but at the same time he had sent some to someone else. I called the florist and discovered that he had sent flowers to a woman in a country he had recently traveled to. I left. Two weeks later, I spoke to him about it, and he made the same promises as before, so I went back to him once again. When I thought about all this, I realized that I had married him because I thought he was the ideal person, and I would do everything possible to make our marriage work. I was aware that he made me feel invisible and insignificant; I was his wife although I did not feel like I was myself.

Despite all this we tried again. We went to therapy as individuals and as a couple, but we did not solve anything. We continued with our routines and that was when I started to write. I realized that in the midst of all this pain, I could write and I could express everything I felt, so I wrote a few poems. I showed them to him and he responded only by saying, "They're beautiful!"

I kept them. I now understood how small minded he was and how disappointed I felt because of the things he did.

I kept writing and time passed - three years. Time flew. Things did not improve in our marriage, but we stayed together. We got on well and we did not fight. After three years I still felt that the relationship was not how I wanted it to be. We got together a lot with my family; my brother was always there, and on one occasion, he asked me whether I thought my husband was having an affair. I suddenly felt as I had three years earlier. I said nothing, but I started to spy on my husband again. At that moment I felt very indignant; my female pride had been damaged. I started to observe Juan. I saw changes in the way he dressed. He was constantly on his cell phone, and his general behavior had changed. On one occasion I called his secretary, who was my best friend, and she told me that Juan had borrowed her car during the work day and had been absent for several hours. I started to check the calls on the phone and discovered that in one single day he had made eleven calls to the same number. Things began to happen very quickly.

At that time I went with my family to visit our homeland; he was supposed to come over a few days later, but to our surprise, when we went to pick him up at the airport, we found he had not gotten on the plane. I called his cell to ask him what had happened, and he asked angrily why I had called. He was very defensive.

My holiday continued all the while knowing that something was going on. When we returned, he collected us from the airport, but he was very cold. His appearance had changed, and he was wearing a necklace, like a teenager. That evening I asked him if he was having an affair, but he emphatically denied it.

On July 4th, I was not well, but my husband went out with some friends without a care in the world. I felt terrible because I felt betrayed. I saw his discomfort and desire to create distance. Things were very tense. It was a friend's birthday, and I wanted to write something in their card, so I found my book of poems and begin to read it. These were the poems I had written three years ago, and I began to cry, as I realized that nothing had changed in that time. I found myself asking, if anything at all had improved in this marriage? No, nothing had changed.

When my husband came in, he passed by my door and found me writing the card. Supposedly he had just got back from therapy, so I asked, "Did you go to therapy?" He replied, "No therapy will help us!"

"No," I replied, "Especially if you are seeing someone else."

"Yes, I am seeing someone and I like her a lot," he finally admitted.

"If that's the case, we can get a divorce, today," I replied.

And so that day we finally decided to divorce. He wanted me to disappear, so we started negotiations.

What hurt me most, more than losing him, was the fear that I would not be able to cope. The fear of being officially a divorced woman and thinking about what would happen made me feel a little lost. Despite the fact that my marriage was not working, I liked the idea of being married, the nice perfect image it portrayed. I was afraid of everything; the future looked black, and I wondered what would happen next, as if he were the only thing in my life. I spent a lot of time fixing legal problems.

He slept in another room in the house until, finally, he left. When we spoke, it was always a very tense situation, and we argued lot. I was no longer submissive, and I became more assertive and would not allow him to have things all his own way. It was my turn now, and an inner strength I never thought I had was flowing out of me.

I admit that I had to go through a lot of anguish and fear to reach this position of safety. I knew that once I had worked through the fear I would be fine. I became more assertive; if I had to talk to someone I did not know. I went to the lawyer's office and sat in front of my husband and listened to him say, "I don't love her."

I heard things that annoyed me, but I did not care. It didn't matter. At that point I knew he couldn't hurt me.

Right at that time, I found an angel of an accountant who fought for me, who gave me strength, and convinced me that divorce was only paperwork; that it would end and that I would move on. I thought that all of it would be horrible, but I realized, little by little, that it was not so bad. In my marriage, I had felt very alone, distanced from life, but slowly, I was becoming a woman, a divorced woman, with a new identity. Another thing that helped me a lot were my friends, family, and people who I started to meet, like my accountant. The lawyer I finally found was also an angel. Many people who stood by me helped me tremendously.

And so, after many months, I began to see everything in multicolor. Driving the streets, I was surprised to see what I had not previously been aware of; everything was so beautiful and green!

I now have no one, I thought, so what will I do when I travel?

I thought about material things that I would miss and believed that I would not have without Juan. But at the same time I felt free and saw the world differently; the people looked different. I think that I did not care about people previously; they were there but not really there. They gave me a lot more than I could have gotten from my marriage. Now I had everything I needed emotionally. I had my family, people calling me constantly, and I was almost never alone. I believe that I have always been able to be alone, so did not need to always be with people. But now when I was with my friends and family, I felt that I became more alive. I remember once talking with a friend I knew through another person. When I asked him why he had not spoken to me before, he replied, "I did not see you before."

And, after that, I realized that I did not even see myself before! I was the wife of someone I had put on a pedestal, and now I wondered why. I had in fact, been at his side making his life easier, but not my own. And then gradually I began to leave the shadows and move into the light. I think that the loss of my marriage made me what I am now. If this divorce had not happened, then I would have remained in the shadows.

Now I feel that I am a person with other aspects of my life far more important. I am more communicative with my friends. Now I know it is not a crime to go through a loss in this way; you leave because there is no love. When I was first divorced, I hated my job, but now I appreciate and like it, and I know I can do it. I started to realize I had control over things. We should not be passive or take life as it comes. No! We have to change it; we must have the ability to have the life we want.

I wanted to be married, but not if I do not feel accomplished as a wife or a woman. Now I feel realized as a woman, as a friend, as part of a workforce, part of a company, not like before, in the shadows. In that I have changed my life.

A MESSAGE OF STRENGTH AND HOPE

It is important to feel the pain created by loss. Honor it and know that, in time, that pain will bring positive results: the rebirth of a person who was in a place where they should not have been, or that if they had to be, the moment would pass. It is important to know that in the future, good things will come from a painful experience. It is necessary to be present at all of the stages and use them for the future.

LOSS OF A JOB

WHEN A DOOR CLOSES, GOD OPENS A WINDOW
Maricarmen
62 years old

I am originally from Cuba. I came to Miami as a fifteen-year-old girl. I did not speak English, and it was a problem for me to go to school. I was not fortunate enough to learn English as I was already married, and I had to work to create a home. It was very difficult to make a living in those days.

Immigrants had to work hard. After a few years in Miami, I started going to night school to learn basic English with a Cuban teacher. I then started with an American teacher. I have always been a forward thinker and never feared anything, so I progressed well with my English classes. The jobs I held down got better and better until 1978 when I divorced the father of my children (one of my daughters decided to go to live with him).

According to a psychologist, I had to make a decision, or that is what they told me. I had to decide whether I was a mother or woman. So I decided to be more woman than mother for a while, and I signed up at a college. I told myself that if I was going to get a divorce, I did not want to be working in a factory for the rest of my life. I had to progress in life, and so I went to college. I worked and studied all the time. My week started on Saturday.

To be able to go to college, I cleaned houses all morning and got to class at one o'clock in the afternoon, where I took two classes. I went to college four days a week. I finished my degree in four years. I studied business administration, and I am now an accountant. I was thirty-seven and had very limited English. I spent a lot of time studying; a lesson that for someone else took three hours took me six and a half. It was very difficult for me, but I was focused, and when I finished, I graduated *magna cum laude*.

I left my job where I was earning ten dollars an hour as I did not want to continue working in a factory and went to work in an office at the very lowest level.

When I finish my degree, a friend got me a job with a Cuban doctor who paid me minimum wage, but it was an opportunity to learn how to run an office. Within six months, I decided to leave that and, through my cousin, had the opportunity to get a job in a bank. I took the job and three or four months later I tried to get a promotion. Six months later I was in the Accounting Department. I went on to the Department of Certificate of Deposits, and I kept climbing the ladder, first as a cashier, then as a manager, and finally Head of Public Services. I kept working and saw the opportunity to become Office Manager. That is where I met my ex-husband. I worked for many years at a highly recognized bank in Florida. I was earning $123,000 a year in 1999. However, the bank was taken over and the new policy did not accept workers with matrimonial ties. My former husband and I were working together. I received a proposition from the Latino bank and I took it. After six months, I was laid off because a friend of the owners was brought into the bank and was given my job. I received a compensation package to keep me quiet. My husband at that time still worked in the bank, so I decided not to take any legal action. I signed a paper agreeing to keep my mouth closed, and I was given four months' salary. I was so traumatized by what had happened that that I could not look for any other work. I trembled at the idea, and I had to seek medical help. I was in a hole and could not get out. At that time, the economic situation was very difficult because there were many problems in banking, and work was not easy to get. I started to look but found nothing. Then my daughter offered me a job in her insurance agency. Three years later she decided to sell the business and entered the restaurant franchise world. I ran their stores. I went from being a bank executive to running a sandwich shop. I was in charge of everything, from preparing the sandwiches to cleaning the toilets. When one is the boss, one must lead by example. Therefore, if I saw that the toilets were dirty and the girls were busy making sandwiches, I cleaned them. I was not embarrassed because I take pride in my work.

Then I broke my foot and started having problems with my legs, so I went back to working in an insurance company for three years. Quite quickly I began to work as an accountant for a really nice person; I earned half of what I earned in the bank, which was something I had to adapt to. I remembered what the judge told me when I filed for bankruptcy: "You will never earn the same." The judge saw my gray hair and advised me to dye it so as to be able to find a job. Even now, I have never forgotten those words.

All I have lived through has been, above all, a spiritual journey. God does not abandon us, and God is always with us. The great faith that I hold helped me at all times. Without faith my faith I could not have moved forward. Sometimes it is hard to see when you are doing well...and have many friends. If things take a turn for the worse, very few people will remain at your side. The phone stops ringing. People forget about you. This has a great effect on a person; it passes but hurts a lot at the time. I never again contacted those so-called friends. Some people see that you are going through a tough situation, and they create distance through pity. They do not talk about it and do not realize the damage they do to that person. Being present is very important. The knowledge that someone will come round and say, "I'm here" is very important!

A MESSAGE OF STRENGTH AND HOPE

Keep in mind, first and foremost, your faith. God is with you. Never forget to find people to help you, either via support groups, be they professional, family or friends. Do not face it alone! Give all the love you possess to others, and always give thanks to God for what you have, and for what you have not yet received at that moment in time. The time will arrive...not when you want, but when He wants. And remember that that as long as your attitude is positive, loss will make you grow, and growth increases your humility and wisdom, which in turn gives you happiness.

IF ONE DOOR CLOSES, ANOTHER OPENS
Cristina
28 years old

On December 22nd, after my company's Christmas party, I received one of the hardest blows to my life. My brother-in-law and boss, Carlos Alberto, tried to kiss me in the building's elevator. Shocked, I pushed him away and asked him what he thought he was doing and had he forgotten that I was his wife's sister. I told him he had gone too far and that he should calm down. He reacted by trying to kiss me again, and telling me that he had felt something for me for a long time, and that was why he offered me the job. Not believing what he had said, I ran out of the building swearing never to see him again.

Upon arriving home, I threw myself on the bed and cried. How would I face my sister? Christmas was in two days time at her house. I did not sleep, outraged, and at the same time hurt for my sister, for being married to a man like that.

And what about work? What was I going to do? I did not want to go back there! But I had to pay off my university loan, the apartment, my car, and I had all my living expenses!

The next morning I got up very early and decided that, come what may, I would never return to that company. I thought I could get a new job. It would take from now until the end of the year, to find another job. However, I did not know what to do about the family situation.

I went to the gym, raging and fearful for what was about to happen.

That morning my sister called me and asked me to help with the Christmas Eve dinner. I pretended to be ill and that I had a fever like the start of the flu. I had planned not to attend the family reunion. I did not want to see my brother-in-law, and I did not know how to disguise my feelings. I did not want to spoil the family dinner. After the dinner and the holidays, and the New Year began, I did not return to work.

On Tuesday morning, Carlos Alberto called me to see what had happened. I told him that I would never return to work for him and that if he called again, I would tell my sister. He got very upset and assured me that he would personally make sure that I would not get another job. I took no notice, but his words read like a prophecy...I sent out over eighty CVs, and called about many job placements. Initially I received invitations to interviews, but they got canceled. Three months went by, and I was desperate as my savings were running out. I needed to pay the rent next month and did not know where to turn. I was frustrated, depressed, and had no desire to get out of bed. I began to spend the day in front of the television. I did not want to talk to my family or my friends. Another week went by until I woke up early one morning, I looked at myself in the mirror, and I said to myself, "You have to get out of this. You can do it."

The next morning I called a friend who worked at Mary Kay, the beauty company, and although I had no experience in sales, decided to try it. I was not going to limit myself. Thus I began a new career; I slowly pulled myself out of the hollow I was in. I felt a lot of support among my colleagues, and I received emotional support from them. I learned all the names of all the products and what they offered, practicing day and night in front of the mirror, and after three weeks I made my first sale. That was what I needed. From then on I felt sure of myself, and I soon exceeded my goals. Today I feel competent and capable of overcoming any difficulty. Now I am able to confront my brother-in-law and tell my sister what happened. I know it will be very difficult, but I have to do it for both her and myself. I realized that never again will I fear any man or adversity. I learned that I am capable and can fight for what I desire.

A MESSAGE OF STRENGTH AND HOPE

Never let fear dominate you, and always believe in yourself. Sometimes we close a door but a larger one opens. Losing a job need not be the end of the world; it may in fact be the beginning of a greater world.

LOSS OF ONE'S HOMELAND

JUST LIKE THE WORLD, LIFE KEEPS TURNING
Cecilia
64 years old

I believe that the greatest loss that I have suffered was when I left the country where I was born and raised forty-four years ago. At that time I was three months pregnant, and I went with my husband to Brazil. I was only twenty years old, and I left my entire family behind, including my parents, siblings, and grandparents. It was very difficult for me because I missed my family and was extremely lonely. I had no friends and I did not speak the language. I waited on the balcony for the postman to arrive to receive the mail. I was eager to hear from my parents and other relatives. I wanted to talk to someone about spiritual things. My belly was growing, and I talked a lot with my baby because it helped to sooth the great loneliness. But as time went by we slowly started to find friends.

Despite the fact that I was only twenty years old and had a strong character, I had agreed to live in a foreign country with my husband, as we were expecting a child. Others had done what we were doing, so I could too. (After some time I returned to my homeland, but after two years left again.) My husband with his wonderful spirit managed to fill the loneliness when he arrived home, and when my daughter was born, it was a very exciting time. I went home to give birth to her and be with my family.

Today as a grandmother, I am fulfilled by my life as it has made a beautiful story.

Currently I have no problems because I am used to living abroad, and life keeps going round. I now live alone with my husband. My children and grandchildren have left the country. With all these experiences, I learned that the day that my children left home, I would not suffer as I did when I left my country. Life is like a wheel; everything keeps turning; it comes around again.

On leaving my home, my life was transformed in a way that each time I returned to my land, it touched my soul. But now I have my adopted homeland that I love, as my grandchildren were born here.

A MESSAGE OF STRENGTH AND HOPE

Have strength and courage, because life keeps turning like the world, and you have to be strong to cope with the comings and goings. If you have someone at your side who supports you, stay together. You will have great strength. The world will be yours although your loved ones are far away.

MEMORIES OF AN EXILE
Gabriel
66 years old

The greatest loss I have experienced in my life is possibly not being able to return to Cuba, the place where I grew up and enjoyed my youth, because I cannot go back. I left in 1972 because it was then that I had the right to leave legally. Previously my departure had been suspended for thirteen years. I tried to get out the first time in 1960, but I finally managed it in January 1972 as a civil servant. I loved my house but I made the necessary arrangements for my departure from Cuba. I left by plane when I was thirty-one years old. I left with my mother, my wife, and my wife's aunt. I still vividly remember the moment of departure. The international airport in Havana is twenty-five minutes from the city. My father drove very slowly, contrary to usual; it was the only time I saw him driving slower than everyone else. I realized he was trying to stretch out the time for as long as possible; it was the last time we were going to be together. I understood this, but did not talk about it.

I said, "I'm going... I'm never coming back! This is the last time...!"

Now, we grew up in a very rigid emotional environment... Things were experienced, but not mentioned. My parents were divorced, and my father had re-married and was staying in Cuba with his wife.

We had to be at the airport at 6:20 a.m. Sitting in the car, despite all the enthusiasm of leaving, I felt I had no right to tell my father to rush and that we were going to be late. Upon arrival at the airport at seven o'clock, we were moved to the "fishbowl," a room surrounded by glass, where we were given back our passports and our luggage. The only things we were allowed to take were one suitcase, eleven inches long, eight inches wide, and eight inches high, and whatever fit into it, but no more. This meant one pair of tights, one pair of underwear, a shirt, and if it fit, a pair of trousers.

We left the "fishbowl" at 2:45 p.m. without even a sip of water. We got on the plane and took off at three in the afternoon. I said goodbye to my father by a glass door, and I remember stopping, not knowing what to say and with a lump in my throat, both perfectly aware that it was likely that we would never see each other again. Speaking by telephone, perhaps, but meeting, never! We were both very aware of that. He put his hands on my shoulders and said, "I want to ask you a favor."

"What will the old man say now?" I wondered.

"The only thing I ask is that you never come back as a tourist."

"As a tourist?"

"No! Never come back as a tourist," he said.

I knew what he was saying. I could return but not as a visitor. I could only return to live. I knew that he would not have received me in his house. I remember taking off at three in the afternoon on January 9th and arriving in Madrid the next day. At that time there were only three places where one could go: Jamaica, Mexico, or Spain. I did not know where we were going. I knew I had bought tickets for a round trip, because we left on a tourist visa and on arrival in Spain we had to seek political refugee status. I understood that I had left my country when the landing gear went up. I cried non-stop until we passed over Puerto Rico. I was not hysterical, but it was something like uncontrollable laughter. I had collected everything I had bought and known for thirty-one years, put it in a box, and thrown it into the sea. I was leaving Cuba with only the clothes on my back....In those moments I did not consider my memories, only I was not happy because I was leaving. I did not want to go. But things were complicated and I had to seize the opportunity.

My mother at seventy-one was in bad health and died a year after leaving Cuba. She is now buried in Spain.

When we arrived in Spain, my wife's sister had booked us two rooms in a hostel.

The pain was so great that it was like carrying a scar on my face.

I remember when I arrived in Madrid; it was one of the saddest days that I had lived. Immediately we asked for permission to stay, not as political refugees; that was an administrative thing you did later. We left Spain on October 9th, 1974. After two years and nine months we went to New Jersey, as we could enter the U.S. through a cousin of mine who lived there. In those days you had to live where the person claiming you lived. We lived there from October 9th, 1974, to January 8th, 1977, and then I came to Miami. There were many Cubans here. I moved to Miami because the costs in the North were very high.

I only came to look at a job I was offered, but I started to work immediately. I did not come with a desire to be in Miami because every time you change the environment from where you have been living for a while, be it Australia, New Zealand, Argentina, or Miami, wherever you go you are always a foreigner.

The only place I thought that I was part of society was in Madrid. I did not feel like a foreigner. Foreigners are tourists. I dressed like Spaniards, talked like them, and thought like them.

Upon arriving in Miami I made some friends and managed to talk with them.

When I left Cuba I did not come to the United States with the intention of making a new life. What I have done is survive life.

Being an emigrant is different from being an exile. I think that many people who arrive in a foreign country to start a new life are economic migrants; most of them did not leave their country due to political beliefs. It is different leaving for economic reasons because one is trying to achieve a better life. I did not come to the United States seeking a better life. What I remember is that upon my arrival in Spain I was able, after much time, to sleep in peace at night.

For me emigrating was all very unpleasant, but I understand that it was like the heat used to forge iron. I have not chosen to be where I am; I have traveled a path, and life has taken me by the hand.

I think I have managed, thanks to my religious faith. I believe in a Supreme Being; I speak with him all the time. I call him God, but you could call Him anything. I know that there is someone who is above me, someone who perhaps can solve my problems, someone to whom I can complain, and thank. I complain and I give thanks in the same way that children ideally talk to their parents. This has helped me, having someone to speak to, because there is nothing more unpleasant than to feel alone.

A MESSAGE OF STRENGTH AND HOPE

If there is something that I want to communicate to people who are in situations like mine, it is that while you are away from home, never forget where you came from, because it is the only way to know where you are going.

A CELEBRATION OF LIFE
Baldo
51 years old

My greatest loss, which I am currently suffering, is the loss of my homeland's future. This loss initially started legally through the presidential elections in Venezuela. I never thought, as did the large majority, that things could get worse. I realized that life is a state of perpetual change, so things are always going to change for the better or worse, depending on factors and results of decisions or positions taken.

When the new situation arose, I was discomforted, annoyed, and frustrated, and I shared this with my family. I felt a lot of tension and nervousness at the same time.

On the spiritual and religious side, I was shocked to see that the strong values and principles that I consider sacred, such as freedom, came into open conflict with the practices of the new regime. This caused me deep sadness and made me feel a sense of loss and emptiness.

But I understand that one learns to live with these moods day by day as they are only chapters of an unfinished book.

233

What has helped me through this loss was keeping up to date with the developments, and to discuss and talk about alternatives for the future.

I realized that I was going over the same things in my mind and investing time in analyzing and understanding why things happen, but yet I had no control over them.

I have learned that when and how one faces things will determine, to a greater or lesser extent, the learning that one receives from them.

The transformation that I experienced in my life from this loss is that my power of observation has increased, as well as knowing how to interpret and analyze conflicting or divergent positions.

A MESSAGE OF STRENGTH AND HOPE

Anything can happen; you can see it with different hues, depending on factors such as the time and space from where it is observed.

Life is short and we have to celebrate it. Therefore, I propose, regardless of any personal loss, to always be able to take advantage of the way we go through life and our time in the world.

LOSS OF A PET

MY DOG PINKY
Myriam
44 years old

I met my dog Pinky in 1988. At that time I lived in Coconut Grove, a beautiful neighborhood in Miami. It was about five in the afternoon when I went for a walk with a friend and saw Pinky. She seemed lost. I mentioned it to my friend, and she urged me to keep walking. I did so, although I did not want to. I looked back at the dog, and I was struck by its honey-colored eyes; it seemed sad and desperate.

That night I went to a barbecue at a friend's house and got some leftover food for the dog, in case I saw it again. As I expected, upon arriving home, I saw her running around the outside of my house. I let her come in and gave her the food. I adopted her there and then. At the time I was feeling down. I was suffering from a dreadful alcohol and drug addiction. This dog, which I named Pinky (I was a fan of Pink Floyd), awoke the fibers of my being that had lain dormant for some time.

From that moment we became inseparable. Pinky began to fill my empty, emotionless heart. Our friendship gave some meaning to my life. All my life I had suffered from loneliness.

Little Pinky, right from the very beginning, became my unconditional and exceptional teacher and friend. She came into my life to teach me to love and forgive, to care about others, to laugh and play, and to take things lightly. She forced me to enjoy the open air, to walk and talk with neighbors; to smell the freshly cut grass; to feel privileged to be alive and able to enjoy such experiences. Pinky loved to swim in the lake, to run and roll around in the grass and rub her back in it. She enjoyed it so much that I joined in with her, and I could understand why she enjoyed it so much! Pinky enjoyed trying to catch squirrels, bugs, or anything that moved, as she had an instinct to recover things. She loved children and they loved her back. She was the key in helping me overcome my addiction.

After a few years, Pinky developed a hip displacement, which made it difficult for her to walk. Both of her hips were operated on and she recovered well. This increased her quality of life, but after five or six years the symptoms returned. She became so bad that a friend suggested, "putting her to sleep." I was infuriated by such an idea, but over the days and with a worsening prognosis from the veterinarian, I had to think from the heart and consult my God. I concluded that I could make the decision that I had so strongly resisted. Pinky had lost total movement in her hind legs; she could not even relieve herself without covering herself. I was embarrassed for her, seeing her lose her dignity; it tore into my soul.

I struggled with much conflict but finally decided that she could not live like this. During the days preceding her euthanasia, I cried over our inevitable farewell.

I started grieving in the final days of her life until, finally, came the much-feared day. Patricia, my close friend, accompanied me to the veterinarian's and held my hand while I let Pinky go. It was a very sad and unforgettable Saturday, September, 22nd in 2002. It took me months to overcome my sadness over the loss of my unique friend with whom I shared so many years. Every dog I saw reminded me of Pinky, and if it looked like her, I started to cry.

I felt connected with her soul, which shimmered in the moonlight and in the splendor of the grass on which I sometimes laid and rubbed my back.

A very dear artist friend of mine, who specializes in ceramics, gave me a container where I placed Pinky's ashes. I decided to give Pinky a send off, so I met with some friends who had known her, and we spent a whole afternoon recalling stories of "my girl." God has her in his glory forever, and my memory of her even today still brings tears and smiles.

A MESSAGE OF STRENGTH AND HOPE

If you've suffered the death of a pet that was very dear to you and you still suffer this loss, I suggest you develop a ritual in their memory, as this act may help a lot in the healing process. Do not erase your feelings; instead, share them with people you like and who understand your loss.

ON LIFE AND DEATH
Belkis
64 years old

There is never a better time than Christmas, amid the joy of the celebrations of the birth of the baby Jesus, to reflect on life and death, fate, family, and God.

To some people it may seem disproportionate, and even absurd, that I speak of my dear dog, a dachshund (a sausage dog) called Pattern, who has inspired me even in death. He spent nine years at my side day and night, even sharing at times the chair where I sit in front of the computer. When we are suddenly deprived of the presence of something so near and dear, our heart responds with a strange mixture of grief, distress, and disbelief that over time gives way to another feeling Oh, the painful, forced resignation, but never forgotten. It is the moment that the saying "from dust we have come and to dust we shall return" is revealed with all its biblical meaning.

But are we just that, dust? Do we return to dust to continue living in nature, to make us trees, rivers, fruits, wind, and snow; to make clouds?

Pattern died in my arms, of a heart attack on Thursday, November 30th at noon. Outside, there was still ice on the streets, and the veterinarian's clinic was a few blocks away. I had no more time than to try to give him life with my desperate cries and my tears. He died; I could do nothing! The most terrible thing was living through his death, his agony; feeling him shake, his heart exploding, his head finally fell, sprawled onto my chest. I couldn't believe it. I do not believe in death. I do not accept it, and maybe never will.

That is why I believe in the resurrection of Christ, in heaven, wherever it may be; it is a place of eternal peace in which we live under God's glory. Most religions deny that animals have souls. However, in my personal experience, living with dogs for so many years makes me think that if they exist and breathe. They also have a soul, a word that ultimately comes from the word "animate," which means breath, energy, life.

"They are angels, Belkis," a dear friend said, not so much to comfort me, but due to his conviction—which I also share. Yes, dogs and cats, and perhaps others like them in the animal kingdom, are angels that God sends to share our lives and help us. In my case, I can assure you that Pattern heard, on my behalf, those sounds that I have not been able to hear since 1968, when I lost a lot of my hearing.

Before he died, with tears rolling down my cheeks, I put Pattern on my bed and took several photos. But I have not had the courage to look at them yet. I have still kept some photos taken over the years; I wanted to retain the last image of my dear companion. In a photo, coming home at two months old, he appeared next to me in the summer issue of *Linden Lane Magazine*, helping to illustrate my poems (ww.lacasaazul.org; go to where it says *Linden Lane Magazine*).

Like the rain and frost, everything happened suddenly; I decided to ask for help from the neighbor across the street to bury Pattern in my yard, at the bottom of the steps, next to my other beloveds, Lucky and Jackie, and my cat Chiquita.

I did not know Glen, as he was new in the neighborhood. But armed with a shovel and dressed for the intense cold, he did not hesitate to dig a grave for Pattern, without any complaints. To my surprise, Boomer, my husky, suddenly appeared and approached the lifeless body of Pattern. He prodded Pattern's body with his snout, perhaps giving him a farewell kiss.

Glen asked me if I wanted to say a few words before covering the grave and helped me down the ice-covered steps. It was beautiful and sad at the same time: a ceremony of celebration for the life of Pattern, a prayer of thanks for having had him sent to me, and for the love he showed me. I gave thanks to the heavens, and still shaky from my tears, I climbed the steps and went back into the house. It was a great moment of sadness, only disturbed by the expectant look of amazement I received from all my cats, who oversaw the bizarre ritual. Did they know what was happening? Sure, their eyes told me so.

A MESSAGE OF STRENGTH AND HOPE

Most religions deny that animals have a soul, but I think they do. If they live and feel, express joy and sorrow, why would they not have a soul? Our pets are angels that God sends to accompany us in our lives and to help us.

LOSS OF CHILDHOOD

AN UNFORGETTABLE LOSS
Jessica
37 years old

When I think about the greatest loss that I have suffered, I could start talking about death, as it is something I always associate with the word "loss." It could be the death of my grandparents or the death of my best friend, which happened four years ago, that really made me feel very bad. But it is not that story I want to tell.

I would like to talk about childhood; I think this is the greatest loss that I have personally suffered.

I remember this as the best stage of my life, although there is no doubt that each stage of life has its own delights. When you are young, you are at the age when you enjoy everything; when you study, you have great opportunities; when you marry, you create a family; when your children are born, because you really enjoy them; when your children grow up, you teach them; when you work, it gives you security; when you mature, you become wiser; when you get older, you are in a stage of tranquility; and when you die, it is a fact of life.

I remember when I was a little girl, I passed all the day with a smile on my face and I truly enjoyed that smile. From early in the morning until I went to bed, I thought that life was a game; I met with my friends every day which was the best of the best.

My life with all its complications was still wonderful.

Thanks to God, I always had everything. I think there was never anything I was missing. At least I thought so until now; what I did not have, I did not miss. Although I had lots of toys everywhere, I didn't allow this to limit my big imagination.

I used everything I had around me (sand, sticks, old bottles and cans, tree leaves and many other things from my surrounding environment). I do not know how, but I always managed to find their best use for everything, and all I had to do was spend my afternoons having fun with my friends.

The best month of the year was December because the little baby Jesus came to give gifts. At many meetings we had to recount the good things we had done during the year! It was clear that those who had not been good would have few surprises waiting for them at Christmas.

I think it was a beautiful childhood that gave me the luxury of saying that if I had any bad times, I do not remember them. I grew up in an atmosphere of love and affection and hid anything that might obscure the greatest treasure of man, innocence.

I think with these few words I have made it clear that every person has a path to walk, and that they will leave behind many things. If one day a Genie were to come out of a lamp and grant me one wish, I would safely say, "I wish to return to my childhood," because as my father always said to me, "childhood only happens once."

Today I am a woman in every sense of the word, with a nice home; beautiful children, although they give me headaches at times, but they are also my greatest pride and joy; and a husband about which, fortunately, I have no complaints.

It may seem like a fairy tale as everything is very nice, but the truth is, to get here I gained a lot, but I have had to leave many things along the way.

Childhood is something that we all leave behind; it is a cycle of life. But in my case, I get the best out of applying it all to the present.

Each of the endless pranks I pulled when I was small serve as an example to me today.

Even today, I still to try to keep that smile that I always had as a child, because in difficult situations it keeps me afloat. The best thing is that my smile rubs off on the people by my side.

The "no shame" attitude that overtook me when I went skating in the evenings is what I now use to get what I want.

The set of crowns, sticks, sand, leaves, and branches that used to give free rein to my imagination are what taught me to be a hard worker; to keep going when trying to cope with problems and to always look for a positive side, even when one may not exist.

I still sing in the shower, at karaoke, or when I am with friends. I still think that on Christmas Eve the baby Jesus arrives. Who cares if it is a lie or not! The belief in something makes one happy!

A Message of Strength and Hope

I have learned to overcome very tough situations. I feel that being alive gives us this great opportunity. It is enough to give thanks for what we have. If one starts from this thought, then everything around us is shaped by our doing and, above all, we must remember that life in itself is a great gift.

LOSS OF FRIENDSHIP

TO BE A GOOD FRIEND REQUIRES EFFORT
Isabel
20 years old

Among the most valuable qualities we can have in a friend are honesty and support, but these qualities are hard to find.

It is always difficult to be the new girl at high school, suddenly faced with hundreds of new faces. When you finally get to talk to them, you ask yourself if they might actually become your friends. Apart from getting to know all these people, you are trying to find ways to adjust to the new school, including the buildings and the amount of work.

I entered the ninth grade with a positive attitude, eager to meet new friends who could help me adjust to my new life in high school. Almost immediately I met a nice group of nice girls, but it took me almost two weeks to learn all their names, and it was not helped by the fact that there were triplets in my class! The friendliest girl I met was also the fussiest; her name was Sarah. We shared the same classes, ate together every day, and we slept at each other's house every weekend. In other words, we immediately became best friends, sharing secrets, gossip and talking on the phone for hours.

It was fantastic to have a friend like her, and when I failed my first chemistry exam, she was at my side telling me that other people also failed and it did not mean that I was not able to cope. If I had any serious problems that I thought I had to solve immediately, otherwise it would be the end of the world, she was ready to stop everything she was doing to talk to me. Similarly, I was at her side every time she fought with her family; trying to give her courage to talk to the boys she liked, and I went to all the school plays she performed in and always applauded with great enthusiasm. I was at her side when she fought against her body image and low self-esteem.

Being a good friend requires much effort. You have to be willing to sacrifice a lot for that person and not have an ounce of selfishness to be able to be a support, and above all, to be adaptable. It is not easy at times, and everyone makes mistakes. When I started dating my new boyfriend, Sarah started to express hostility towards me. I assumed this was her way of adjusting to the new situation or perhaps even a little jealousy. I thought that maybe she was bitter because her boyfriend had just dumped her. The time passed and I it was clear that Sarah had problems with me.

She made up rumors and constantly lied behind my back. My other friends started to believe her, which made the situation much more stressful, and I started to consider our friendship. Was it worthwhile trying to fix things between us? She made it clear that things were never going to change after the fifth or sixth time that I confronted her and asked her to be understanding. She had promised, as always, that she was going to support me. But the lies increased and then finally I realized that Sarah was no longer the person I had been friends with. This was made obvious when she turned to other recreational activities that I was not attracted to, due to their dangerous and harmful nature. I no longer had anything in common with her. In addition, she began to develop an urge to draw attention to herself, which culminated each day at lunchtime when she presented her personal monologues in the middle of the class. Things that the old Sarah would never have said or done and everyone began to notice.

The closer we got to the end of the year and graduation, the happier I became, because I would not have to see her any longer. The fact that I felt that way about someone I had previously considered my sister, filled me with much sadness. Sometimes I wonder if perhaps I had chosen the wrong person to be my friend in the ninth grade. I think that if I had seen any indication of this personality trait then I might have seen what was going to happen. However, when I look back to ninth grade, I am surprised as to how different she was. I simply could not have perceived these horrible things in Sarah. She was a different person; people definitely change.

Fortunately, during my first year at university in North Carolina, I found a wonderful friend who supported me in everything, consoled me when I was homesick, and who showed me she was devoid of selfishness. She erased any doubts about my ability to choose good friends. Instead of seeing the situation of Sarah as a negative experience with regard to making friendships, I now see it as an opportunity that gave me the strength to determine who I can trust.

I think it is extremely difficult to find a good friend you can trust. If you do find it, do everything you can to keep that relationship strong and healthy. When someone loves you, they will be at your side under any circumstances. Losing a friend is very painful; two years later and I constantly think about the original Sarah and how she betrayed me and how much I wish that everything had been different. I miss our long talks on the phone, our jokes that made high school so much fun and our Friday nights, eating popcorn and chocolate while watching silly love movies.

A MESSAGE OF STRENGTH AND HOPE

The loss of friendship makes us stronger and teaches us to take greater caution in choosing who we let enter our life. This experience taught me that the most valuable thing that I can bring to a friendship is my support when a friend needs it.

LOSS OF INNOCENCE

THE BEST ACTRESS IN THE WORLD!
Lucia
36 years old

My biggest loss has been my innocence. This happened when I was six years old and lasted for a period of two years. I lost my innocence while I was playing in my doll's house, which was in the garden of my house. I remember that day was filled with joy at first as I was playing housewife and was getting ready to give lunch to my dolls. Suddenly, the gardener of many years and husband of my nanny entered my house after knocking on the door and asked me if I would invite him to eat with us. I was playing and played along with him. But it was at that moment that I realized that there is evil in the world. I understood that something bad was happening and the worst was…that I had allowed it to happen. Suddenly I heard my nanny, the gardener's wife calling me. When she came to the doll's house, she knew something terrible had happened. I could see it on her face when she saw her husband was with me. I remember I felt very bad at that moment…I pretended I was playing so that she would not find out. I avoided looking directly at her face. It was then when I learned how to pretend and hide my pain to appear as if everything was fine....I was....the best actress in the world!

Because of that event I became withdrawn and quiet. I started to distrust everybody. I knew I had a secret and was afraid people would know about the sin I had committed. I felt very ashamed for what happened. I remember my chest hurt due to the painful emotion I experienced, but I couldn't show it. I felt very bad when I had to see the gardener working at my house and started to lower my head. Some people noticed I was a quiet girl with sad eyes. At times I noticed that sadness at the heart of my childhood because I had a great weight on my soul and I didn't feel happy.

Although time has passed, I still have to deal with the issue of distrust. I say to myself I will be okay, that things in my life will be okay, and that I will be fine. I give myself the message that not only do I encounter bad things, and that I am able to keep on going. Although time has healed most of this memory, at times I feel a great pain in my chest and a great sadness. I cry without an apparent reason. I know the pain is in my sub-conscience, but I have learned to be a survivor. I have learned that our thoughts are everything and that if one chooses to be a victim, one will be a victim. The fact that one suffers bad things doesn't mean one will remain a victim. When one is an adult one has the opportunity to choose the life one desires.

A MESSAGE OF STRENGTH AND HOPE

Smile, because life is too short to live with pain. Fill your surroundings with good people who love you...and smile, smile, smile...because the smile is the flowing spring of the soul.

LOSS OF SECURITY

A PERMANENT MARK
Danilo
57 years old

Shortly after eight o'clock in the morning on Tuesday, September 11th, 2001, I was in front of my computer writing a newspaper article, and at the same time, intermittently watching the TV, when suddenly there was a news flash that stated that a commercial plane had just crashed into one of the World Trade Center buildings in New York.

The news hit home when an image of the towers in lower Manhattan came on. I immediately went to the TV and turned up the volume to be able to concentrate on the news report, and I saw live images of Tower One in flames, like a huge torch of fire and black smoke. I felt a pain in my heart and kept watching avidly. Like a special effect, I saw a plane approaching at high speed and then a terrible explosion filled the air. I thought it was amazing how quickly emergency personnel had reacted to try to put out the fire. They had sent a fire plane like the ones they use for forest fires that use foam to smother the fire. Even the TV broadcaster did not realize what was happening, "Was it another plane?"

A headline at the bottom of the screen began to appear from right to left, "A second plane has hit the Twin Towers in New York!"

I could not believe it! What was happening? Was it a joke from the TV channel? How had this happened in just a few minutes? It was understandable that due to the volume of air traffic in and around New York City, a commercial airliner could collide with these buildings because thousands of flights go in and out of New York daily. Every hour hundreds of aircraft fly around the city. I was not alone; millions of North Americans were asking the same question.

Again the newsflash was stating, "Several planes have apparently been taken hostage and are off course at this time!"

I could not concentrate on my work, watching these Dantean images of the Twin Towers ablaze. I stopped everything at that moment and started to make calls to New York, with the intention of finding out about my friends and co-workers, but the lines were congested and there was no possible way of communicating. This greatly increased my anxiety, and I plunged into a terrible state of tension and anguish. It is indescribable the powerlessness that I felt, not being able to do anything for the people who were burning in the flames, burning alive, throwing themselves out the windows, spinning in the air and trying to cling to life with hands and feet dancing around only to face certain death.

I thought of everyone I knew working in lower Manhattan, including personal friends who worked in the Twin Towers. I could not imagine what they were experiencing or if they were already dead; I thought of their families and children.

I could not contain myself, my God! I was alone, no one to talk to and without even realizing it my eyes were streaming with tears. I could not contain the mist of pain and despair I felt.

Everything that was happening was a nightmare, the kind you want to be just a bad dream, but no, it was real! A little stupefied, I went out on the balcony of my apartment to get some air. My apartment faces Collins Avenue, Miami Beach, a tourist attraction, which is always crowded with tourists from all over the world, as it is next to the famous South Beach. But there was nobody in the streets or on the beach! Everyone had disappeared as if by magic. I went down to the hotel in front, the Florida Beach, and in the lobby was a giant screen showing live pictures of New York. I looked at the faces of the people, and everyone was stunned. Some could not contain tears; others who had come there let out screams. Children not understanding what was happening asked their parents what was going on. Everywhere there was an atmosphere of uncertainty and fear.

To complete the drama, the news could not be worse: the Pentagon had been attacked as well! And another plane was missing. It was like a scene from a horror movie in which everyone was hugging and waiting for something terrible to happen to them.

That event on September 11th, 2001, had changed the history of humanity forever; things could not remain the same.

After the September 11th, 2001 events, I was in a state of total and absolute desolation. I simply stood behind the curtains and occasionally went out on the balcony to watch from the twelfth floor, the total solitude; there were virtually no cars or people on Collins Avenue in Miami Beach. Everybody was in shock. I could not turn off the TV and I watched continuously to see the latest news of what was happening. The same images of the Twin Towers collapsing in a huge cloud of dust and people running in a disorientated manner through the streets of Manhattan ran hundreds of times. Those streets were so familiar to me as I had traveled them extensively, and I could identify individual images, buildings and outlets of my beloved city of New York!

I had lived there in my youth, and I had had the best experiences of my life there as a student and as a professional. This could not be true. I could not believe it; it was the typical denial. Unfortunately, it was true, and there were thousands of people trapped under rubble in the subway; in elevators; in shopping malls under the ground; in their offices and in restaurants. At the time it happened, it was customary to have a coffee and some toast before entering the office. One still could not estimate the number of victims, and there was just simply speculation about figures without any basis, just trying to keep pace with the news.

The awakening of a new day brought thousands of questions: Could it be that we were going to be victims of anthrax and we were all going to die? What would happen now? Who was going to travel by plane now? How would business survive? Would we be able to keep the dollar as an international currency? Would American multinationals be terrorist targets around the world?

In the following weeks things went slowly, the lethargy of the economy, a feeling of mourning, and the disruption of air travel. The attack had dealt an almost fatal blow to all of the productive areas of the country and the world, compounded by the continuing threat of anthrax, which in the past, had already caused several casualties.

In my personal case, I canceled all my international commitments and was assigned to a crisis management intelligence team to give support and aid in severe cases. I was also on the frontline of a red alert, because no one knew for sure where the next attack would be.

The world changed radically after the September 11th attacks. However, despite these events and restrictions, the world remains determined to eradicate this threat. The most important thing is in knowing what we can do as individuals to contribute positively to the recovery process. Firstly, to be up to date with information, and secondly, to keep up to date professionally, and finally, to educate ourselves on computers and the Internet.

A MESSAGE OF STRENGTH AND HOPE

Although we have been "technified" and "industrialized," the emotions and feelings of humans prevail over everything that is generated. To be leaders in what we do, we must never forget our roots and not believe that we are infallible or irreplaceable. We are much more fragile than we think, but sometimes the lack of evidence enables us to assess our true beliefs about our weaknesses and strength.

PART THREE

TRANSFORMATION

THE ELEVEN PRINCIPLES OF TRANSFORMATION™

As You Transform Your Loss You Can Change Your Life

> *Probably you do not choose to suffer, but you can choose the option to transform your suffering into a meaningful life.*
>
> SAMET M. KUMAR

What would you think if I told you that the grief and unhappiness you carry within you could be significantly reduced? And that the day would come when you would be free from this enormous pain that you feel in your heart, and that you would be able to pick up the pieces of your life after your loss? Would you like this to become a reality? Then, I have good news for you. <u>You</u> can make it happen!

Within you resides an unlimited power to change the current course of your life and achieve what you desire so much—to be happy! Because in reality we all want to be happy. Dr. Isabel Goméz-Bassol, in her book, *Los 7 pasos para ser más feliz* (*Seven Steps to Happiness;* 2006), assures us that happiness is actually the most coveted desire in the world. Despite the trauma of losing a loved one, facing a divorce or losing a great job, I believe we all desire and deserve happiness. So we should try not punish ourselves with negative attitudes. Let's relinquish all sense of doubt and fear and make the decision to find meaning in our loss. Let today be the day you make the decision to transform your loss. With all my heart I offer you these tools to help you make this transition from grief and loss to peace and happiness.

But please understand that I do not assume to know the reason or reasons for your loss; I only speak from my own experiences and those of the many people who have shared theirs through the stories in this book. With this said, I must also mention that these tools for transforming your loss have been tried and tested by the numerous people I have worked with, through private consultations as a counselor, and through workshops and seminars. Using the eleven principles presented here, these people have indeed transformed their losses, and the lives of those around them by using these guiding principles.

My purpose, as I share some of my own losses with you, is to let you know that I too have been on a similar path to yours, and that I once believed that all was lost. But moving on is possible! I did and so can you! Remember that transforming your loss can change your life!

PRINCIPLE I – ACCEPT YOUR LOSS

Your vision will become clear only when you can look into your own heart. Who looks outside, dreams; who looks inside, awakes.

CARL JUNG

Come out of the shadows toward the light. Yes, the bright sun can initially be blinding, but little by little you will become used to it, and you will see better and more clearly. Acceptance is the first principle and the basis for your transformation process. Within us resides the power to choose to have a positive attitude in life. Although it is common knowledge that the great majority of people deny having suffered a loss, it is necessary to have courage and have confidence in our capacity to love and overcome these hardships.

I say love, because I believe that is where all the goodness and marvelous things in our lives and the world originate from. If we love ourselves and the people around us, we will give the best of ourselves, and this implies that we want to get out of the difficult situation we are facing and start a process of growth. However, although we may have the best intentions, the pain we suffer from a loss may be so great, we may fail to be aware of the transformative power of love, especially when confronted by the death of a loved one. With this message I don't mean to devalue your pain or to suggest that you distance yourself from it. Although I wish I could make it disappear, that wouldn't be the best course for you because you may still need to go through those moments of despair and those sleepless nights. You will experience grief but in order to see the light, when the time comes, you need to go through that valley of darkness. As I have mentioned, it is common for many people to deny their loss. Often because the pain is so great, it seems impossible to accept it. The person thinks that the loved one is still living, or that the divorce is not final; another may believe that they will one day get back the job they just lost. We constantly hear about the stages of grief, and although I have already mentioned them, it is necessary to analyze them once again. It is of the utmost importance that we remember these universal concepts and use them as a starting point to really understand them.

The concept of denial introduced by Elizabeth Kübler-Ross in her book *On Death and Dying* (1969) embodies the five stages one lives through when confronted with death. These five stages of grief apply to a number of situations:

- Denial
- Bargaining
- Rage
- Depression
- Acceptance

Dr. Kübler-Ross, the Swiss-born psychiatrist, was one of the pioneers in thanatology, the study of death. Thanks to her, the taboo of talking about death was broken, and we started talking about the necessity of accepting and confronting death. The problem with this theory is that many believe that one must pass through all the stages of grief. The other problem is that people assume that these stages are linear, when in fact they can be circular.

For example: One can overcome depression, pass on to anger, only to return to depression. It is important to understand that there is no predetermined order of the stages of grief. Occasionally someone suffering a loss expects to go through these stages in a specific order, which causes further pressure and at the same time, anxiety.

Every now and then new theories on grief are introduced, for example, those of William Worden in his *Four Tasks of Grief*, which were covered in the section on grief. Still, denial is the predominant stage among the bereaved because it is a natural human reaction to experience unwillingness to accept change, primarily when facing the loss of a loved one or something very close to our hearts. "I can't believe it!" is a very common reaction to the news of a friend or family member's misfortune. It is quite possible that when we face the tragedy ourselves, we choose not to believe it, because while we are in denial, we think we avoid suffering. Quite often we find ourselves in need of a certain amount of time to assimilate our loss. Even so, it is important to face up to our new reality, and not to reside indefinitely in this stage of denial. Once you are able to internalize your loss and accept it, you will have taken the first step in your transformation process. This reminds me of something a friend once told me:

"The most important thing in a long journey is taking the first step." Do not worry if this takes some time; the important thing is to start the journey. Entering into the process of transformation does not mean it has to occur quickly. You are unique and so is your individual process. It is not important that some people take longer than others; it is fundamental, however, that you never lose hope, and take all the time you need. In his book *The Wisdom of the Ages* (2002), Dr. Wayne Dyer reminds us of the value of patience in our lives. The desire to rush causes us to stumble, and not really go through the processes we need to go through.

Nonetheless, dealing with the death of a loved one requires us to first face up to the situation.

A MOMENT OF REFLECTION

Now please take a break, place your hand on your heart and recite the following affirmations:

- I am starting a new stage in my life without (the name of your loved one, your homeland, your job).
- Loss is a part of life.
- I embrace life.
- I will have small successes every day.
- I have a great capacity to confront loss.
- I can raise my world.
- Darkness is not eternal.
- I accept the challenge of living with my loss.

MEDITATION

By confronting my loss and accepting that I am starting a new stage in my life, I have been able to acknowledge that I have the capacity to keep loving and to transform my life. I understand that I have painful memories and moments of doubt; however, I do not fear them. They are not easy to confront, but I will embrace them and make them mine. They are a part of the process of accepting this new dimension in my life. I have realized that I suffer such pain because I have a great ability to love and feel.

PRINCIPLE II – LIVE YOUR GRIEF

Tell your heart that the fear of suffering is worse than the suffering itself. And no heart has ever suffered when it goes in search of its dream.

PAULO COELHO

If you are grieving, you may find yourself swept up in different emotions. Like ocean waves, they repeatedly sweep you into a sea of grief and despair and cast you on the shore again, feeling battered and hurting. You may be in an ocean of confusion, so enormous that you do not even know exactly what you feel anymore, be it pain, frustration, affliction, fear, depression, or the lack of hope. But from the moment you hold this book in your hands and wish to know more about how others—who have suffered like you—managed to overcome their loss, you are demonstrating that you want to move forward. You are showing that you want to put all your effort into continuing to embrace this precious gift that is your life.

But this book is only a lifeline to give you hope. It is you who must grasp this lifeline and slowly pull yourself to shore and resume you life. You may still slide backwards, but hold this lifeline tight until you finally pull yourself to shore. With each strong effort you make, you will gain in confidence in the future, and hope will once again be reborn in your life. The moment will arrive when you are able to go beyond your grief and you will have transformed your loss. Again, please remember not to expect your grief process to be the same as another person's, which includes family members. We have already commented that everyone expresses their grief differently and that the period of mourning can vary. Sometimes we think this period went too quickly, at other times too slowly and that we have taken far more time than necessary to go through this stage.

This reminds me of a metaphor the Reverend Dale Young used during a bereavement workshop we did in Miami, Florida[13]. In this workshop he stressed the importance of taking into account the personal clock each of us has for experiencing grief. I thought this was a marvelous concept as everyone in effect has their own clock, or amount of time needed, for the mourning period. One person can feel ready to re-integrate into society within three months, whereas another may take a year, not feeling ready for social interaction.

For this reason I recommend that you have some self-compassion, and take all the time you need to grieve. It may be that according to your "grief clock" you are not yet ready to even imagine any kind of transformation of your loss, which is perfectly fine, and understandable. Maybe you are still in the acute stage of grief, be it realization or transition, and do not feel ready to be fully engage in this process. The only thing I would still suggest is to slowly go through the principles in the book at your own pace. There is no rush. You may wish to do some of the exercises that I have suggested in the *Moments of Reflection* as they may help you in this stage of your grieving process. Try the ones that you think could help you process your grief. But only you know for certain when you will be ready to try them.

What you can do first is read the exercises and consider trying one of them. The first could take you a while to do, but keep in mind how much it could help you to get in touch with your emotions. There will be many times that you think it is impossible to confront such sorrow and affliction throughout your grieving process. You may even want to give up at some point, to run away, escape reality, and maybe resort to less effective or damaging methods, such as permanent denial, isolation, alcohol or other drug abuse (I will touch on this later). All of which will only help you escape the reality of your loss temporarily, only to re-confront your grief once their effect has worn off.

Do you ever try to avoid what you are feeling in your heart? It is common that when you are dealing with a loss, you avoid confronting or experiencing your feelings, as they can be too painful or even ambivalent. To deal with your emotions may be so painful that you avoid talking about your pain. But it is necessary to search deep within yourself until you are somehow able to experience your real feelings.

I want to emphasize that the grieving process is not a linear process. Some days will be harder than others, but the important thing is to just keep going. In trying to avoid pain, many people ignore the situation, and just bury the pain deep inside themselves, never speaking about it. They continue their daily lives as if nothing has happened. But after awhile they may suffer a series of disorders, from the emotional to the psychosomatic, having no idea why they feel down or ill. Getting through the grief, the painful sensations, as observed in a previous section, is not limited to dealing with the emotions; grief can eventually manifest physically or spiritually, or both. It is possible that the repressed pain caused by a difficult situation comes to light several years later, having become what is called a *complicated grief.*

Since it is important to know the tools we can use to deal with and transform our loss, it is also important to recognize the methods that may throw us off course and bury us deeper in the state of grief we are already in. The following series of behaviors can damage your spirit and delay your growth as a human being instead of helping you.

UNHEALTHY WAYS TO DEAL WITH LOSS

Eagerness to overcome grief or to shrug off the grief process causes people to fill up their time by making sure they are constantly distracted and busy. The things they do are probably not very important, but they keep them occupied, thus preventing them from paying attention to the most important thing: themselves.

Therefore, once you understand and recognize that there are no immediate solutions, that everything takes time, you can embrace the opportunity to slow down and observe yourself and your life. Little by little, you are being transformed, and you are finding an inner strength which you may have had no idea you possessed. What you may have thought was impossible starts to become a reality.

The problem with distractions is that many people lose themselves in their work or leisure activities. They may constantly go out in the evenings to make sure they do not have to face the lonely night, or they may seek another type of escapism. With certainty, they do not wish to face their new reality and process their affliction.

Another way people contend with a loss, which does not help the healing process, is by abusing alcohol or drugs. Many people think or hope that by drowning their problems in alcohol, they will feel better. Of course they may manage to relax for a short while, and they can even manage to forget for a while, but...what about the following morning when the reality appears at their window again? What happens when they wake up with that sinking feeling, that feeling of emptiness and guilt? Will they feel more depressed and unsatisfied? They run the risk of getting trapped in a vicious circle, as each day they may drink more and more to numb the pain and forget their situation.

Sometime ago, when I was dealing directly with alcoholics, I had one case, Sandra, a woman of 38, who had lost her partner. She could not escape her sadness; she was unable to share her feelings with anyone around her. She isolated herself from her family and friends, and compulsively devoted her life to her job. At night, on her way home, she would stop at a bar on the corner, to have a couple of drinks to help fill her void. This was the case for four months, until one day she collapsed at work, and her boss smelled alcohol on her breath. She was not only drinking in the evening after work, she became so desperate to choke her pain, she began drinking first thing in the morning. Her boss sent her to rehabilitation, and it was then that she began to share her feelings in the group sessions, started to work on her grief, and began her recovery process.

Grief work brings to the surface feelings that are sometimes difficult to recognize or accept as they are painful. It is necessary to go through them to be able to heal the wounds, or at least assuage them. Therefore, do not take refuge in drinking or eating to excess. Face the situation, confront your loss, and try to get to the root cause of what is happening. Try not to stifle your pain with addictions or compulsions as they are not healthy, as in the end, you will become more depressed.

Don't forget that, although you have a weight on your soul, life goes on and we continue with it! When you recognize that your pain is present, stop and observe it. Be mindful of your pain. I strongly recommend this. As you reflect on what you feel physically, mentally, emotionally, and spiritually, you will become more aware of what you are experiencing overall. Perhaps you will be able to recognize what led to this state of mind. Your thoughts could simply be an expression of memory.

Whatever it is, observe it, reflect on it, process it, and embrace it.

A MOMENT OF REFLECTION

What am I feeling at this moment, physically, spiritually, and emotionally? What made me feel this way? How do I try to hide my feelings: With alcohol or drugs? With excessive work or exercise? By slumping in front of the TV or computer for hours? Or by just not talking about the loss?

How do I feel confronted with this new reality?

AFFIRMATIONS:

- I can get to the bottom of my pain.
- I am conscious that while facing the situation, some days will be harder than others.
- I choose to let go of the pain.
- I dedicate a part of each day to feeling my grief.

- I am free of drugs or alcohol.
- I can avoid becoming excessively distracted.
- I can take hold of my pain.
- I know my pain is not forever.

MEDITATION

The transformation process requires confronting my pain, not avoiding it. In the moments that I feel pain in the depths of my soul, I will receive and embrace my pain. It is part of me. Each day, I will take a moment to write about what I feel and why I am feeling that way. If I need to cry, I will, because little by little, I will start to feel better. I will become stronger and my life will take on more meaning.

PRINCIPLE III – GO DEEPER INTO THE SPIRITUAL DIMENSION

Our time in the wilderness, or the dark cave, may be long and tortuous. We may never find satisfactory answers to all of these questions, but at some point - if we are going to live - we will have to push back the stones and move on. We will emerge from our cave or from the "muddy waters of the Jordan" with a new understanding of life, and new resolve. Hopefully, what we have lost in physical or emotional prowess we will have gained in wisdom, determination, purpose, and spiritual strength.

SYDNEY WILDE

For the majority of humankind, spirituality seems essential in their lives. For this reason I will expand on it as my third principle for transforming loss because I consider it to be one of the most powerful tools we have to overcome and transcend our loss. Faith or a strong belief is very powerful when confronting the loss of a loved one. You may have ascertained this from some of the stories in Part Two of this book. As for example, Zig Ziglar, renowned author and speaker, in his book *Confessions of a Grieving Christian* (2004), tells how his faith in God helped him find comfort when he lost his daughter Suzanne. Ziglar wrote this book while he was going through his grief process. He states that he was able to process his grief and come out of mourning through prayer, and because he believed his daughter could be found next to God. Additionally, he found joy on his path of mourning and grief. His grief was very painful, as he describes it:

> It is impossible to describe fully the grief that overwhelmed my family and me at the death of our beloved firstborn daughter. Nothing had prepared me for the intensity of pain and sorrow I experienced....There is no grief that I had experienced that has come close to my grief over the loss of our child. Throughout our months and years of grieving, faith has been the redeeming force that has enabled us to bear the pain and continue to live on victory....God uses grief as a process to show His compassion toward us, to teach us, and to bring us into greater wholeness.[14]

These words are from a man who loved his daughter profoundly, and at the same time loved and trusted God. It was this love and his deep faith that helped Ziglar transform his loss as shown through his positive, loving, and spiritual message. In Principle X you will find Ziglar's testimony repeated, with his message of hope that opens doors of possibility for us.

Finding answers through spiritual or religious beliefs can give us the necessary means to find significance in our loss. This is what happened to my client Carla at her husband's death:

> I think that, from the very first moment, during my grief, I felt that if God permitted me to go through something, it was for a reason, even if I did not know what is was. On the second day after the funeral my little brother said, "Sis, don't be angry with God. I don't want your relationship with him to be damaged."
>
> I answered him, "No, I'm convinced that if God permitted it to happen, it is because my children and I have to live it…as well as the soul of Javier, my deceased husband."

If you feel you are in the need of spiritual guidance, go to your religious leader or teacher, depending on your religious persuasion. If you are not religious, seek a person that you believe to have deep spiritual and human values. Use meditation and silence periods. Reading inspirational books can be of great help. L. B. Cowman, in his book *Streams in the Desert*, reminds us that through misfortune we can find powerful gifts that we would otherwise not have found. These are some of his words:

> We cannot see what loss, sorrow and trials are accomplishing. We need only to trust. The Father

comes near to take our hand and lead us on our way today.[15]

Re-read the previous lines, and once more pause and reflect. It could be that as you go deeper into your feelings, you will discover gifts that can give meaning to your life and transform your grief. Do not fear going deep into your soul. You may cry, but remember the well-known saying, "Tears cleanse the soul," which I believe to be true. This natural catharsis is necessary to release stress and pain and to realize that we are human. We do not have to repress what is happening to us.

If you have just gone through a divorce, I recommend that you take a reasonable time before getting involved in another relationship again. You need time to accept your new situation, work through the grief, and reintegrate your life. After any loss, life is not the same. We can overcome a loss, but our life has been touched by it. Therefore, let's give it the time it deserves and not run from it, as sooner or later, it will catch up with us. Faith very much helps many people to deal with loss as you have seen in the majority of our stories. If there is an iota of faith in you, embrace it, and pray with fervor, as the power of prayer and faith are mighty. Or use another form of spiritual practice that is of comfort or provides a means of self-reflection.

I recently spoke with a friend, Jorge Córdoba, author of *A Line Between Two Numbers* (one of the presentation texts of this book) and a cancer survivor. He is a very religious and spiritual man who had an experience with the Virgin Mary. He tells me he felt her presence while at a prayer group. While saying his Hail Mary's he suddenly noticed a strong scent of roses. He immediately went to his wife Naomi and asked if she too smelled the aroma; she had not, neither had the rest of the group. The leader of the prayer group told Jorge he had been the only one who had noticed the scent and that it sometimes happens when the Virgin Mary comes to people. That same night, in bed, Jorge smelled the same aroma; at the same time he felt warmth in his neck, where his cancer was located. He woke his wife and told her:

"I feel warmth in my neck; I know that it was the Virgin Mary healing me."

What Jorge realized that night was that his faith had healed him.

Most people continuously suffer losses, but many of us have found the answer to our problems through spiritual practices, which allow us to grow spiritually and transform our lives.

I assure you that one often requires a spiritual source to recover from a crucial loss. This can be of a religious nature, such as attending a church, temple, synagogue, or mosque, or reading a religious text or praying. It could be integrated into broader contexts such as yoga, meditation, contemplation, visualization, or inspirational readings. Choose the one that has meaning for you, but above all, keep in mind that you already have the gifts of spiritual love, forgiveness, hope, and gratitude. Probe your soul, discover these gifts, cultivate them, and you will see that your life will change. Then I recommend that you briefly explore these gifts.

I suggest, as proposed by Ira Byock,[16] that you frequently repeat exclamations such as these to help you have a fuller life:

- I love you!
- I forgive myself!

- I forgive you!
- I thank you!

Can you imagine hearing these words more often? Why wait for a misfortune to express our love for everyone and see the value that a few words can have? Remember that forgiveness is a part of love; this includes forgiveness of oneself, which sometimes is the most difficult. Above all, when faced with feelings of guilt, we forget that we are human and as such, we make mistakes.

A MOMENT OF REFLECTION

I propose that you take a break, look at yourself in a mirror and deep into your eyes, then repeat the following assertions:
- I forgive any mistake I made in the past.
- I forgive (name) for having done me wrong in the past.
- I feel free of any grudge or bitterness.
- When I forgive, all resentment is lost.
- I feel liberated.

Another form of apology or forgiveness can be achieved by writing a letter to a person or writing notes in a journal. (In Principle V, dedicated to rituals, I'll give you some ideas to help you find the spiritual peace that your soul needs.) Here are questions for reflection:

Love
- How do you express your love?

- Who do you love?
- Who loves you?

Forgiveness
- Who do you have to forgive?
- Who needs to forgive you?
- Have you forgiven (name) for _____?

Appreciation
- What do you have to be thankful for in your life?
- Who should you thank for their love or friendship?
- What do you feel when you are thankful?

Hope
- What makes you feel hope?
- Who do you give hope to?
- In what areas of your life do you experience hope?

Affirmations:
- I have hope for the future.
- Every day is an opportunity for love, to be thankful and to forgive.
- I love myself and everyone else.
- I have faith that I will end up walking by myself, with expectation and confidence.

MEDITATION

In my times of distress I just need to close my eyes and look inside myself. I seek the deepest part of my being, to charge myself with the spiritual gifts that I possess. Within me reside pure feelings that provide me with peace and hope. I let God penetrate my life and deliver me from my sorrow. I know that my faith on Him will help me move forward, step by step, along the path of my grief.

PRINCIPLE IV – EXPRESS YOUR FEELINGS

A concept that is often used to teach children to express themselves adequately is "emotional intelligence," since psychologists have realized how important it is to express one's emotions in an appropriate manner. I think we would be a very different society and more functional people if we externalized our emotions adequately right from childhood. Channeling them in the right direction is essential for our well-being, as sometimes we show one thing when in fact we feel something totally different. Why do we do this? Why do we defend ourselves so as not to seem vulnerable? Is it to avoid possible wounds? With regard to anger, it's easier to say "I am angry" than to say "I am depressed." It is easier to accept, and perhaps what we should say and do is to admit that we're depressed and expand on our feelings until we find the reason for it, then do something to help ourselves. Do you realize how important it is to understand the root cause of your emotions? We do not have to fear our emotions! We are human beings and as such we can express what we feel.

I invite you now to take your paper and pencil and jot down what you think is the difference between anger and depression.

Once you have identified the two emotions, describe situations in which you have felt anger and those in which you have felt depressed; then expand on each. Remember this, and next time consider whether it is really anger or depression that you are experiencing.

Another wonderful exercise for becoming aware of your feelings is to draw on a sheet of paper the face you present to the world. On a second sheet of paper draw the one that represents how you feel inside. Now compare them.

Are they the same?

What is different? What do you feel inside that you are not expressing?

Sometimes we feel a mixture of feelings, or conflicting feelings, and wonder:

"What is happening to me?

"Am I going crazy?"

"Is this normal?"

"Everyone tells me that it is about time, but I do not feel ready yet. Am I behaving normally?"

There are times when our emotions are mixed and confuse us. Mary, a mother who lost her son, asked:

"Is it feasible that sometimes I wish to laugh and cry at the same time?"

One of the most common feelings when facing loss is guilt. Sometimes we wonder if we could have done things differently, or if the loss could have been prevented, at least for a while longer. It is very common to feel angry and/or experience fear for the future. Anger is a common feeling when experiencing a loss, and as Les Parrott (2004) says, "Many of us feel anger [while grieving] which scares us, and that is why we do not admit it." But if you are experiencing anger during a loss, do not be afraid. Remember that you are human and to accept this requires courage.

Let's return to the example of Mary, who shared the story of her son's death. She admitted in public to having initially felt angry toward God and told how she went about eradicating this feeling, to the point that with the help of another mother who had also lost her son, she formed a support group in a church to help others who were experiencing grief and mourning their loss.

A MOMENT OF REFLECTION

Take a break now and answer the following questions as best you can. This exercise will give you the opportunity to delve into your feelings and express them in a beneficial way. If when considering the source of your anger, you have more than one answer, list them all. As you write the answers, examine them, and then try to explore each more deeply. This way you can get to the source of these feelings and can deal with them better.

If you experience anger:
- What is its origin?
- Against whom is the anger directed?
- How do I express my anger?
- Are there moments in which I do not feel angry?
- What are those moments?

Now, in case you are experiencing guilt, explore it:

- What is its origin?
- When do you feel guilty?
- What do you think you could have done differently?

If you feel that fear of the future is dominating your life, I recommend that you answer the following questions:
- What am I afraid of?
- When do I feel most afraid?
- Why do I feel like this?
- How long have I felt like this?

Affirmations:
- I fear no pain.
- I can confront my feelings and accept them.
- I dismiss any delay in my spiritual growth.
- I experience my feelings of mourning.
- I recognize that every day will not be equal.
- I differentiate between anger and depression
- Gradually, I overcome my grief.
- I have the ability to heal my own grief.
- I trust the future.

MEDITATION

Living through the grief process, I have come to delve into the most profound depths of my being and at the same time, I have managed to embrace all of my feelings, including anger, guilt, and fear. I don't need to escape from them or hide them. I understand that when I face them I take a step closer to the transformation process. I understand that some days will be more difficult than others, but it is a process. The days that I want to cry, I will, but that does not mean that I'm going backwards on my journey of healing. I will be compassionate with myself and give myself all the time I need.

PRINCIPLE V – SHARE WITH OTHERS

Attending a support group can be very helpful for those who are going through a loss. By participating in a grief support group you can identify with the loss of other members. And it is very likely that by listening to others' painful stories, you can find strength, and you will know that you are not alone. Being in a group can also help you deal with your pain.

There are different kinds of support groups. Find the one for you and with which you feel most comfortable. Do not judge them with one visit. If the first one you go to is not for you, attend others, until you find one you identify with.

However, it is important to share in an active, not passive manner. At first you may feel shy or embarrassed because you are in a strange place with people you do not know. But as time passes, you will notice that there is something that bonds you all. You will identify with the losses that members of the group suffer; in turn, you will feel little by little, that you can lower your guard and open your heart.

You might even share aspirations and establish specific personal goals with the group. Sharing our ambitions with others forms a commitment, and you feel more motivated to realize what you have shared with others.

After a loss we can feel disconnected from the rest of the world. Perhaps we are surrounded by people but have no connection with them. We may feel empty and desolate. It is possible that you cannot talk about your loss, even with your own family. Perhaps they think that enough time has passed and are telling you to just get over your grief and get on with your life. Maybe your loss is too recent, and you are unable to help each other.

The members of a grief support group can accompany you on your path while you live through your loss. Though each of us has their own pace of recovery, seeing how other people are getting through their pain, what tools they use, and by what means, can help you. Surround yourself with people who understand you, who do not judge, and who may even hold your hand when you need it or just sit with you in silence. As the great English poet John Donne said, "No man is an island," so human beings need the strength of others, friends and family. One needs to know that he or she can count on them in times of need, for a hand to hold, a shoulder to cry on, a softly spoken word, or simply encouragement on those darker days when it is extremely difficult to get out of bed. Your family and friends are part of your helping network. Talk to them, share with them. Do not pretend to feel good if you do not. What counts is that you can communicate honestly and know that you can depend on people who love you and care about you.

Giving thanks is a very important part of this principle of sharing with others. Thank the people who have helped you. Make sure they know they are important in your life. This can be done with a thank you note, a phone call, or a personal visit. Do it! It will make the person feel good and special, and you too!

Write a list of names of the people who have helped you, and take a little time everyday to thank each of them. This should not be an obligation that you do quickly. I suggest that you take time and reflect on this. Remember what each person on the list has meant to you during your difficult moments.

HELP OTHERS

Keep in mind that it is also essential that you put aside your own pain occasionally to help others who need your caring support. Keep an attitude of openness towards life. Learn to love and forgive. Learn to listen and feel the pain of others. Often through assisting others, by setting aside our own suffering temporarily, it is possible to find light at the end of the tunnel of our own grief. If we maintain a constant attitude of self-pity, we cannot be compassionate toward others. It also helps to do something productive. Although there will be days when you can do nothing to help others and need your own space, it is not good to remain focused on your own needs all the time. Remember that you are a special person and that the world needs you. Maybe you can touch the life of another with only a gesture, even during your grieving process.

This reminds me of the conversation I had with Cecilia, a girl who carries out bags at a supermarket. I found her sad. She shared with me how she missed her homeland of Perú. I allowed her to talk, and when she finished, I gave her a hug. To my surprise it was the first hug she had received in two months! At that moment I thought:

"How little is required to give some happiness to another."

Imagine, if every day we gave a little encouragement or a gesture of affection to some one; the world would be a better place. Therefore, I suggest that you not live surrounded by your own pain all the time. Try to shift your focus and by getting out and sharing some love. Most probably someone needs you, without your knowing it. It will help you more than you imagine by being useful to others and doing something productive that gives meaning to your life. There will be moments when you will want to enjoy your solitude, a necessary time, of course. It is important to be alone, as it gives you the opportunity to reflect, plan, or simply explore your feelings. However, avoid making it a way of life. Remember, "No [woman] is an island." This is a great truth because we live in an interdependent world. You need the world and the world needs you! Your family, your friends, and your co-workers all need you. You need yourself! Try not to concentrate solely on your own pain. Think about other people around you who may also be going through a loss.

Maybe you can touch a life with a single gesture.

A life that you succeed in touching is a life that can be helped to change.

Helping others is always an act of love, and giving something of yourself can be part of your healing from grief and loss.

AFFIRMATIONS:
- I find support in others.
- Talking about my pain with my fellow human beings helps me through my trials.
- I realize that I am not alone.

- Helping others shifts the focus from myself.
- If there is someone waiting for their hand to be held, I will offer mine with love and compassion.

MEDITATION

I am blessed because I can count on people who are concerned about me and have offered me their hand. I have learned to share and accept the love of others. My family loves me. My friends love me. My fellow group members love me. I am able to give and receive. I give thanks to God for people whom I have found on my path.

Principle VI – Take Care of Yourself

Why take care of yourself? Because if we live according to the precept "Love thy neighbor as thyself," it implies that to love others you must start with yourself. What does it mean to love yourself? To love yourself means that you must take care of yourself.

And what does that imply exactly? Taking care of yourself involves paying attention to your body and mind, because a healthy body and mind take care of the spirit.

Your Body

Your body is what makes up your physical dimension, and it is essential that you not neglect your health. If you do not feel healthy or if you are suffering from certain ailments, seek medical attention to become better informed, in case you need some kind of treatment. Never assume that something is not physical and that what you feel is caused by your emotional pain. This could be the case, but always consult with your doctor. It is also essential to pay attention to what constitutes a well-balanced, nutritional diet. Sometimes by staying home or just lacking the desire to cook, because of our grieving process, we don't follow a good diet that brings us well-being.

Therefore, we can feel tired and lack energy. If necessary, seek advice from a good nutritionist, or ask your doctor to help you make a plan that best suits you. There are many diets, but yours must be in accordance with your constitution and condition.

Exercise has become an essential component for good health. It is recommended to help combat chronic illnesses such as diabetes and heart disease. There are even exercise programs for the elderly; there is no age limit on improving one's health. Regular exercise also helps tremendously to liberate yourself from anger and depression, especially if you can do it in the company of others. There are many fitness activities. Pick one that interests you and makes you feel comfortable. You can register for a class, become a member of a gym, or simply go for a walk.

Soon after Johanna lost her husband in a plane crash, she joined a gym. She explained that the exercise and the act of attending a gym helped her tremendously with her grieving process and in having the strength to keep going. Any physical activity provides beneficial results for your body and mind, and adds to your capacity for transformation.

YOUR BODY

Our mind is more powerful than we think. It drives or directs our actions. Therefore, it is essential to feed it positive and valuable information. Reading is a fundamental way to stimulate the mind, but take care to select stimulating and appropriate materials that can be of positive benefit. At this moment in time, it would be a good idea to read books of a spiritual nature, of achieving personal feats that overcome grief, and self-help books. Biographies of people who have conquered great challenges and triumphed in life are also very stimulating and uplifting. Choose reading that best fits your personality and concentrate on the subject. Make notes of relevant or important points; or you could just underline the text directly. Really get into the passages, find their profound messages and teachings.

Another very productive way to keep the mind occupied and avert depression is by doing crossword puzzles or playing a game such as dominoes. They are both a form of concentration and at the same time stimulate the brain. It is very important to keep the mind occupied with beneficial activities in order to keep a positive frame of mind. This serves as another step in your transformation process.

Your Spirit

Taking care of your spirit is an essential dimension for leading a fulfilling life, and you do not need a formal religion to do so. Try to dedicate an hour a day to cultivating your spirit in some way; you will realize it is a life-changing decision. This time can be spent in many different "spiritual" exercises. You could read a book; meditate; do yoga; write in a journal; listen to music; go to a church, temple or a spiritual center; go to the beach or to the country; discuss relevant subjects with a friend or relative, or simply take time off to recharge your batteries. If you do a different activity every day, you may realize that it really does not take that much effort. These things could easily become a regular part of your routine that enable you to lead a full and plentiful life. Above all, remember to integrate your gifts of love, gratitude, and forgiveness. Your life will become full of light, hope, and peace.

AFFIRMATIONS:

- My body is my temple, which I lovingly care for.
- I feed my body with healthy nutritious food.
- I participate in physical activities for the health of my body and mind.
- I feel healthy and full of energy.
- I want to grow spiritually.

MEDITATION

With every passing day, my body feels stronger and healthier. I feed my body with high quality nutrition, and I exercise regularly, which makes me feel good and full of vitality. I feed my mind with meaningful information so that I can evolve as an individual. I have the power to decide the type of life I want to live. I choose a healthy life with high objectives.

Principle VII – Use Rituals

Rituals can help to restore sense of balance to life.

ALICE PARSONS ZULLI

During our lives we engage in many rituals. We celebrate birthdays, anniversaries, graduations, and religious festivals and holidays. We go to our temples, churches, or meet for a family Sunday meal. A ritual is a ceremony that holds some special personal or community meaning.

Many rituals are religious, others secular. But they generally have one common element in terms of meaning and purpose: to make us feel good, and in many cases, to maintain family traditions. In fact, many families have different kinds of rituals. Some have shared rituals, while others are more personal. An example of a ritual of great significance for many Catholics is praying the Rosary. Participating in a ritual often equates to an action of special significance or meaning for us.

In the specific case of loss, rituals help to process it and give us meaning for that precise event. However, we must be aware that rituals can become obsessive acts if we do not focus on the purpose of our behavior and what motivates us to carry them out. As mentioned, a ritual is the execution of a specific significant action, but if such action becomes a repetitive act that we need to do many times to feel satisfied, we may be developing an obsessive compulsive disorder. If we suspect that this action wields a power over us, it is important to know and recognize that we must seek help, because it can become something that interrupts the regular flow of our lives and our behavior. If this happens to you, my advice is to find help, talk to someone, open your heart, and you will find the help you need to prevent such a disorder or misuse of ritual.

The purpose of carrying out rituals, among other things, is to assist people in solving emotional problems and to find meaning in their lives. Rituals can be very significant, and in cases of the loss of a loved one, funerals and memorials are rituals that greatly help those who are beginning the grieving process.

RITUALS FOR DIFFERENT KINDS OF LOSSES

There are many kinds of rituals for observing the death of a person. These follow the cultural and/or religious customs of the deceased, or some other observance befitting the person and according to the wishes of the survivors. Personal rituals can also mark different kinds of losses besides the death of a loved one.

THE FUNERAL

When someone dies, we usually have an opportunity to attend the person's funeral or memorial service and share our loss with close family and friends. Yet many people avoid attending these services, as they prefer to remember the beloved person as they were in life. However, the funeral has a *raison d'etre*; it is an effective way to internalize the fact that the person has died and that they are no longer with us, and usually to honor them and their life and contributions. Additionally, "...the funeral is a time to publicly commemorate a life that has ended, as well as to put the complex experience of death into a framework of meaning" (A. Parsons Zulli, 1998).[17]

Parsons states that there are different ways to conduct a funeral depending on the religion or belief of the person as to how it is conducted.

A common type of funeral or memorial service is known as a *celebration of life*, a ceremony that celebrates the person and their lifestyle. For example, if a person felt a great passion for tennis, mementoes of tennis might be displayed, from a tennis racket to pictures of the deceased and fellow players.

Diana, the manager of a funeral home, told me that their staff pays special attention to conducting the kind of funeral that meets the specific requests and needs of families to honor their loved one. Funeral and memorial services reflect the culture and religion of the family, in addition to honoring the life of the deceased.

PERSONAL RITUALS

I would like to suggest a series of rituals that can be done in accordance with the loss you are facing. You can do them all, if you so wish, since all of these rituals can give you peace and a feeling of profound well-being. A ritual can be enhanced with the use of candles. Candles create a spiritual and peaceful atmosphere when combined with prayers, certain rites, or simply ambient background music. There are many types of candles - long, round or floating – and they can be used according to the ritual that is to be performed. The following are rituals for specific losses, but suggest ways you can create your own for your particular loss.

LOSS OF A LOVED ONE

Take a picture of your loved one and place it on a small table with a white candle. When you light the candle, say a prayer or intention on behalf of your loved one (e.g., for peace or release from suffering), give thanks for the love you had and the eternal love you will always feel for them. If you are religious, you can make the following request:

> Dear God, I ask You to fill me with white light and let my whole soul be in communion with my loved one. Give me the peace that I need and may this feeling of peace stay forever in my life.

LOSS OF HEALTH

Set candles of different colors on a table and assign them a different kind of energy, such as vitality. Then take a couple of drops of lavender oil and rub them on your temples, the palms of your hands, and your heart. Then, as you light the candles, imagine that your whole body is surrounded by a celestial blue light, a color that is known for its healing and spiritual powers. With faith, call for the restoration of your health.

LOSS FROM A DIVORCE

Light a purple candle, which represents spirituality and wisdom. Then take a pen and paper, and write a letter to your former spouse. Include in this letter whatever leftover feelings you still have within yourself, including resentment and anger. If you need to forgive or ask forgiveness for any past act, do so. Then tear up the letter you have written and burn it in the candle flame. In doing this, you can get rid yourself of all those negative feelings that are still hurting you and impeding your progress toward recovery from your loss.

WRITING A PERSONAL JOURNAL

Writing a journal is another activity that can be a ritual. The process of writing is in itself a form of personal expression and, in turn, is healing, because when we write what we feel, we cleanse our soul.

A journal can hold an account of our experiences and what is important to us. It is a way to explore our feelings and reactions to certain circumstances.

If you start writing a journal to process your grief, you will realize that it is a powerful tool to help you become aware of the changes within yourself throughout the grieving process, because we may not even realize this happening.

If you re-read your journal regularly, you will notice your increasing progress and that you are undergoing a transformation. The changes occur even if you do not perceive them.

Your family may have noticed that you have learned to give more of yourself, by being more compassionate or patient. We are often so engaged with the pain caused by our loss that we do not perceive the small changes in our lives.

I think of Lucia, the woman who, after having gone through a painful divorce, had not been aware of the positive changes in herself. She had emerged from the shadow in which she lived, behind her husband, to shine on her own. She was like a caterpillar who became a butterfly. She did not fully comprehend this until one day while we were talking, I reminded her about the early days after her divorce and how she acted when she was married. It was her wake up call. She is now a woman, sure of herself and full of happiness.

You can write your journal in different ways: either freely or by categories, for example. Do what you prefer, but I recommend that whenever you write, to remember to include the date and time.

Choose your topics, ideas, or experiences as you please. You can write about your day's experiences in a general manner or under specific headings. Find a list of items that can serve as starting points, such as these:

- I am sad about…
- I feel guilty about…
- I fear…
- ….bothers me
- I miss…
- I am grateful for…
- I hope….

These starting points are basically to put you in touch with your feelings. Express them freely and without hesitation. After carefully reading each entry in your journal, examine what you feel. Over time, especially if you date the entries, you can appreciate the gradual evolution of your state of mind. If you notice that you are stuck with certain issues, I recommend that you look for professional help or visit your spiritual advisor.

WRITING A LETTER

Writing a letter can help you express feelings that remain in your heart and which you need to release. This happens when we could not express what we felt, or were not able to say goodbye to our loved one. The idea of writing a letter is not always for the purpose of sending it as though the person was still alive, but to express what you feel. A letter can help bring closure to any loss.

You may wonder,"How do I write a letter that I am not going to send?" I respond: "Write it from your soul."

Take a notebook and start the letter however you wish, but express what you feel. Perhaps, if you are a widow(er), you may want to tell your husband or wife how much you miss them.

Letters can be used to process other experiences. You can write a letter to your former boss, expressing your anger for having dismissed you without notice. You can write to the father or mother of your children, for having left you for another person, after your divorce. You can even write a letter to your pet that has passed on. The idea is to express fully what you feel. You can either save the letter or get rid of it. That is your choice.

Marta Felber in her book: *Finding Your Way After Your Spouse Dies* (2000)[18] tells us how writing letters to her deceased husband—which she now keeps in a special folder—helped her during her grieving process. If you have lost a spouse, this idea could serve you as well.

AFFIRMATIONS:
- Lighting a candle brings peace to my soul.
- Lighting a candle lets me feel closer to my loved one.
- Writing in my diary helps me cleanse my soul.
- Writing in my journal is a way to express what I am feeling.
- Prayer brings me peace and inner strength.

MEDITATION

If I feel sad or nostalgic, I know I can find peace and serenity by venturing into the depths of my being and establishing contact with my feelings. I will sit relaxed in a room, light a candle and experiment with my feelings. If I wish to write in my journal, I will do so freely and without interruption. Once I connect with my emotions, I will allow my sorrow to be released and open my heart to new experiences and sensations.

PRINCIPLE VIII – LIVE THE PRESENT

Do not dwell in the past, do not dream of the future, concentrate the mind on the present moment.

THE BUDDHA

Have you noticed that you often live your life, thinking about what has happened or hasn't happened yet? We tend to look back and lament about the past as those were better times. When facing a loss, it is very common to think nostalgically about our loved one, the good job we lost, or the homeland we left behind. The feelings we are trying to address are all very normal experiences. The problem is that when our life is only focused on these thoughts, lamenting about what has been or what is still to come means we are not living for today.

What if you decide to live each day with absolute purpose in all your actions? Does this seem difficult?

Eckhart Tolle, in his book *The Power of Now* (2004), reminds us how necessary it is to be aware of each action and thought. This means being present to ourselves and others. You may ask what does the phrase "being present" mean. It infers that whatever we do, we do it conscientiously, mindfully. Whether you are eating or just sitting, you should be aware of what you are doing. By entering into a state of mind where you are paying full attention to everything that happens, you will enhance the experience. When you are talking to someone, listen to that person; do not become distracted by other thoughts. Being present and alert truly facilitates the confrontation of loss, since it forces you to get to the bottom of your feelings, in a state of absolute consciousness. Do not despair if at first you find this difficult to do. It is normal, as this type of behavior is not the norm in our society. We rarely take time to be just by ourselves and to listen to our thoughts. When we eat, we usually do it in a hurry and do not enjoy the flavor of the food. When we cry, the tears come to us and we feel regret, but perhaps we are not really aware of what is making us cry. Take your time. Be present in your own thoughts and get to know yourself a little more.

On the other hand, by understanding the concept of "now", you will realize that each moment is a "now." What is now the present, tomorrow will be the past. Our life is a succession of "nows." Still, as I say this, I don't mean we should live without thinking about tomorrow. What I propose is, that you be concerned about tomorrow, but be aware that this will only materialize according to your attitude and actions today. Therefore, it is worth building the future you want to live by living in the present in a meaningful way to anticipate tomorrow.

A Moment of Reflection

Sit comfortably without closing your eyes and get in touch with your inner self. Be aware of your breathing and perceive your surroundings. Look around and discover the colors that you have not previously noticed and smells you haven't perceived. In this moment, as you are absolutely present and experiencing fully each second, feel how the universe surrounds you.

Affirmations:
- I live in the present.
- I embrace the future.
- I am present in every moment.
- I live fully and completely for today.

Meditation

Learning to live in the present is not easy, but it helps me to live fully. I have discovered that I have a source of wisdom and strength not known to me before. I appreciate every experience of every day. I listen to my inner self, my worries and intrusive thoughts are allowed to escape. Living to the full each today makes me feel alive.

PRINCIPLE IX – MODIFY YOUR THOUGHTS

I cannot always control what goes on outside. But I can always control what goes on inside.

WAYNE DYER

In life we go through difficult situations, but everything depends on our response to them. We must learn to accept losses because, as the Dalai Lama said, this opens the possibility of seeing the pain of others and not just focusing on our own.

Initially the feelings of grief and anxiety are a natural human response to loss. But if you allow these feelings of loss and concern to persist, there is a danger. If these feelings are left to run free, they can lead to a kind of "self-absorption," a situation where you become the focus of yourself. When that occurs, you feel overwhelmed by emptiness and feel that you are going through this situation alone. But, in reality, there are others who are going through the same.[19]

I suggest you re-read these words of the Dalai Lama and realize the danger of falling into "self-absorption," because then we become passive victims rather than active agents. Usually this is caused by the way we think, and this affects our feelings.

Usually people hold a monologue (sometimes a dialogue with themselves.) We are constantly sending out many different messages or are trapped in a particular way of thinking. If you are going through a lot of pain, you probably think you are the only one and that your pain is greater than anyone else's. But stop and look around you! Many people are also suffering.

THE TRANSFORMATIVE POWER OF OUR THOUGHTS

Beliefs are rooted in thoughts. Of course, in the case of loss, mainly the loss of someone we love, feelings also have a great influence on our beliefs. I am not referring to the emotions you experience, but to the messages that you give yourself with your thoughts.

The feelings for your loved one will never cease. I still love my father thirty-six years after his death, but I have emerged from my state of hopelessness and the thinking that I could not get out of the sad state of mind I was in. But gradually I began to forge my life, inspired by my father's life. From the moment I changed my way of thinking about his death, my life changed. It took me many years to accomplish this, which is why I wish to share this message with you: to help you avoid being in such a state of mind for an extended time.

Only when I had the opportunity as an adult to do a regression to the time of his funeral, and relive the painful situation, was I able to release the feelings I had buried in my soul, and reckon with my loss and change my life.

In the first pages of this book I shared with you that when my father died I did not use any of the tools that could have helped me in the grieving process. I did not use support groups, counseling, rituals, or journaling. In fact, for many years I was stuck in the first stage of grief, denial.

For many years I carried this pain inside my soul, and that is why today I am offering you this guide so you can focus on transforming your grief. When negative thoughts go through your mind, try to convert them into a positive message.

If you are continually saying:
I cannot live without my beloved.
Repeat the following:
I will learn to live without my loved one.

If you've said this many times:
I cannot move on.
Say the opposite with conviction:
I can move on!

If you have thought that:
Life is no longer worth anything.
State with conviction:
Life is a great gift!

Now, take some paper and a pencil and do the exercise below.

A MOMENT OF REFLECTION

Think of three things that make you feel guilty.
Think of three things that make you feel afraid.
Think of three things that make you feel upset.

Affirmations:
- I am free of any guilty feeling.
- I embrace life.
- I have to let go of anger.
- I have a lot to give to life.
- I love myself and everyone else.

After each negative thought below, write a positive one. Convert negativity into positivity.

MEDITATION

From this moment on, I will not allow any negative thinking to strip me of harmony. I see my thoughts becoming a source of strength and hope. Life is beautiful and I want to live it fully. Despite pain and adversity there is a capacity in me to transform and grow. I believe in myself.

PRINCIPLE X – REBUILD YOUR WORLD

As we consider Principle X, we may find rebuilding to be an innovative concept that is incorporated into the other principles on how to process grief and find meaning in loss. Psychologist Robert Neimeyer (2006)[20] considers this concept to be a necessary and constructive proposal. He tells us that "... trying to rebuild a world of meaning is the central process in the experience of mourning" (*Lessons of Loss*, p. 83). He reminds us that the process of making sense out of a loss, especially the death of a loved one, is very personal, and that the reconstruction of our life can be extremely difficult. Even so, Neimeyer believes that...

> Grieving is the act of affirming or reconstructing a personal world of meaning that has been challenged by loss... It requires us to reconstruct a world that again "'makes sense,'" that restores a semblance of meaning, direction, and interpretability to a life that is forever transformed (p. 92).

Initially this may seem impossible, especially when confronted with the loss of a loved one. A mother who lost her nine-year-old child to leukemia, once asked me:

"How do I find meaning in the death of my son?"

In reply, I asked her,

"Would you like to create a charitable organization in honor of your son? Do you want your child's death to be a legacy for others, who perhaps are suffering from the same disease he suffered from?"

The most important thing was that this mother not feel that her son's death was in vain. Take the example of MADD (Mothers Against Drunk Drivers), which was founded twenty-five years ago on the promise a mother made to her thirteen-year-old daughter, who died as a result of a drunk driving accident. Other mothers who had lost a child to drunk driving joined her to help keep this promise. Presently, MADD is a national organization in the United States that has more than two million members. MADD develops programs and promotes public awareness about the dangers of driving under the influence of alcohol.[21]

This is a vivid example of how to give meaning to a loss, and at the same time, to transform it into an act of love that benefits many others. Such acts help us to transform what can be unendurable grief into something positive for ourselves and others.

The death of a loved one can lead to many positive changes in the lives of those left behind. I learned more about this when I attended a seminar called *Strange Blessings: Grief and Posttraumatic Growth*.[22] The conference elaborated on the possibility of achieving a life transformation after confronting a painful loss. The presenter described different types of what have been termed "strange blessings," or beneficial outcomes that may arise when dealing with the death of a loved one. Among the changes that were mentioned were:

- Changes in oneself, such as living a more meaningful life.
- Changes in relationships, forgiving someone and letting go of resentment.
- Changes in the philosophy of life, to appreciate every single moment and thinking that life is a gift.

These changes include the reassessment of our priorities. Sometimes, we focus on less important or less significant things in our lives, and may not place value on truly meaningful things, such as family, friends and acquaintances; helping others and giving ourselves time. Occasionally we live without taking others into account enough, but when faced with the death of a loved one, or the diagnosis of a fatal disease, we realize that we need to spend more time on what is really important in our lives. The familiar quote "You do not realize what you have until you lose it" is all too true. This can also manifest when dealing with a divorce, if one realizes in retrospect that perhaps they could have worked on the relationship; or after losing a job that all they did was complain about its circumstances.

Similarly, this can happen when our parents die, and we regret not giving them the love or the time they merited. All these are human reactions and sometimes, only because of the loss, do we understand them.

Although not all people grow from suffering as everyone reacts differently, in most cases the changes are significant, especially at the spiritual and existential level. Along these lines, here are questions to consider:

- Can you think of something to do that will honor the memory of your loved one?
- Would you like to found an organization in their memory?
- Could you conduct a charitable event or offer your services as a volunteer in honor of your loved one?

A MOMENT OF REFLECTION

Take a break and finish the following statements:

My loved one…
fought for_____

loved_____

expected_____

dreamed_____

Which organization did they contribute to or wish to contribute to?

_____

How can I make a contribution to the lives of my peers so as to honor my loved one?

_____

_____

_____

_____

Do you remember that in Principle III I mentioned the case of Zig Ziglar and how his faith helped him use his loss by knowing that his daughter was with God?

Ziglar (2004) also recognizes that a loss can be transformed into a source of love and faith when he tells us:

Out of my grief has come a deeper love for my other children…a love that exceeds the great love I already felt for them. Out of my grief has come a deeper love for other members of my family including my sons-in-law, my daughter-in-law, my grandchildren, cousins, nieces, nephews and other relatives.23

Like Ziglar, several people when sharing their stories in this book agreed on the importance of demonstrating our love for others and to living every day fully. Such a need may be, in your case, a powerful reason to transform your life.

BE GRATEFUL FOR WHAT YOU HAVE

Gratitude is one of the spiritual elements covered in Principle III, as it may be of great help in rebuilding your life.

You might ask:

"What can I be grateful for since if I have suffered a loss?" What I am suggesting is that you can be grateful for what you still have in your life, despite your loss.

Why not focus on what we have? Throughout our lives, we suffer losses of all kinds. But remember that we constantly make gains as well. When we suffer a loss or sadness, despair clouds our vision, but what if we remove that filter and make the effort to evaluate what exists in our lives? It can enrich us if we give ourselves a chance to appreciate it.

A MOMENT OF REFLECTION

Now pause, take a deep breath, and get ready to make a list of what you are grateful for in your life. Once you have listed these, give thanks for each of them. You can make the list using different categories such as social, physical, psychological, and spiritual. Or you can simply make lists of friends, family, personal belongings, personal attributes, and the goals you have achieved. What is important is to recognize that your life still has things for which you are grateful. (Use additional paper or your notebook or journal to continue the list).

I am grateful for:

_____

_____

_____

_____

Similarly I recommend that every night before you go to bed that you write down three things for which you are grateful for that day. Perhaps you unexpectedly received a phone call, or you received a raise, or someone held the door for you, or perhaps someone simply smiled at you in the supermarket. Write down three things that made you feel good during the day. If you have more than three things, even better, write them all down.

It would not surprise me to learn that you have many reasons to be grateful. The next morning, re-read the list before starting the day, and you will see how good you feel. You can then face the day with greater enthusiasm. In the evening, make another list of three new things that occurred to you during that day. Try to do this for three months so as to understand what all you have to be thankful for in life, and all the special things that you have. The more focused you are on what you have, the easier it will be to live with what you have lost.

I am grateful for this day for the following three reasons:

_____

_____

_____

FINDING THE MEANING IN LIFE DURING LOSS

Melvin A. Kimble (2002) states that finding meaning in life is an essential component of spirituality, since the chances of finding the significance [for our surroundings] are always found in life; not even suffering and death can part us from that...Such recognition can renew the spiritual conscience of the individual in relation to their own divinity and value as a person.[24]

It is therefore essential to rebuild our faith and hope, by processing our grief.

When you reach this stage of your grieving process you can ask what the real purpose of life is. It is probable that after having experienced the pain of loss, your values will change, or if they remain the same, they are at least re-enforced. What can be a real help for carrying out your own transformation in loss is in learning what is really important in your life and how you can complete your purpose.

Each of us has a different purpose in life. Therefore, I ask, what is yours? What gives your life meaning? Which of these experiences of transformation have been prompted by your loss?

- transcendence
- legacy
- self-confidence
- love
- contribution to the world
- compassion
- evaluation of values
- acceptance

On finding meaning in loss, listen to Silvia, a sixty-five-year-old who lost her daughter of twenty. She managed to transform her loss through acceptance and great faith:

> It is necessary to live with the loss. When you are diabetic, one learns to live with insulin; if you lose a leg, one learns to live without the leg; if you lose a loved one, one learns to live without them; you have to choose between living and dying, not by being depressed and abandoning yourself to your bed. I do not think this is appropriate. One has to think that life is beautiful because it keeps changing from moment to moment; it is based on cycles. When the cycle is good, we must take advantage of it. I have learned that nothing can trouble me, and I know that because of my faith, every day is better. In the 23rd Psalm it says: "The Lord is my shepherd, I shall not want."

It is very likely that initially you will not understand the "why" of your loss, but if you transform it into something positive, as have many according to their testimonies in this book, it can become a gain.

Rabbi Harold S. Kushner who lost his son Aaron at age fourteen, after ten years of an agonizing illness, said:

> I think of Aaron and all that his life taught me, and I realize how much I have lost and how much I have gained. Yesterday seems less painful, and I am not afraid of tomorrow.[25]

Changes occur after your loss, even if you do not perceive them. Your family might notice you have learned to give more of yourself and that you might be more compassionate or patient. Frequently we are so immersed in our pain and loss that we do not perceive the small changes that occur in our lives.

Remember the case of Lucia (referred to in Principle VII: Elaborate Rituals), a woman who had not noticed the positive change brought on by her traumatic divorce. She emerged like a butterfly from a chrysalis, as a confident woman, full of happiness.

This phenomenon often happens. The inspiring author Barbara De Angelis also clearly expresses this recovery from loss as rebirth:

> When we first achieve a moment of personal transformation we are so busy recovering from the process that we may not realize how much we have changed...what we still have not come to see that we have been reborn.[26]

PRINCIPLE XI – VISUALIZE THE LIFE YOU WANT

What is the biggest lie in the world?
It is: at a given moment of our
existence we lose control of our lives,
and it becomes governed by fate.
This is the biggest lie in the world.

PAULO COELHO
THE ALCHEMIST

Upon our arrival at Principle XI, the last in this guide to the transformation process, I assume you have begun to integrate the previous ten principles into your life and loss. This is why I have presented them to you sequentially. You could never have known how to visualize your life if you had not taken the first step: Accepting your loss.

You have been through the stages of living your grief; your spirituality; gaining the support of others; caring for your persona; appreciating what you have; reconstructing the meaning of your loss, and, finally, you have reach the stage of visualizing how your life will be after the transformation. As Paulo Coelho said, "Choose not to be victims of fate." If you think you can turn your loss into something valuable in your life and for others, you will have succeeded.

Napoleon Hill says in his bestseller *Think and Grow Rich (1996)*, the first step to carrying out a dream or change in your life is desire. [27]

The motivational speaker Robert Allen reminds us that in our imagination, everything is possible. Therefore, we can foresee the reality that we want to live in the future (Allen, 2000). This concept is widely used to better one's life. I want to apply the same concept in the area of the transformation of loss, because now that you have reached Principle XI, you have already processed your grief, so it is healthy to project yourself into the future. Imagine your life in one or two years:

- How do you see your life in a year or two?
- How would you have contributed to humanity, with your family or your own life?
- What goals will you have achieved?

Realize that there will come a time in which you have to re-integrate into your regular daily activities and take control of your life again. If you continue with a passive attitude toward the future, then you will still be in a similar situation to the one you are now in.

Is that what you want?

Do you want to feel better in future years than you do now?

Do you want to feel the same sadness, the same dismay, the same hopelessness? I don't think so! That is why I urge you, once you've gone through the most acute period of mourning, to take control by having an attitude full of hope and confidence for the future. Once you assume control in your life you can develop the great potential you have within.

To achieve what you want in your new life I propose that you define targets in the different areas where you want to perform better. Write them all down and then start with the easiest. Do not become overwhelmed. Choose only one if that makes you feel more comfortable. You'll find that, little by little, you will start to realize all the dreams you want to achieve and you will see that, if you visualize them and commit to them, you will realize them!

Having specific targets is, according to Zig Ziglar (2002), the only way to be able to have a life with purpose, if not, then we will digress. Although the lack of desire and a certain disorientation are normal in the early stages of grief, at some point we need to take back the helm of our life and regain direction with more purpose and meaning.

A MOMENT OF REFLECTION

In the space below describe how you want to be living your life in the future:

_____

_____

_____

_____

_____

_____

_____

_____

AFFIRMATIONS:

- I can build the life I desire.
- I am ready to achieve my goals.
- I will live my life with purpose.
- I deserve to be happy.

MEDITATION

My life is a gift and it has great meaning. I understand that my happiness is the result of my decisions and how I relate to myself and others. Therefore, I choose to be happy. By transforming my loss I have acquired the ability to build a life with a greater purpose. I thank God for my life and for giving me the ability to love and feel.

WITH LOVE, FAITH, AND GRATITUDE!

Remember that to realize our goals it is necessary to find purpose and, above all, the meaning of what we want to achieve. You can do it! The power resides within you! You have come this far in the book because you wanted to undergo this transformation. You could have stopped reading it on the second page, but you decided to continue to the end because you understand that this life is a gift and that it is the only one you have. Do not waste it! With your ups and downs, your joys and sorrows, it is yours and however fragile it may be, it belongs to you. Keep in mind that we are here today, as are the people we love, but we do not know what tomorrow holds. The difficult situation in which you find yourself can inspire you to live more fully and with more gratitude. The more you learn to express your feelings, by telling the ones you love how much you care for them, you will finally succeed in finding purpose and meaning in your life, whatever it may be. When you get to the end of your life you should feel satisfied by what you did with it, from what you dreamed, did, and loved. You have managed to develop your personal strength after passing through calamities and understand the meaning of each event. Only then will you have grown and lived to the full. If we stay at the stage of complaining, we will never be able to move forward.

You can transform your loss! As my friend, Jorge Córdoba says in his introductory words: You can do it! You can mutate your pain into an opportunity for spiritual growth. This may be the chance to do something that benefits the rest of humanity; it can be an opportunity to redirect your life into something that has more meaning, and it could be the threshold for becoming the person you really want to be.

At the end of our journey I wish to bring you this message of hope and ask that you read it with the eyes of your soul... I hope I have inspired you to transform your life using the tools presented in this book, and remember: Live everyday of your life as if it were the last! Live with love, faith, and gratitude!

Evaluation of Your Loss Now

Now that you have read this book I invite you to answer the questionnaire that you answered at the beginning of the book.

Evaluation of Your Loss

Questionnaire II

Please circle the statements that you identify with.

1. I do not want to think about my loss.
2. I will never be happy again.
3. These misfortunes only happen to me.
4. Everyone else is happy.
5. Looking after my health does not interest me.
6. I do not believe in support groups.
7. I do not believe in God.
8. I do not believe in spiritual guides.
9. I feel a lot of anger.
10. I feel a lot of resentment.
11. I will never forgive those who caused this pain.
12. I do not want to talk about death.
13. Life is unfair.
14. If I occupy my time I do not need to think about my loss.
15. I do not have to share my pain with anyone.
16. I need to be strong for others.
17. From now on I will not show my feelings.
18. I do not think I will recover.

19. Nobody understands me.
20. Never again will I see my loved one.
21. Religion does not help to heal a loss.
22. Why did this happen to me?
23. I am guilty of suffering this loss.
24. Someday I will be happy.
25. I will learn to live with this loss.
26. I will get over this loss and transform my life.
27. I would rather be alone.
28. I do not want help.
29. I have internalized my loss.
30. I will be happy again.
31. Losses are part of life.
32. Everybody faces tough times in life.
33. Looking after my health is very important.
34. Support groups can provide help.
35. I believe in the possibility of something stronger than myself.
36. At certain times we need spiritual guides.
37. I have managed to distance my anger.
38. Saving up resentment is not healthy for my soul.
39. I have managed to forgive.
40. It is necessary to talk about death.
41. Sometimes life is not easy, but I still go forward.
42. Although it is difficult, I need to process my loss.
43. There is a lot that helps me share my sorrow.
44. I do not need to feign strength to others.
45. It is important to show my true feelings.
46. There will be a time when I will have recovered.
47. There are people who understand my pain.
48. I always carry my loved one in my heart.
49. The spiritual dimension helps me to find meaning.

50. I am not the only person facing a loss.
51. I am not guilty of this loss.
52. I help others with their loss.
53. I can love, starting with myself.
54. By transforming my loss I can change my life.

FINAL REFLECTION

As I finish writing this book, I am filled with many feelings, hope, and strength. I realize that I have undergone a transformation myself because, while writing what I have shared and connecting with many people at a very deep level, I have understood, once again, that what encourages us and inspires us to move forward after loss is love. That is the force that must prevail in our souls. Love without selfishness, full of compassion and understanding; love gives and does not expect to receive. It is only when we develop this ability to love that we can transform our loss and change our lives for the better.

I sincerely wish you well as you continue to heal and recover from your loss, and encourage you to continue to grow spiritually as transformation is a never ending process. As a way of showing appreciation for purchasing *Transform your Loss: Your Guide to Strength and Hope* and to further assist you in this process I invite you to become a member of The Circle of Healing and Transformation.^{tm} You can do this by visiting www.transformyourloss.com so I can provide you with the code embedded in this book. As a member of this circle you will have the opportunity to receive special promotions applicable to live seminars, webinars, and private consultation.

If you have a story or comment you would like to share about a loss, or any response to this book, you can send it to info@transformyourloss.com   or   visit   my   website www.transformyourloss.com

NOTES

1. Kübler-Ross, Elizabeth (1969). *On Death and Dying.* New York: McMillan.
2. DeSpelder, Lynn & Albert Lee Strickland (2005). *The Last Dance. Encountering Death and Dying* (Seventh Ed.). New York: McGraw-Hill.
3. Viorst, Judith: *Necessary Losses* (1987). New York: Fireside.
4. Kumar M. Sameet (2005). *Grieving Mindfully.* Oakland, CA: New Harbinger Publications, Inc.
5. Doka, Kenneth J., Rev. Ed. (1999). *Clergy to Clergy: Helping You Minister to Those Confronting Illness, Death and Grief.* Hospice Foundation of America.
6. Freud, Sigmund (1976). *Mourning and Melancholy,* in the complete works (V xiv). Buenos Aires: Argentina: Amorrortu Editores.
7. Martin, Terry L. & Kenned J. Doka (2000). *Men Don't Cry, Women Do: Transcending Gender Stereotypes of Grief.* Philadelphia, PA: Brunner/Mazel.
8. Fitzgerald, Helen (1995). *The Mourning Handbook.* New York: Fireside, p. 53.
9. Quoted in DeSpelder, Lynne & Albert Lee Strickland (2005). *The Last Dance. Encountering Death and Dying.* McGraw-Hill.

10. Frankl, Viktor (1984). *Man in Search of Meaning*. Boston, MA: Aventin Press.

11. Beviones, Julio (2006). *Living in the Zone*. Cordoba, Argentina: Editorial Brujas.

12. Klass, Dennis (1993). *Solace and Immortality: Bereaved Parents' Continuing Bond With Their Children*. Death Studies, pp., 343-368.

13. Bereavement Program (2007). Pastoral Care Services Congregational Health Alliance Ministry Program (CHAMP). Workshop to enable group leaders for helping with mourning. Baptist Health South Florida.

14. Ziglar, Zig (2004). *Confessions of a Grieving Christian*. Nashville, TN: Broadman & Holman. pp 11-12.

15. Cowman, L. B. (1997). James Reimann, Ed. *Streams in the Desert*. Zondervan, p. 13.

16. Byock, Ira, (2004). *The Four Things That Matter Most*. New York, FreePress.

17. Parsons Zulli, Alice (1988). *Healing Rituals: Powerful and Empowering*. Kenneth J. Doka and Joyce D. Davidson, Eds. Hospice Foundation of America. *Living With Grief: Who We Are, How We Grieve*, p. 261-275.

18. Felber Marta: *Finding Your Way After Your Spouse Dies* (2000). Notre Dame, IN: Ave María Press, Inc.

19. The Dalai Lama (1998). *The Art of Happiness* (1998). New York: Riverhead Books. Excerpt of the book

20. Neimeyer, Robert A. (2006). *Lessons of Loss. A Guide to Coping*. Memphis, TN: University of Memphis.

21. http://www.madd.org

22. Tedeschi, Richard and Lawrence G. Calhoun (2007). ADEC's annual conference. Indianapolis, IN.

23. Ziglar, Zig (2004). *Confessions of a Grieving Christian.* pp 12.
24. Kimble,Mervin (2002). *Finding Meaning in the Face of Life's Changes: Viktor Frankl on Aging and Self-Transcendence.* <u>ForSa,</u> 2002, vol. 4, no. 1, pp. 2,7.
25. Kushner, Harold S. (1981). *When Bad Things Happen to Good People.* New York: Shocken. p. 148.
26. De Angelis, Barbara (2006). *¿Cómo llegue Acá?* New York: HarperCollins, p. 220.
27. Hill, Napoleon (2003). *Think and Grow Rich.* Los Angeles, Ca: Highroads Media Inc.

ORIGINAL SOURCES

Browne, Sylvia (2006). *Light a Candle.* Cincinnati, Ohio: Angel Bea Publishing.

Byock, Ira, MD.(2004). *The Four Things That Matter Most. A Book About Living.* New York: Free Press, 2004.

Coelho, Paulo (2002). *The Alchemist.* New York: HarperCollins. 10th Anniversary Edition.

Cowman, L. B. (1997). James Reimann, Ed. *Streams in the Desert. 365 Daily Devotional Readings.* Grand Rapids, MI: Zondervan.

NOTES AND SOURCES OF ORIGIN

De Angelis, Barbara (2006). *How Did I Get There? Translated by* Rosana Elizalde. Rayo/HarperCollins.

DeSpelder, Lynn & Albert Lee Strickland (2005). *The Last Dance. Encountering Death and Dying* (Seventh Ed.). New York: McGraw-Hill.

Dyer, Wayne (2002). *Wisdom of the Ages*. New York: Harper Collins.

Felber, Marta (2000). *Finding Your Way After Your Spouse Dies*. Notre Dame, IN: Ave Maria Press.

Fitzgerald, Helen (1994). T*he Mourning Handbook: The Most Comprehensive Resource Offering Practical and Compassionate Advice on Coping with All Aspects of Death and Dying*. New York: Fireside.

Gomez-Bassols, Isabel (2006). *Los Siete Pasos para el Éxito en el Amor*. (Fonolibro CD). Miami, FL: Venevisión Internacional.

Gibran, Kahlil (1982). *El Loco*. Barcelona, España: Ramos-Majos;

_____ (1983). *El Profeta*. Mexico: Edaf, S.A.

Hay, Louise L. (1991): *I Can Do It*. Carlsbad, CA: Hay House Inc., 1991.

_____ (1995) *A Garden of Thoughts: My Affirmation Journal*. Carlsbad, CA: Hay House Inc.

Hill, Napoleon (1996). *Think and Grow Rich*. New York: Ballantine Books.

Houben, Ligia M. (2009): *Aging and Spirituality: The Fourth Dimension*© Ebook. www.ligiahouben.com

Keyes, Ken. Jr. (1987). *Your Life Is a Gift*. Coos Bay, OR: Living Love Publications.

Kushner, Harold S. (1981). *When Bad Things Happen to Good People*. New York: Shocken.

Kumer, M. Sameet (2005). *Grieving Mindfully*. Oakland, CA, New Harbinger Publications.

Doka, Kenneth J. & Joyce D. Davidson. Ed. (1998). *Living With Grief. Who We Are. How We Grieve.* Hospice Foundation for America. Bristol, PA: Brunner/Mazel.

Maxwell, J. C. (2003). *Actitud 101. EE. UU.* Caribe-Betania Editores.

Meyer, Joyce (1995). *Battlefield of the Mind: Winding the Battle in Your Mind.* New York: Warner Books.

Martínez-Houben, Ligia (2004). La Virgen María y la mujer nicaragüense: *Historia y tradición.* Managua, Nicaragua: Imprimatur.

Neimeyer, Robert A. (2006). *Lessons of Loss. A Guide to Coping.* Memphis, TN: University of Memphis.

Staudacher, Carol (2006). *Tiempo de duelo. Pensamientos para consolarse ante la perdida de un ser querido.* New York: HarperCollins.

Tolle Eckhart (2004). *The Power of Now.* Novato, CA: New World Library.

Worden, William J. (2008) *Grief Counseling and Grief Therapy. A Handbook for the Mental Health Practitioner.* New York: Springer.

Ziglar, Zig (2002). *Goals: Setting and Achieving Them on Schedule.* Audio CD, New York: Simon & Schuster.

CARENOTES by Abbey Press

Baldwin Kathyln S.(2004). *Taking the Time You Need to Grieve Your Loss.* St. Meinrad, IN: Abbey Press.

Diehl, Erin (2004). *Finding Your Way After the Death of a Spouse.* St. Meinrad, IN: Abbey Press.

Stout, Nancy (2004). *Five Ways to Get Through the First Year of Loss.* St. Meinrad, IN: Abbey Press.

Wheeler, Eugenie G.(2004). *Finding Strength to Survive a Crisis or Tragedy.* St. Meinrad, IN: Abbey Press.

ABOUT THE AUTHOR

Ligia M. Houben, MA, CT, CG-C, ACCP, is a specialist in issues of life transition, with experience as a consultant, coach, counselor and lecturer. She has degrees in Psychology and Religious Studies from the University of Miami. Ligia has a Master of Arts degree in Religious Studies, and did graduate studies in Gerontology and Loss and Healing. She is also a fellow of the American Academy of Grief Counseling.

As a certified thanatologist and a certified grief counselor, she specializes in helping people who suffer losses or challenges, using a transformation process, *The Eleven Principles of Transformation,*[tm] that is designed to generate spiritual rebirth and subsequent personal growth. The consequent outcome is to, integrally, achieve a higher quality and deeper appreciation of life.

To learn more about Ligia's professional background and experience and the educational and professional services she offers, visit her website (www.ligiahouben.com.) There you will find complementary information, such as her statements in the media (CNN in Spanish, among others); reviews of her national and international conferences, and information on her articles, some of which have appeared in international publications.

Her teaching as a university professor (in Death and the Process of Bereavement, Religion, and Ethics) in traditional classrooms and virtual spaces, as well as her social work, are aimed at all ages. She gives special attention to older persons, especially their spiritual well-being, as featured in her e-book *Aging and Spirituality: The Fourth Dimension*™. Ligia has also integrated meditation as a powerful tool for transforming any loss, or just to achieve spiritual well-being. Her guided meditation CD, *Momentos de Reflexión*©, is a complement to the Spanish edition of this book, *Transforma tu pérdida: Una antología de fortaleza y esperanza.*

Programs of Ligia M. Houben

Seminars and Workshops

Ligia offers national and international seminars and workshops on a host of topics, all with the objective of human enrichment through a guided process of growth and transformation. For full details go to www.ligiahouben.com or call 305-666-9942.

Transformation Coaching

To receive assistance with any transition that limits your personal or professional development, visit Ligia's website www.ligiahouben.com. In a consultation with Ligia, you will find a personalized response to achieve, through a process supported by successful and meaningful results, the enrichment of your unique human experience. You can use her coaching services in person, via e-mail or telephone.

Publications

Ligia is also the author of *La Vírgen María y la Mujer Nicaragüense: Historia y Tradición* (*The Virgin Mary and Nicaraguan Women: History and Tradition;* 2004) , which is based on her masters thesis and explores Marian devotion with a direct and easy style to understand. She was selected to participate, with other well known authors and speakers, in the book *Success is a State of Mind* (2008), which offers time-tested strategies for success in frank and intimate interviews.

CONTACT INFORMATION

If you want to learn about the Integral Enrichment and Transformation Program, you may contact Ligia M. Houben

By telephone:
(305) 666-9942 and (305) 299-5370

By email:
info@ligiahouben.com

Through these websites:
www.ligiahouben.com
www.transformyourloss.com

Connect With Ligia M. Houben Through:

Facebook:
www.facebook.com/profile.php?id=765995712&ref=name

Twitter:
www.twitter.com/ligiahouben

Ligia's Life Transitions Blog:
www.ligiahouben.wordpress.com

IF YOU ARE INTERESTED IN LIGIA'S SPANISH PRODUCTS PLEASE VISIT THESE WEBSITES:

The book in the Spanish version "Transforma tu pérdida: Una antología de fortaleza y esperanza."
www.transformatuperdida.com

The CD on Guided Meditation: "Momentos de Reflexión"
www.momentosdereflexion.com